Indigenous Social Security Systems in Southern and West Africa

Published by AFRICAN SUN MeDIA under the SUN PReSS imprint

This publication was subjected to an independent double-blind peer evaluation by the publisher.

The editors and the publisher have made every effort to obtain permission for and acknowledge the use of copyrighted material. Refer all enquiries to the publisher.

Views reflected in this publication are not necessarily those of the publisher.

First edition, first print 2018

ISBN 978-1-928357-90-2
ISBN 978-1-928357-91-9 (e-book)
https://doi.org/10.18820/9781928357919

Set in Warnock Pro 10.5/16
Cover design, typesetting and production by AFRICAN SUN MeDIA

SUN PReSS is a licensed imprint of AFRICAN SUN MeDIA. Scholarly, professional and reference works are published in print and electronic format under this imprint.

This publication can be ordered directly from:
www.sun-e-shop.co.za
africansunmedia.snapplify.com (e-books)
www.africansunmedia.co.za

INDIGENOUS SOCIAL SECURITY SYSTEMS

IN SOUTHERN AND WEST AFRICA

Ndangwa Noyoo & Emmanuel Boon

EDITORS

SUN PRESS

TABLE OF CONTENTS

CONTRIBUTORS

Editors

Ndangwa Noyoo is an Associate Professor and the Head of the Department of Social Development at the University of Cape Town, South Africa. Previously, he worked for the University of Johannesburg in the same capacity of Associate Professor in the Department of Social Work and before that, for the South African Government as a Senior Social Policy Specialist/Chief Director in the National Department of Social Development. Prior to this, he was a Senior Lecturer in the Department of Social Work at the University of the Witwatersrand. He has published widely in the areas of social policy, social development and related fields, especially, in the context of Africa and Southern Africa. He has also presented papers at various symposia in Africa, as well as abroad. He holds a Doctor of Philosophy (PhD) from the University of the Witwatersrand, a Master of Philosophy (MPhil) in Development Studies from the University of Cambridge and a Bachelor of Social Work (BSW) from the University of Zambia. He was a Post-Doctoral Fellow at the Fondation Maison des Sciences de l'Homme, Paris, France.

Emmanuel Kwesi Boon is a fulltime Professor at Vrije Universiteit Brussel (VUB), Belgium. He graduated with a BA Honours in Economics and Geography at the University of Ghana in 1979. In 1981, he received a Master's in Industrial Location and Development from VUB. He obtained an MBA from University of Antwerp in 1983 and was awarded a PhD in Economic Sciences by VUB in 1986. Prof Boon also lectured at University of Ghana Business School from September 1987 – July 2007. He was also awarded an Honorary Doctorate Degree by Sumy State University, Ukraine, in 1998. He is a Visiting Professor to several universities and institutions in Africa, Asia, Europe and South America. He enjoys applying multidisciplinary methods to teach his courses which include: Advanced Business Policy and Strategy, Human Resources Management, Environment and Development, Communication and Leadership Skills and Research Methods and Practical Skills. He has published several scientific papers and textbooks. In 2005, Prof Boon was appointed the President of UNESCO's International Commission for developing "Theme 6.150 – Wildlife Conservation and Management in Africa" within the framework of the Encyclopaedia of Life Support Systems (EOLSS).

Authors

Albert Ahenkan is a sustainable development expert and Senior lecturer at the University of Ghana's Business School. He obtained his PhD in Human Ecology from the Vrije Universiteit Brussel (VUB), Belgium in 2011. His areas of expertise include sustainable development, environmental management, public policy, social protection, local economic development and decentralisation. He has published several articles in international peer reviewed journals. Albert Ahenkan is the co-editor of two books on *Public Administration in Ghana: Selected Contemporary Issues* and *Health Services Management: Readings from Ghana.* He has consulted for many organisations including the Ministry of Environment, Science and Innovation, Ministry of Lands and Natural Resources, Environmental Protection Agency (EPA) - Ghana, World Bank, United States Agency for International Development (USAID), Gesellschaft für Internationale Zusammenarbeit (GIZ), The New Partnership for Africa's Development (NEPAD), Food and Agriculture Organisation (FAO) of the United Nations, Oxfam, etc., on social protection, poverty reduction, climate change and disaster risks reduction.

Agnes Ebotabe Arrey holds a PhD in Social Health Sciences from the Vrije Universiteit Brussel, Belgium. Previously, she studied law in the University of Yaoundé, Cameroon, graduating with an LLB in 1982. She worked in the Treasury Department of Cameroon, holding different posts of responsibility from 1983-2002. Agnes also has five years teaching experience. After her eighteen-year career as a cadre, Agnes decided it was time for continuous improvement. She moved to Belgium in 2002 and obtained an MBA in Leadership and Change Management in 2003 and in 2004 she obtained a postgraduate diploma in Entrepreneurship and New Ventures from the United Business Institute, Brussels. She later obtained an MA *magna cum laude* in International Politics from Université Libre de Bruxelles (ULB) in 2005. In 2009 she obtained an MSc *cum laude* in Cultures and Development Studies from Katholieke Universiteit Leuven (KU Leuven) and a postgraduate diploma, *cum laude* in International Educating from Groept T-KU Leuven. She also obtained a certificate on Sexual and Reproductive Health, an online course organised and accredited by the United Nations.

Justice Nyigmah Bawole is a Senior Lecturer and Head of Department of Public Administration and Health Services Management, University of Ghana Business School, Legon. He obtained his PhD in Development Policy and Management from the Global

Development Institute (formerly known as the Institute for Development Policy and Management), University of Manchester, United Kingdom, 2013. He holds an MPhil, BSC, Administration (Public Administration Major) and Diploma in Public Administration degrees from the University of Ghana, Business School which were obtained in 2006, 2003 and 1999 respectively. His research interests include ethics in public administration, public performance management, sustainable management, sustainable development, particularly environment-poverty relationships, poverty reduction, Non-Governmental Organisation (NGO) management and state - third sector relationships.

Clement Dlamini holds a Masters in Social Work which he obtained from Stephen F. Austin State University School of Social Work, USA. He is currently the President of the Monitoring and Evaluation Association of Swaziland (MEAS), Deputy Chair of the National Human Development Report (NHDR) Steering Committee and a Faculty member of the Bristol Myers Squibb Foundation, Secure the Future Technical Assistance Programme (TAP), where he currently serves as the country leader for Swaziland in Technical Support. He currently works at the University of Swaziland in the Department of Sociology and Social Work where he also lectures.

Edwell Kaseke was Professor of Social Work and Chair of Social Work at the University of the Witwatersrand, School of Human and Community Development, South Africa. He was a renowned scholar in Social Security and had published extensively on the same subject. Sadly, he passed away on 24 August 2017.

Lungile Mabundza is a social work lecturer at the University of Swaziland. She has a Ph.D from the University of KwaZulu-Natal, Master's Degree in Social Work from the University of Kansas, USA and a Bachelor of Arts Degree from the University of Swaziland. Her research interests include gerontology, social policy, social security, HIV and children.

Zitha Mokomane is an Associate Professor in the Department of Sociology at the University of Pretoria (UP). Before joining UP in 2015 she was a Chief Research Specialist in the Human and Social Development research programme at the Human Sciences Research Council of South Africa (HSRC) and a Senior Lecturer in the Department of Population studies at the University of Botswana. She holds an MA and a PhD in Demography, both from the Australian National University. Dr Mokomane has extensive research, policy and programmatic expertise in the fields of: Family studies with specific interest in work-family interface; social policy analysis; as well as poverty reduction and social protection. She published widely in her areas of expertise and presented papers at both local and international conferences.

Mildred T. Mushunje has a keen interest in women and children's rights issues. She is affiliated to the Justice for Children in Eastern and Southern Africa. She works on issues of social protection and gender. She has researched and published on women and children's rights and social protection. She is highly experienced in gender sensitive programme development, livelihoods and social protection.

Beatrice Mutale Sakala is a social worker. She obtained her undergraduate degree from the University of Zambia (UNZA) in 2008. She has worked with various private institutions as a Research Assistant. In 2015 she obtained a Masters in Clinical Social Work from the University of Johannesburg, South Africa. She is currently working for the Ministry of Health and is based at St Francis' Hospital, in Katete, Zambia. At St Francis' Hospital she is a Social Worker and also a co-ordinator for the Gender Based Violence Survivor Project, which is managed by World Vision with support from United States Agency for International Development (USAID) and United Kingdom Aid (UKaid).

Boitumelo Seepamore is a lecturer at the University of KwaZulu-Natal's Department of Social Work and a recipient of the prestigious National Institute of Humanities and Social Sciences/the South African Humanities Deans Association (NIHSS-SAHUDA) scholarship. She is currently registered for studies towards a PhD in social work where she is researching distance parenting. Boitumelo's work experience includes being a researcher in the Speaker's Office at the City of Johannesburg and one of her highlights was establishing an employment equity forum. Also, she co-ordinated the employee counselling and psychosocial support programme at the Perinatal HIV research unit at Chris Hani Baragwanath hospital, where she developed and carried out the first ever in-house HIV Counselling and Testing service for staff. She obtained her Bachelors and Master's degrees in Social Work at the University of the Witwatersrand.

Laura Weidmann is currently a PhD candidate in the Department of Human Geography, University of Fribourg, Switzerland. She holds an MA in Social Anthropology and Interdisciplinary Ecology (IKAÖ) from University of Berne, Switzerland. She has an in-depth knowledge of Namibia and Southern Africa, accumulated through qualitative research and analysis over the past seven years. In her current PhD project she focuses on the Communal Land Reform in north-central Namibia with regards to its socio-political implications on various scales, especially on an informal level. The PhD was initiated through a project funded by the Swiss National Research Foundation, focusing on the 'Communal Land Reform in Namibia' - more generally (Project No 140433).

FOREWORD

I am delighted and proud to contribute a foreword to this tremendous effort and share my thoughts on this matter. This book entitled: *Indigenous Social Security Systems (ISSS) in Southern and West Africa*, is another addition to the base on human service literature for Africa and Southern Africa in particular. It is to be hoped that the authors will continue in this noble task of contributing to literature that is so urgently needed for teaching and practice on the continent. Indeed, to date, scholarly texts which are being used by African academics and students alike, at the different universities on the continent, are predominantly written by Western scholars. Arguably, some of these texts still miss out on the African realities – no matter how noble the writers' intentions may be. This is simply because African conditions are best expressed by those who were born and bred on the continent and have, and continue to, experience its triumphs and challenges. Therefore, the book comes at a time when Governments throughout the world, especially in developing countries and Africa in particular, are seriously thinking about developing strategies and mechanisms that can be used to effectively and efficiently address the basic needs of their various population segments.

Several reasons account for this resurgence in public spiritedness including the desire by Governments to provide for those who are on the fringes of society. There is also the desire to employ more inclusive approaches in the redistribution of resources among citizens. This book is therefore, not only essential, but also timely. One of the prominent features of this publication is its origin and the process involved in its development. It is a result of deliberate, conscious and focused conceptualisation of ideas whose origins are located in an academic International Workshop. The richness of the book is justifiably associated with the variety of contributions that gave impetus to its production. The book's utility is extensive and includes titles that capture many essential and current topics that have an appeal to academicians, policy-makers and analysts and practitioners in the field of social welfare and also the donor community. Perhaps, another attractive feature is that the materials enhance the ability of the reader to compare and contrast both indigenous and formal social security systems in several countries of Southern and West Africa. This book will be a very pragmatic and expedient tool for human service practitioners and any enthusiast of broadly social security systems and Indigenous Social Security Systems in particular.

On a personal note, the co-editor of the book, Ndangwa Noyoo, is a person I have known since he was a student. So Bravo Ndangwa! You have done it again! Ndangwa has and continues to elicit tremendous energy for academic work – since I have known him as a rising star in my class at the University of Zambia (UNZA), in the late 1980s and early 1990s. He is also one of the most enthusiastic contributors to the base on human service literature for Africa and Southern Africa in particular. Hence, what we see now in terms of his high rate work is not incidental, but natural to him. I am proud to be associated with this endeavour.

Lengwe-Katembula J. Mwansa (PhD)
Professor, Department of Social work, University of Botswana
Former President of Southern African Social Sciences Conference (1994-1999)
Founding member of the Association of Schools of Social Work in Africa (2005-2010)
Former Head of Department of Zambia and
Botswana Schools of Social Work Gaborone, Botswana

ACKNOWLEDGMENTS

We would like to thank all our colleagues who participated in this academic initiative, from its inception to this product – the text of *Indigenous Social Security Systems in Southern and West Africa*. We would like to particularly thank the University of Johannesburg's Faculty of Humanities and Department of Social Work that supported the project through seed funds that went towards the convening of the International Workshop on Indigenous Social Security Systems in Southern and West Africa, in Auckland Park, Johannesburg in 2016. The said Workshop was instrumental in laying the basis for the research processes in respective countries of Southern and West Africa, which formed this book's chapters.

DEDICATION

This book is dedicated to the memory of
Professor Edwell Kaseke (09/10/1954 - 24/08/2017).
May his soul Rest in Peace.

ACRONYMS

AfDB	African Development Bank
AIDS	Acquired Immune Deficiency Syndrome
ARB	Association of Rural Banks
AU	African Union
BEAM	Basic Education Assistance Module
BFI	Block Farming Initiative
BIG	Basic Income Grant
BNSAF	Botswana National Sports Appeal Fund
BOCAIP	Botswana Christian AIDS Intervention Programme
BoG	Bank of Ghana
BSAC	British South Africa Company
BUCA	Botswana University Campus Appeal
CAADP	Comprehensive African Agriculture Development Programme
CBOs	Community-Based Organisations
CBRDP	Community Based Rural Development Programme
CBRP	Community-Based Rehabilitation Programme (for the Disabled)
CEDC	Children in Especially Difficult Circumstances
CHHs	Child Headed Households
CLRA	Communal Land Reform Act
CSG	Child Support Grant
CSO	Central Statistical Office (Zambia/Zimbabwe)
DACF	District Assemblies Common Fund
DFID	Department of International Development

DPMO	Deputy Prime Minister's Office
EC	European Commission
EPWP	Expanded Public Works Programme
ESAP	Economic Structural Adjustment Programme
ESPP	Enhanced Social Protection Project
EU	European Union
FAO	Food and Agriculture Organisation
FBOs	Faith-Based Organisations
FCBE	Free Compulsory Basic Education
FNGOs	Financial Non-Governmental Organisations
FSSP	Financial Sector Strategic Plan
GAWU	General Agricultural Workers Union
GCSCA	Ghana Co-operative Susu Collectors Association
GDP	Gross Domestic Product
GEAR	Growth, Employment and Redistribution
GES	Ghana Education Service
GETF	Ghana Education Trust Fund
GHHs	Grandmother Headed Households
GLST	Ghana Luxemburg Social Trust
GNSPS	Ghana National Social Protection Strategy
GOG	Government of Ghana
GPRSs I & II	Ghana Poverty Reduction Strategies I &II
GPRSI	Ghana Poverty Reduction Strategy Initiative
GPRTU	Ghana Private Road Transport Union
GSGDA	Ghana Shared Growth and Development Agenda

GSOP	Ghana Social Opportunities Project
GSS	Ghana Statistical Services
GSSSs	Ghana Statistical Service Surveys
HIV	Human Immunodeficiency Virus
ICESCR	International Covenant on Economic, Social and Cultural Rights
ICSW	International Council on Social Welfare
IKS	Indigenous Knowledge Systems
IMF	International Monetary Fund
ILO	International Labour Organisation
INGO	International Non-Governmental Organisation
INS	Institut National de la Statistique
ISALS	Income Savings and Lending Schemes
ISSS	Indigenous Social Security Systems
LEAP	Livelihood Empowerment Against Poverty
LIPW	Labour Intensive Public Works
MDGs	Millennium Development Goals
MESW	Ministry of Employment and Social Welfare
MFIs	Micro Finance Institutions
MIS	Management Information System
MLRGH	Ministry of Local and Regional Government and Housing (Namibia)
MMD	Movement for Multi-Party Democracy
MMDAs	Metropolitan, Municipal and District Assemblies
MOFA	Ministry of Food and Agriculture
MoGCSP	Ministry of Gender, Children and Social Protection
MoH	Ministry of Health (Swaziland)

MoLSS	Ministry of Labour and Social Security (Swaziland)
MSMEs	Micro, Small and Medium-scale Enterprises
MSSEs	Micro and Small-Scale Enterprises
NBFIs	Non-Bank Financial Institutions
NBSSI	National Board of Small-scale Industries
NCPs	Neighbourhood Care Points
NEPAD	New Partnership for Africa's Development
NGOs	Non-Governmental Organisations
NHIA	National Health Insurance Authority
NHIS	National Health Insurance Scheme
NPRA	National Pensions Regulatory Authority
NPS	National Pensions Scheme (Zimbabwe)
NRC	Northern Rhodesia Congress
NSIF	National Social Insurance Fund
NSPS	National Social Protection Strategy
NSSA	National Social Security Authority
NYEP	National Youth Employment Programme
OAG	Old Age Grant
OECD	Organisation for Economic Co-operation and Development
OVCs	Orphans and Vulnerable Children
PF	Patriotic Front (Zambia)
PPPs	Public Private Partnerships
PWC	Public Works Component
RBA	Rights Based Approach
REP	Rural Enterprise Project

RFSP	Rural Financial Services Project
RNFU	Rhodesia National Farmers' Union
SADC	Southern African Development Community
SAP	Structural Adjustment Programme
SDGs	Sustainable Development Goals
SEC	Securities and Exchange Commission
SEDCO	Small Enterprises Development Co-operation
SFP	School Feeding Programme
SIF	Social Investment Fund
SILCs	Savings and Internal Lending Communities
SMEs	Small-to-Medium Enterprises
SNPF	Swaziland National Provident Fund
SPS	Social Protection Strategy
SSNs	Social Safety Nets
SSNIT	Social Security and National Insurance Trust
SSA	Sub-Saharan Africa
Stats SA	Statistics South Africa
TAs	Traditional Authorities
TAA	Traditional Authorities Act
UBLS	University of Botswana, Lesotho and Swaziland
UIF	Unemployment Insurance Fund
UN	United Nations
UNAIDS	United Nations Programme on HIV/AIDS
UNCEB	United Nations Chief Executives Board
UNDP	United Nations Development Programme

UNICEF	United Nations Children's Fund
UNIP	United National Independence Party
UNRISD	United Nations Research Institute for Social Development
USAID	United States Agency for International Development
VDC	Village Development Committee
WB	World Bank
WCIS	Workers' Compensation Insurance Scheme
WFP	World Food Programme
WHO	World Health Organisation
WSPR	World Social Protection Report
ZANU – PF	Zimbabwe African National Union – Patriotic Front
ZIMSTAT	Zimbabwe National Statistics
ZNPF	Zambia National Provident Fund

INTRODUCTION AND BACKGROUND

Ndangwa Noyoo & Emmanuel Boon

This book brings together a collection of papers on Indigenous Social Security Systems (ISSS) in Southern and West Africa. The chapters of the book are written by various researchers and policy-makers who have an interest in ISSS matters in Africa. The authors contend that ISSS should constitute an important basis for the formulation of public policies in Africa. The background to this book involved a process of conceptualising a research project on ISSS in several countries in Southern and West Africa followed by the implementation of a research phase and thereafter, documentation of the findings. This introductory chapter of the book retraces the stages that led to this final product.

On the 8th and 9th of March 2016, several researchers and policy-makers from Southern and West Africa assembled in Auckland Park, Johannesburg, at an International Workshop to deliberate on ISSS in their respective countries. The presenters of papers at the workshop were from Botswana, Cameroon, Ghana, Namibia, South Africa, Swaziland, Zambia and Zimbabwe. The ISSS initiative emanated from a desire of the researchers and policy-makers in the two regions to investigate possible linkages or synergies between Indigenous Social Security Systems and government policies in Southern and West Africa. Researchers from the two sub-regions of Africa presented papers on on-going scientific investigations on ISSS in their countries during the workshop. After the workshop, the resource people and participants spent some time analysing the main issues that emerged to facilitate mapping the way forward for follow-up discussions and action. The two principal issues that were identified are the following:

➤ ISSS in Africa needed to be discussed by the participants on an on-going basis, culminating in an annual event for at least a period of five years.

➤ The participants also took cognisance of the fact that the two sub-regions should not be the sole participants in this endeavour. They agreed that an invitation should be extended to countries from East Africa to participate in future activities.

Rationale for the initiative

During the last decade, there has been an upsurge of initiatives calling for the elevation of social security or social protection (as it is sometimes broadly referred to) in Africa at the academic, policy, practice and service delivery levels. This drive comes on the back of the perceived absence of formal social security systems on the continent. Several researchers and policy-makers in the region and abroad have decried the absence of social security systems in Africa or their abysmal weakness and have called for concerted efforts from state and non-state actors to crystallise social security efforts on the continent. In the same vein, there have been several continental initiatives that sought to deepen social security initiatives in Africa. For example, the ground-breaking Livingstone Social Protection conference which was hosted by the Zambian Government in 2006 is a case in point. This meeting brought together Ministers and Senior Representatives from 13 African countries, namely: Ethiopia, Kenya, Lesotho, Madagascar, Malawi, Mozambique, Namibia, Rwanda, South Africa, Tanzania, Uganda, Zambia and Zimbabwe. Other parties in attendance were from Brazil, development partners, agencies of the United Nations (UN) and Non-Governmental Organisations (NGOs). The conference discussed, among other issues, measures to protect Africa's poor populations against chronic poverty. It also noted with concern the high levels of poverty in Africa and the likelihood that the Millennium Development Goals (MDGs) would not be achieved on the continent unless development strategies incorporated direct actions to enhance social development in Africa in line with the 2004 Ouagadougou Outcome *(Summit of African Union's Heads of States and Governments on Employment and Poverty Alleviation)* and the African Union social policy framework.

According to the resource people and participants of the March 2016 Auckland Park Workshop, there is a dearth of actions directed at mainstreaming ISSS into the development agenda of African countries despite the on-going advocacy on the need to improve the social security systems on the continent. The main social security systems that are currently being envisaged and championed in Africa are largely the formal and Eurocentric ones. With the foregoing notwithstanding, there seems not to be many intellectual forays in ISSS in Africa and how they can be interlinked with governmental formal programmes. The work by Devereux and Getu (2013) casts some light on this issue by seeking, among other things, to analyse the synergy between informal and formal social protection systems. This essentially examines how both systems function and supplement each other in a transparent and effective manner, whilst avoiding duplication of effort, wastage, abuse and misuse of scarce resources. Nevertheless, the characterisation of Indigenous Social Security Systems as 'informal' by the former authors does a disservice to the mainstreaming of ISSS into public policy formulation by African Governments. To this end, the resource people and participants of the March 2016 Auckland Park (Johannesburg) Workshop all concurred that referring to Indigenous Social Security Systems as 'informal' only cements their peripheral status. They all thus agreed to use the term Indigenous Social Security Systems as opposed to 'informal' social security systems.

Nonetheless, the findings of Devereux and Getu (2013) are crucial for the on-going debate on social security systems in Africa, but differ in some ways from the perspectives of the current research on ISSS. The contention of the different academics and policy-makers from Southern and West Africa is that those who are researching on ISSS issues in their regions find their research still being treated as peripheral and not even considered for formal policy inclusion. ISSfS are called 'informal' or even pejoratively referred to as 'insecurity' regimes, at times. In the context of the Southern African Development Community (SADC) some research has already been undertaken in the area by Olivier, Kaseke and Mpedi (2008). These researchers argue accordingly: "Attempts to link informal and formal social security require a proper understanding of informal social security arrangements. There is a need to understand and appreciate the reasons for the existence of informal social security arrangements, the different kinds of informal social security arrangements, the role and importance of informal social security arrangements and the nature of the (current) relationship between informal social security and formal social security arrangements." (Olivier *et al*, 2008: 5) The authors further assert and stress:

> There is increasing evidence that in the SADC region informal arrangements are
> not merely an expression of African cultural values, but, for the reasons advanced
> above, serve as substitutes for the formal arrangements (Olivier *et al*, 2008: 5).

Purpose and scope of the study

The research project sought to establish the extent to which African Governments endeavoured or not to mainstream ISSS into their formal policy regimes. The researchers from Southern and West Africa who participated in the project recognised the fact that in most African countries, the Eurocentric version of social security still predominates and seems to be the most preferred form of social security that is provided by African Governments and propagated by their development partners in the name of donors and international non-governmental actors. Thus, despite ISSS serving as a substitute for such formal arrangements in Africa, anecdotal evidence still seems to paint a different picture and even indicates that ISSS are playing crucial roles in staving off abject poverty and destitution in most African countries. Due to the foregoing, the researchers were concerned that there was no compelling evidence that showed that African Governments are making efforts to incorporate these indigenous approaches into their formal policy mechanisms. Thus, the identified gap motivated the researchers to embark on this study. The research also moved from a normative position, asking whether states should adopt indigenous practices and not merely whether they did (Metz, 2016).

Research objectives

The research was guided by the following four objectives:

- ➤ To determine the existence of Indigenous Social Security Systems (ISSS) in Southern and West Africa.
- ➤ To find out how ISSS are being used by ordinary people in the two sub-regions.
- ➤ To investigate and determine whether Governments in the two sub-regions have incorporated ISSS in their public policies and public policy responses.
- ➤ To make recommendations on how ISSS could be incorporated into mainstream public policies in the two sub-regions.

Methodology

The research process that culminated in this text was basically an exploratory study that sought to ascertain the extent to which ISSS are embedded in formal government public policies or social protection policies in Southern and West Africa. The research was also based on desktop research of existing literature and the findings were augmented by fieldwork investigations where possible. The empirical investigations involved the following:

- ➤ Where possible, sampling of at least three Government officials working at the national level from relevant Ministries or Government Departments. This was to determine whether Government officials ever considered indigenous knowledge in policy development.

▷ Where possible, sampling at least three ordinary people in the respective countries to ascertain if first, they had any knowledge of ISSS and second, how they used their indigenous knowledge in dealing with shocks and insecurities relating to lack of income, assets and similar issues.

The primary tool for gathering data was an interview guide. Fieldwork had already commenced before the Workshop was convened in Johannesburg in March 2016. The Workshop brought together key resource parsons who participated in the research project. After the presentation of papers focusing on the theoretical underpinnings of the wider study, the following issues were discussed and agreed upon: Empirical data collection methods, the writing up of chapters and the organisation and publication of this book.

Structure of the Book

PART I   The Southern African Segment

The book has two segments which cover the two targeted sub-regions in Africa, namely Southern and West Africa. Chapter One introduces the topic for discussion and here Ndangwa Noyoo and Emmanuel Boon bring to the fore the key issues that are examined in the book by the different authors from the two regions. In Chapter Two Zitha Mokomane focuses on Botswana. She argues that the national principle of self-reliance provides the framework within which ISSS in Botswana operate. Drawing her insights from reviewed literature and documents, the chapter provides an overview of key ISSS in pre-colonial, colonial and post-colonial Botswana. The chapter also spends some time discussing ISSS in contemporary Botswana and concludes by assessing the extent to which these systems remain relevant and how they can be strengthened.

Laura Weidmann picks up ISSS in the context of Namibia in Chapter Three and casts some light on that country's Traditional Authorities (TAs) and their roles *vis-à-vis* the Central Government's development agenda. The Oukwanyama Traditional Authority, which was the subject of her case study, informs the discussions of the chapter. Weidmann argues that the former has a long history of knitting power and social services tightly together. She also observes that the TA served as a tool for promoting personal or collective legitimisation even during the colonial period. The chapter's discussions are further reinforced by answers to the question: "How do TAs adjust their local 'traditional' social security systems to the national government's development projects (and changing local interests)?"

In Chapter Four, Lungile Mabundza and Clement Dlamini discuss ISSS in Swaziland. They argue that ISSS still exist in Swaziland, even though they might have slightly changed as they have had to accommodate changes in society due to colonialism, migration, education, modernisation and globalisation. Their research, which informs the chapter, notes that ISSS are at the forefront of meeting the needs of Swazis in present times. They argue and conclude that Swaziland needs to have a definition for social security that encompasses both the formal and ISSS if effective service delivery is to be achieved in the country.

Ndangwa Noyoo and Beatrice Mutale Sakala examine ISSS in Zambia in Chapter Six. Their chapter investigates whether ISSS are considered in the public policy-making agenda of the country. The chapter's discussions are informed by findings from an empirical research which was undertaken by the authors. The research had sought to find out if the Government of Zambia had considered incorporating indigenous knowledge from ISSS when it formulated public policies. The research established that ISSS were not considered in the public policy-making process. The findings of the research study also confirmed that the Zambian Government did not consider indigenous knowledge in its overall policy development, but rather still adhered to Western knowledge and Eurocentric approaches inherited from the British colonial system. The chapter concludes that, *inter alia*, the Zambian Government should consciously support ISSS, through the development of specific policies. This is particularly important because most developing countries such as Zambia have an informal sector, where ISSS predominate, and which is larger than the formal sector.

The Southern African segment of the book ends with Chapter Seven which focuses on ISSS in Zimbabwe. Based on a review of secondary literature, Mildred T. Mushunje and Edwell Kaseke discuss ISSS in Zimbabwe. Their chapter explores how ISSS have been incorporated into the mainstream public policies of Zimbabwe. The two authors conclude that ISSS remain limited in their scope of coverage in the country. They also note that ISSS discussed in their chapter have in common, characteristics such as promoting solidarity and commitment, among other things. Such ISSS also rely on benevolence and the pooling of resources to meet the needs of the poor. The authors also observe that although they are very progressive and respond to the needs of the vulnerable, ISSS are negatively impacted by external economic forces. After their examination of the ISSS in Zimbabwe, the two authors proffer recommendations on how the former could be strengthened.

PART II The West African Segment

This second segment of the book has four chapters and begins with Albert Ahenkan reviewing ISSS in Ghana in Chapter Eight. He also endeavours to determine whether ISSS is even considered at the formal policy level in the country. In the chapter, he first describes the formal social security system of Ghana and how it evolved from the colonial era to the present time. He then discusses in detail the ISSS in Ghana and shows how they help to protect vulnerable Ghanaians, who cannot access formal social security, from external shocks.

In Chapter Nine, Emmanuel Boon and Elizabeth Yeboah examine the relevance of ISSS in promoting the development of Micro and Small-Scale Enterprises (MSSEs) in Sub-Saharan Africa (SSA) and Ghana in particular. Although MSSEs constitute a significant part of the economy of Ghana, they are confronted by a complex maze of challenges, including poor access to social support systems. Most of these enterprises have over the years not benefited from formal social security. Consequently, after retirement, most employees of MSSEs become a burden on their families, communities and society at large. The authors emphasise the importance of widening access of MSSEs to the formal social security system as a strategy for improving the welfare of their employees and capacity to significantly contribute to the sustainable development of the country. After a brief review of the definitions of social security, the existing indigenous and formal social security systems in Ghana are examined in detail. Recent reforms in Ghana, such as the National Pensions System, which seek to widen access by all to social security in the country are given some thought. The authors then identify and discuss the key challenges of social security systems in the country that must be redressed to enable MSSEs to have wide access to social security systems for sustainable growth. The authors conclude that MSSEs have the potential to contribute to improving social security and human development in Ghana.

In Chapter Ten, Justice Bawole discusses the important role of Non-Governmental Organisations (NGOs) in providing social security in the Ghanaian context. For him, social protection and social security started in Ghana during the ancestral era where indigenous or traditional forms of social protection predominated. He argues that formal forms of social protection supplanted the indigenous ones, thereby placing huge responsibilities on the Government, especially in the post-colonial era. Due to the limited capacity of the formal social security system to cater to the whole population, as well as the population's over dependence on the Government for social protection, NGOs have become a major social safety net for poor families, especially those that are unable to provide the required support to their members during periods of uncertainty and shocks. Bawole concludes with suggestions for NGOs and the Government such as establishing a workable rapport; learning lessons from previously implemented programmes; building the capacities of stakeholders at all levels; and the need for international development partners to play a more supportive role in this arena.

In Chapter Eleven, Agnes Arrey discusses the problems of access to social protection by HIV/AIDs infected people. She observes that the changing dynamics of the population and household structure in Sub-Saharan Africa (SSA) is impacting on the access to social protection. Apart from Mauritius, Seychelles, Kenya, Botswana and South Africa, most countries in SSA do not have social security schemes that cover people with HIV/AIDS and other vulnerable populations. She observes that in most SSA countries, formal social security programmes scarcely reach the rural or urban poor. Using Cameroon as a case study, she reveals that most HIV/AIDS affected people in the country resort to ISSS, where the typical African tradition relies on family members to provide for the sick, ailing and aging relatives. She identifies several challenges that hinder HIV/AIDs affected people from accessing social security systems. She recommends appropriate interventions such as strengthening the health systems, indigenous social security schemes and those that enhance behavioural change to facilitate a reduction in the spread of the pandemic.

The author notes that the family, social and ethnic networks, as well as community and church-based organisations, are the main forms of ISSS in Cameroon. She concludes that the Government should effectively mainstream HIV/AIDS issues and introduce a supportive policy and institutional framework that prioritises people living with HIV/AIDS rather than overlooking them.

Ndangwa Noyoo and Emmanuel Boon then conclude the book's discussions in Chapter Twelve.

Value sharing and follow-up programme

This book is an outcome of desk and exploratory empirical research on Indigenous Social Security Systems (ISSS) in Southern and West African countries, spanning a period of two years. It will be disseminated widely to inform continental, regional and country-level development policy makers and other relevant actors. As has already been mentioned, this research project will be continued for at least five years and its coverage will be extended to East and Central Africa.

References

Devereux, S. & Getu, M. 2013. The conceptualisation and status of informal and formal social Protection in Sub-Saharan Africa. In: S. Devereux & M. Getu (eds.). Informal and formal social protection systems in Sub-Saharan Africa. Addis Ababa: *Organisation for Social Science Research in Eastern and Southern Africa (OSSREA)*. 1-8.

Metz, T. 2016. Recent philosophical approaches to social protection: From capability to Ubuntu. *Global Social Policy*, 16 (3): 1-19. https://doi.org/10.1177/1468018116633575

Olivier, M.P.; Kaseke, E. & Mpedi, L.G. 2008. Informal Social Security in Southern Africa: Developing a Framework for Policy Intervention. Paper prepared for presentation at the International Conference on Social Security organised by the National Department of Social Development, South Africa, 10-14 March, Cape Town.

I
THE SOUTHERN
AFRICAN SEGMENT

01

INDIGENOUS SOCIAL SECURITY SYSTEMS IN BOTSWANA

Zitha Mokomane

Introduction

When it gained independence from Britain in 1966 Botswana was one of the poorest countries in the world with a per capita Gross Domestic Product (GDP) of about 70 USD. It was a predominantly rural population of just over 500,000 people. Botswana had an agrarian economy that was heavily dependent on foreign aid and also had rudimentary and inadequate education and health sectors (Mwansa, Lucas & Osei-Hwedie, 1998; Malema, 2013; World Bank, 2016). The agricultural sector, particularly cattle rearing and beef production, accounted for 43 per cent of the country's GDP while water and electricity contributed only 0,6 per cent (World Bank, 2016). The only tarred road in the country was the five kilometres stretch from the train station to the British High Commission in the small town of Lobatse, which is about 75 kilometres from the capital Gaborone.

In the years that followed, diamond mining, sound governance and accountability mechanisms, as well as prudent macroeconomic and fiscal management saw the country transform into an upper middle-income state (Mwansa *et al*, 1998; Leite, 2014; World Bank, 2016). The average real GDP growth of nine per cent achieved between

1965/66 and 2005/06 was, according to Leith (2005: 4) "an outstanding and uncontested economic performance record of any country in the world." In addition, the adoption of decentralised health services and primary health care system led to positive health outcomes in areas such as child and maternal health, reproductive health, nutrition, HIV and AIDS care, support and treatment and life expectancy according to the World Health Organisation (WHO) (2016). By the same token, the adoption in the 1980s, of the principle of universal nine-year basic education led to the introduction of free education and an exponential increase in the number of community junior secondary schools (Mwansa *et al*, 1998). This was followed, in subsequent years, by an increase in senior secondary schools and tertiary institutions. Because of this, the country's literacy rates among adults (15-65 years) increased notably in the past two decades, from 68,9 per cent in 1993, 81,2 per cent in 2003 and 88,6 per cent in 2014 (Statistics Botswana, 2015).

Over the years, Botswana has also witnessed significant declines in the incidence of poverty (for example, from 30,6 per cent to 19,4 per cent between 2002 and 2010), as well as in the depth and severity of poverty (World Bank, 2016). In addition to impressive economic growth and the foregoing investments in health and education, the decline in poverty can also be attributed to the country's long-standing commitment to state-led social protection. Overall, against the wide consensus that broad based economic growth is a necessary condition for poverty alleviation, it is not entirely sufficient (Seleka, Siphambe, Ntseane, Mbere, Kerapeletswe & Sharp, 2007). The Government of Botswana has, throughout the post-independence era developed and implemented many agricultural and labour-based policies and programmes "to wage a direct assault on poverty" (Mwansa *et al*, 1998: 62). A detailed discussion on these policies and programmes is beyond the scope of this chapter, suffice it to state that they have included social protection programmes such as family support programmes (such as provision of food, clothing, education and protection for orphans and assisting the terminally ill through home-based care); public works schemes; nutrition programmes; supplementary feeding programmes for vulnerable groups and primary school children; active labour market programmes; and social pensions such as the old age pension and the World War I veterans grants (Seleka *et al*, 2007; World Bank, 2013).

All the foregoing programmes, as well as other national strategies for poverty reduction, are integrated into the country's broader National Economic Development Planning which, since independence, has been guided by the four national principles of: *democracy, development, unity and self-reliance* (Maipose, 2008: 3). Indigenous Social Security Systems – defined as those self-organised indigenous safety nets that draw their membership from a group or community, including, but not limited to family, kinship, age, group, neighbourhood, profession, nationality, ethnic groups and so forth (Dlamini & Mabundza, 2016) – have also been an implicit component of the National Economic Development Planning. According to Gsanger (1999: 3), cited by Dlamini and Mabundza (2016), indigenous social security rests on the following pillars:

- Individual provisions based on individual economic activities (self-employment, subsistence farming, casual agricultural labour of informal sector jobs);
- Membership of traditional solidarity networks (family, kinship, neighbourhood, etc.);
- Membership of co-operatives or social welfare associations (self-help groups, rotating savings and credit clubs, cultural associations, etc.);
- Access to public benefit systems (targeted transfers, donations, social services provided by voluntary organisations, churches, trade unions, etc.).

It can thus be argued that the national principle of self-reliance provides the framework within which Indigenous Social Security Systems in Botswana operate. This chapter provides an overview of key Indigenous Social Security Systems in pre-colonial and colonial times (referred hereafter as 'traditional Botswana'). The types of these systems in contemporary society are then discussed before the chapter ends with a concluding section that assesses the extent to which these systems remain relevant and could be strengthened. It is noteworthy that while other chapters in this book use empirical research findings to inform their discussions, this chapter draws solely from the systematic review of literature and documents and desktop analysis. This could have limited the chapter's arguments to a certain extent.

Indigenous Social Security Systems in traditional Botswana

As in many other African societies Batswana traditionally relied on primary institutions of social support such as the extended family, the chieftaincy system, benevolent neighbours, as well as community members (see Mokomane, 2013). The traditional society provided a sophisticated social security system in times of adversity, need and crisis, such as when there was food insecurity, hunger, sickness, death, old age, unemployment etc. (Mwansa *et al*, 1998: 55). Overall:

> Tswana societies, before contact with the Europeans were relatively self-sufficient agricultural economies. The sense of community obligation was very real and most needs were addressed within the family and tribal framework. Children, the aged and the disabled were cared for by various members of the family in a fixed order of responsibility. Provision of such essential services as housing was the responsibility of household heads assisted by relatives, neighbours and other members of the community. The poor members of the community also benefited from affluent members of society though institutionalised systems... The chief who was the highest political authority among communities, occasionally collected levies from his subjects which were used for public undertakings and sustenance of communities in times of hunger and economic strife (Mwansa *et al*, 1998: 57).

Table 1   Components to some of the key Indigenous Social Security Systems that were prevalent in traditional Botswana

System	Description
Masotla (tribal fields)	These fields were prepared by tribal age regiments on a voluntary basis before the rest of the community was permitted to plough the land. Produce from the fields (typically sorghum, maize, beans, millet, cowpeas and groundnuts) was stored in tribal granaries and was distributed to the community whenever there was a drought or in times of other natural disasters. Disadvantaged people such as orphans, the destitute and chronically ill individuals were from time to time fed from the granaries.
Kgamelo cattle (milk paid cattle)	These were occasionally given to poorer members of the community by the chief as a means of livelihood, but more commonly, they were entrusted to prominent members of the tribe who would herd them. The responsibility of the herdsman was to milk the cattle on behalf of the chief. The milk was then put daily into a milk sack to thicken and then brought to the chief to be distributed. Besides providing for his wives, it was a common practice for the chief to supply milk to the poor, orphans, or other vulnerable groups in the community.
Mafisa (lending cattle to the poor)	This system was a form of special contract by which well-off relatives or members of the community placed one or more cattle into the keeping of a destitute person. The recipient herdsman took care of these cattle for an indefinite period and had the right to use them as draught animals and as a source of milk and transportation to fetch water or firewood. If the cattle multiplied, it was common practise to reward the herdsman with a heifer together with any offspring that they may subsequently produce. Ownership of the cattle remained with the original owner who could claim back the cattle after an agreed period.

Table 1   Components to some of the Indigenous Social Security Systems that were prevalent in traditional Botswana (...continued)

System	Description
Majako	The system allowed poor people to sell their labour and work in the fields of the rich in return for a share of the harvest.
Bo-tshwarateu or *bodisa*	Provided able-bodied poor people with an opportunity to break out of poverty by looking after other people's cattle and in return receiving a payment of a cow each year.
Letsema	Allowed members of the community to perform voluntary work on behalf of a deserving family. For example, if a family wanted to clear a field to be ploughed, the family would invite neighbours and other people in the community to a *letsema*. Any neighbour who refused to participate was made aware that she/he should not expect to be assisted when she/he called a *letsema*.

Source: Seleka *et al.* 2007

To the extent that traditional Botswana typically survived on subsistence crops and livestock farming, it is not surprising that the ISSS were almost invariably focused on agriculture. There were, however, systems that operated in other areas, particularly in health services and education. These were, to a large extent, initiated and spearheaded by missionaries and tribal authorities. For example, between 1921 and 1923, regiment labour, with funding from the *Bakgatla* ethnic group, built the *Bakgatla* National School, which until after World War II was the largest building in the country. The school offered primary and junior secondary education at various periods of time – between 1923 when it opened and 1975 when it was closed. It was reopened in 1977 as a community museum that stores many artefacts related to the *Bakgatla* culture and history and it also houses civic education materials and craft centres (Grant, 2015). By the same token, Moeng College, in the central district of the country was built in 1947 – as one of the first secondary schools in the country – with funds (approximately 100,000 British Pounds) donated by members of the *Bangwato* ethnic group (Kubuetsile, 2009). The King George V Memorial Hall/School in the Southern District village of Kanye was similarly built in 1941.

Indigenous Social Security Systems in contemporary Botswana

It was largely against the implicit recognition of how much had been achieved by the self-help efforts of communities that the Government of Botswana adopted self-reliance as one of the four national pillars at independence (Grant, 2015). In line with this, Botswana's first National Development Plan, which was developed soon after independence, focused on accelerating rural development using the spirit of self-reliance to create basic social infrastructure such as primary schools, health clinics, rural roads and village dams, among other things, through the Department of Social Welfare and Community Development (Rankopo, Osei-Hwedie & Modie-Moroka, 2006). Among the number of remarkable self-reliance initiatives, which took place just before and within the first decade of independence, was the construction of the National Stadium in Gaborone through the Botswana National Sports Appeal Fund (BENSAF) and the establishment of the University of Botswana through the Botswana University Campus Appeal (BUCA). According to Hermans (2006: 165) the establishment of BENSAF was spearheaded by some members of a local football club in Gaborone:

> ... to generate resources, in cash and kind, for the development of sports facilities throughout Botswana, but especially at the national sports centre in Gaborone... BENSAF faced formidable obstacles. Botswana was still desperately poor. There were no 'natural' commercial sponsors to underwrite the development of sporting facilities in Gaborone... in those early days. There were no diamond mines, no breweries, no motor vehicle dealerships or prosperous franchises. However, by 1965, BENSAF had raised sufficient funds from local and overseas sources to enable it to embark on its first and only project, the construction of the National Stadium. Several construction companies... had been awarded contracts for the construction of various components of the Capital Project... some contributed money or contributed in kind... Others helped to design or built sporting facilities without charge... The National Stadium subsequently became the venue for many sporting and official occasions and was the venue for the Independence Day celebrations on 30 September 1966. For many years, Botswana was probably the only country in the world whose national stadium was financed entirely by voluntary contributions, not by the national government.

In the same vein, the BUCA was spearheaded by the late President Sir Seretse Khama, the first president of the country. In 1976 Lesotho suddenly decided to pull out of the jointly shared University of Botswana, Lesotho and Swaziland (UBLS). BUCA, also known as the "One Man, One Beast" fundraising campaign, was launched to raise money for the construction of the Botswana Campus of the University of Botswana and Swaziland. The campaign saw nationals across the country making all types of contributions that included cash, cattle and other livestock, grain and even eggs. In a relatively short time the target of one million South African Rands, the currency then used by Botswana, was reached. By 1982, the University of Botswana became a reality (Morolong, Lekoko &

Magang, 2015; University of Botswana, 2016). The spirit of self-reliance is still persistent in contemporary Botswana and ISSS that continue to play a major role in this area, and the country, include the extended family and kin obligations, mutual aid associations and community support networks (Mupedziswa & Ntseane, 2013; World Bank, 2013). Since 2008, the Ian Khama Presidency has deliberately incorporated self-reliance into national programmes to eliminate poverty and uplift the poor.

Family and kin obligations

As stated earlier, the extended family – which is comprised of generations of close relatives – was for years a source of social security and support during times of crisis and adversity (Mokomane, 2013). Although various socio-economic transformations have stretched its capacity to continue playing this role (Dintwa, 2010; Mokomane, 2013), this institution continues to draw on principles of solidarity and reciprocity to play a significant role in providing social, economic, psychological and financial support, through for example urban-rural and inter-household income transfer assistance, when individuals encounter lifecycle crises (Mupedziswa & Ntseane, 2013). As in many traditional African societies, it is still common that: "When crops fail, family members in town will send food and cash to needy relatives in rural areas. "A relative in town who becomes unemployed will receive food from the rural areas or be received back into the rural homesteaded." (Mupedziswa & Ntseane, 2013: 88)

The extended family is also still a major source of reciprocal caregiving relations between younger and older family members (Mokomane, 2013). For example, kinship care which is defined by Testa and Rolock (1999: 557) as "the full time nurturing and protection of children who must be separated from their parents by relatives, members of their tribes, clans, godparents, stepparents or other adults who have a kinship bond with a child," provides care for at least 95 per cent of children who have been orphaned by the AIDS epidemic in the country (Maundeni, 2009; Malinga-Musamba, 2013). By the same token and similar to many developing societies where older adults tend to live with, and be cared for by kin and where two-generation and three-generation households remain the norm, the 2011 Botswana population census showed that only 12,6 per cent of older people aged 65 years and above in the country lived alone, while 50,4 per cent lived with their children and 53,8 per cent lived with other close relatives (Bainame, Burnette & Shaibu, 2011).

Mutual Aid Associations

Mutual aid associations are formed to respond to specific contingencies as determined by members in the spirit of humanity, reciprocity and solidarity. Common among these are burial societies and informal savings and borrowing schemes known as *metshelo*. Burial societies have been a part of the Botswana sociocultural landscape for years and their origin can be traced back to the recognition of the labour-intensive nature of Tswana funerals that also require massive mobilisation or resources and a social division of responsibility based on age, gender, social status, etc. (Ngwenya, 2003). The burial societies' members – majority of whom are women – typically contribute an agreed regular subscription fee and rely on their members' contributions to build a collective fund and fluid capital that is used to provide members with emergency relief in the case of a relative's death. Each member typically nominates between six and ten 'beneficiaries' for which they will receive funeral support. These often include the member, parents and parents-in-law, the members' children and spouses and other close relatives of the members' choice. Although the relief is mostly financial, it can also be non-monetary entailing the provision of labour during the funeral process (Ngwenya, 2002; 2003). Available evidence shows that older people and other individuals routinely use their monthly pensions and cash transfers from the Government's safety net programmes to pay for burial society subscriptions (World Bank, 2011). The contributions and funeral support provided are regularly revised in line with the ever-increasing cost of mass funerals in Botswana (Ngwenya, 2002-2003; Mupedziswa & Ntseane, 2013).

Metshelo, on the other hand, are essentially rotating savings and credit associations, akin to *stokvels* in South Africa which are informal group savings schemes in which members voluntarily agree to contribute a fixed amount to a common pool on a regular basis: such as every month, fortnightly or quarterly (Matuku & Kaseke, 2014: 505). The members also mutually agree upon the order or cycle of receiving the pooled funds. Overall, the funds can be given to a member on a rotational basis or shared equally at the end of the year (Radipotsane, 2007). *Metshelo* became popular largely against the background of many obstacles that made it difficult for many low income and poor households to access formal financial services. Members (the majority of whom are women) also join either because they are not covered by any formal social protection scheme, or are covered, but the level of protection is not adequate (Matuku & Kaseke, 2014). In addition to supplementing income, funds from *metshelo* are used to build up reserves against unforeseen contingencies: Enhance the ability to meet basic needs, as well as to save and invest; provide easy access to credit and mini-loans for members; empower women; provide moral support and mutual assistance; and create social capital (Radipotsane, 2007; Matuku & Kaseke, 2014).

Community Support Networks

Community support networks, are characterised by the existence of an organisational, hierarchical management structure, with recognised membership and official registration (Rankopo *et al*, 2006). These also play a critical role in meeting the spiritual, social and economic needs of Botswana that experience crises by providing a wide range of services including material aid; psychosocial support; education, advocacy and activism in gender with HIV and AIDS issues; and planning of local social development activities (Rankopo *et al*, 2006; World Bank, 2016). Examples of these are Faith-Based Organisations (FBOs), Community-Based Organisations (CBOs) and village development committees. With over 80 per cent of the country's population belonging to one religion or another, the Government of Botswana identified FBOs as strategic partners in its multi-sectoral HIV and AIDS response (Togarasei, 2011). The Botswana Christian AIDS Intervention Programme (BOCAIP) is an example of an FBO that has made great strides in this regard. Through its 11 centres and six satellite centres across the country, BOCAIP continues to mobilise and co-ordinate the Christian community to make an impact by implementing HIV-related behavioural change interventions, providing material assistance to needy people infected and affected by HIV and AIDS, as well as implementing a range of cross-cutting community mobilisation activities (Haron, Jensen, Mmolai, Nkomazana, Sebina & Togarasei, 2008; BOCAIP, 2011).

The guidance, counselling and spiritual therapy offered by many FBOs to children orphaned by AIDS have also helped to address their psychosocial and emotional needs and enabling them to cope with orphanhood, as well as improve their academic performance (Maundeni, Dinama & Boikhutso, 2012). Since independence, Botswana has also promoted public participation for local level governance and service delivery (Sharma, 2010). One community participation structure that continues to link communities and central Government authorities is the Village Development Committee (VDC) which was established by a Presidential Directive in 1968 (Ngwenya, 2003; Serema, 2002). These committees now exist in virtually all villages across the country and have membership of between 10 to 12 villagers (with the councillor and chief/headman being ex officio members) democratically elected during a community meeting (*kgotla*). The functions of the VDC as outlined by the Botswana Government in its District Planning Handbook (1996: 56) are to:

- identify and discuss local needs;
- help villagers to prioritise their local needs;
- formulate proposals for the solution of identified local needs;
- determine the extent to which the people can satisfy their identified needs on a self-help basis;
- develop a plan of action for their village area;
- solicit the assistance of donors and other development agencies;
- mobilise the community and its institutions for development action;
- provide a forum of contact between village leaders, politicians and District Authorities to enhance the flow of development information; and
- represent villagers in development matters and act as a source and reference point in matters pertaining to village development.

In the 1970s, VDCs mobilised communal labour for the construction of schools, roads and civil servants' houses. Currently, despite challenges, such as limited capital and human resources constraints, the committees mainly advocate for the redistribution of village resources to vulnerable groups such as destitute people, orphans, victims of a natural disaster and people with disabilities. The committees are also active in natural resource conservation issues, as well as in issues related to access to portable water, health, the preservation of cultural sites (such as burial grounds), early childhood education and undertaking a range of income-generating projects to build traditional community assets (Ngwenya, 2008: 71). VDCs are thus a central element of Botswana's local Government (Sharma, 2010) as they also "provide a forum for the articulation of village-level priorities, which are subsequently incorporated through a district planning system, ultimately filtering through to the overall National Development Plan" (Ngwenya, 2008).

Recent presidential initiatives

When he assumed power in 2008, the fourth President of Botswana, Ian Khama, explicitly absorbed self-reliance into his administration's priority programme of 'poverty eradication' (Grant, 2015). According to the former author, to do this, However the presidency "has had to rearrange and adjust those old notions and values so that what had been in the past a community-based bottom up ideal, has now become a Government directed top down strategy" (Grant, 2015: 194). In the past – as seen in the foregoing sections – the principle of self-reliance was used to serve many different needs and purposes. The Ian Khama Presidency applied it to a large-scale Government programme of social relief whose participants, it claimed, were involved as part of their individual efforts to help themselves (Grant, 2015: 194). Presidential initiatives such as *Ipelegeng*, the Presidential Housing Appeal and Backyard Gardening initiative implemented by the Ministry of Agriculture are some of the most well-known components of the Ian Khama presidency's Poverty Eradication Programme.

The *Ielegeng* programme existed for many years largely as a labour intensive public works programme aimed at providing social protection against poverty and the impacts of drought. Due to the recurrence of unfavourable hydro-climatic conditions and scarce employment opportunities the Government decided in 2009, to run the *Ipelegeng* programme on a permanent basis in both urban and rural areas to provide relief whilst at the same time carrying out essential development projects that had been identified and prioritised through the normal development planning process. Beneficiaries of the programme are largely women who are poor in that they own little in terms of assets and have low or no education (Sekwati, 2010: 24). A 2012 review of *Ipelegeng* (UNICEF, 2012) found that 82 per cent of the participants felt that the programme had assisted them to improve their welfare because, among other things:

- Beneficiaries can buy food for themselves without depending heavily on relatives and the Government.
- Beneficiaries, like others in the community, are recognised as workers by small shop owners and as credit worthy.
- Beneficiaries' dignity has been enhanced through their participation in *Ipelegeng*.
- In a somewhat unstructured manner the participants have gained some skills by observing work being done.

The nationwide backyard gardening programme, that was launched in 2009, targets households and individuals who live below the poverty line. They receive basic infrastructure and skill development with the goal of small-scale production of vegetables (Mosha, 2015). Beneficiaries also receive shade netting, rain barrels to collect roof water, drip irrigation tubing, seeds, tools and extension services (Moseley, 2016). The initiative has been criticised in the local press for being impractical due to water shortages, the high cost of water, as well as for not being a priority for some recipients (see, for example Mmegi, 2011; The Patriot, 2014). Indeed, the Government's poverty eradication agency reported that as of 2015, only 317 people had embraced and benefited from the programme around the country – way below the Government's target of establishing approximately 12,800 backyard gardens by the end of 2011/12 (Mosha, 2015). The Presidential Housing Appeal was set up to provide shelter for the needy with donations ranging from cash and building material to complete and fully furnished structures made by private companies, churches, organisations and individuals. To the extent that people benefit variously as individuals, couples or families, the exact figure of beneficiaries are difficult to know. However, in March 2015 the co-ordinator of the Poverty Eradication Programme in the Office of the President stated that "to date, 406 houses have been donated, benefiting an estimated population of 2,436… Currently 75 houses are under construction and if all falls into plan, the fund will at the end of the year boast 150 houses with 50 more expected from donors" (Mmegi, 2015).

Discussion

The purpose of this chapter was to provide an overview of Indigenous Social Security Systems (ISSS) in Botswana. The chapter began by highlighting the country's socio-economic development in the post-independence era. Before linking this to ISSS, the chapter discussed such systems in traditional Botswana. It was essentially shown that the welfare of individuals, families and communities has, for years, been embedded in a culture of collective orientation which underscored the need for community members to provide socio-economic support and assistance to each other and the community and nation at large, as well as to provide intergenerational altruistic assistance (Mokomane, 2017). The chapter further showed that, taking cognisance of how much had been achieved by the self-help efforts of communities, the Government adopted self-reliance as one of the four national pillars of independence. It is largely through this pillar that Indigenous Social Security Systems in contemporary society operate, with those playing a major role being the extended family and kin obligations, mutual aid associations and community support networks. Some of the key presidential initiatives implemented over the past few years were also discussed.

While the effectiveness of the latter has been generally criticised, it is evident from this chapter that, as in many African societies, ISSS continue to play a critical role in addressing poverty and improving the general welfare of individuals, families and communities. The overall conclusion, therefore, is that ISSS should become explicit and integrated components of Botswana's broader National Economic Development Planning process and mechanisms. In line with Olivier, Kaseke and Mpedi's (2008) propositions, first steps in this regard should entail making efforts to obtain a proper understanding of the characteristics, range and dimensions of existing ISSS. As Oduro (2010) argues, in so far as the extent that formal social security arrangements are being introduced and implemented in a social system that already has its own ISSS, it is critical that research is undertaken to understand better the effect the former is having on the latter. Strengthening existing linkages between these systems and formal social security arrangements and promoting the involvement of the indigenous systems in overall social security provisions through, *inter alia*: training, subsidies and technical assistance are also crucial. This can both enhance service delivery among vulnerable groups and address the needs of the poor and vulnerable more effectively (Mupedziswa & Ntseane, 2013).

References

Bainame, K.; Burnette, D. & Shaibu, S. 2011. Socio-demographic correlates of older adults' living arrangements in Botswana. *Botswana Notes and Records*, 46: 106-120.

BOCAIP. 2011. *Home.* http://www.bocaip.org.bw/bocaip-contentphp?cid=1 [Accessed 24 August 2016].

Botswana Government. 1996. *District Planning Handbook.* Gaborone: Ministry of Local Government.

Dintwa, K.F. 2010. Changing family structure in Botswana. *Journal of Comparative Family Studies*, 41(3): 281-297.

Dlamini, C.N. & Mabundza, L. 2016. Indigenous Social Security Systems in Swaziland: Community resilience and empowerment. Paper presented at the International

Conference on Indigenous Social Security Systems and Government Policies: Perspectives from Southern and West Africa, 8-9 March 2016, Johannesburg.

Grant, S. 2015. Boipelego and Ipelegeng before and after independence. *Botswana Notes and Records*, 45: 189-194.

Haron, M.; Jensen, K.; Mmolai, S.; Nkomazana, F.; Sebina, L. & Togarasei, L. 2008. Ditumelo secondary literature review: HIV prevention and faith-based organisations in Botswana. *Boleswa Journal of Theology, Religion and Philosophy*, 2(1): 1-64.

Hermans, H.C.L. 2006. The Mafikeng legacy. *Botswana Notes and Records*, 38: 160-170.

Kubuetsile, L. 2009. *Moeng College 60th Anniversary*. http://thoughtsfrombotswana. blogspot.co.za/2009/09/moeng-college-60th-anniersary.html [Accessed 7 September 2016].

Leith, J.C. 2005. *Why Botswana prospered*. Montreal & Kingston: McGill-Queen's University Press.

Leite, R. 2014. Child-and family-focused policy in Botswana. In: M. Robila (ed.). *Handbook of Family Policies Across the Globe*. New York: Springer. 47-57.

Maipose, G.S. 2008. *Institutional dynamics of sustained rapid economic growth with limited impact on poverty reduction*. Geneva: UNRISD.

Malema, B. 2013. Botswana's formal economic structure as a possible source of poverty: Are there any policies out of this economic impasse? *PULA: Botswana Journal of African Studies*, 26(1): 51-69.

Malinga-Musamba, T. 2013. The nature of relationships between orphans and their kinship carers in Botswana. *Child & Family Social Work*, 20(3): 257-376.

Matuku, S. & Kaseke, E. 2014. The role of *stokvels* in improving people's lives: the case in Orange Farm, Johannesburg, South Africa. *Social Work/Maatskaplike Werk*, 50(4): 504-515.

Maundeni, T. 2009. Care for Children in Botswana: The Social Work Role. *Social Work and Society: International Online Journal*, 7(1): 13-27.

Maundeni, W.; Dinama, B. & Boikhutso, K. 2012. How Faith-Based Organisations Assist HIV/AIDS Orphans with their Academic Work: Botswana Perspective. *Research on Humanities and Social Sciences*, 2(3): 17-27.

Mmegi. 2015. *President's Housing Appeal leaves footprint*. http://www.dailynews.gov. bw/news-details.php?nid=18606 [Accessed 10 September 2016].

Mmegi. 2015. *Botswana dismiss backyard gardening as 'a big joke'*. http:// www.mmegi.bw/index.php?sid=1&aid=1058&dir=2011/May/Monday23 [Accessed 10 September 2016].

Mokomane, Z. 2017. The Developing World. In: International Social Security Association (ed.). *Megatrends: Family and gender dynamics.* Geneva: International Social Security Association. 27-42.

Mokomane, Z. 2013. Social Protection as a Mechanism for Family Protection in Sub-Saharan Africa. *International Journal of Social Welfare,* 22(3): 248-259.

Morolong, B.; Lekoko, R. & Magang, V. 2015. Dynamics of public training in a university setting: Promoting excellence through leadership. In: O.M. Modise (ed.). *Cases on Leadership in Adult Education.* Hersley: IGI Global: 281-295.

Moseley, W.G. 2016. Agriculture on the brink: Climate change, labour and smallholder farming in Botswana. *Land,* 5(3): 21-35.

Mosha, A.C. 2015. Urban agriculture in Botswana. *Commonwealth Journal of Local Governance,* 18: 42-67.

Mupedziswa, R. & Ntseane, D. 2013. The contribution of non-formal social protection to social development in Botswana. *Development Southern Africa,* 30(1): 84-97. https://doi.org/10.1080/0376835X.2013.756099

Mwansa, L.; Lucas, T. & Osei-Hwedie, K. 1998. The practice of social policy in Botswana. *Journal of Social Development in Africa,* 13(2): 55-74.

Ngwenya, B.N. 2008. *Invisible upkeep: Local Institutions and the Democratisation of Development in Botswana: A Case study of Village Development Committees in Ngamiland.* Gaborone: Bay Publishing.

Ngwenya, B.N. 2003. Redefining kin and family social relations: Burial societies and emergency relief in Botswana. *Journal of Social Development in Africa,* 18(1): 85-110.

Ngwenya, B.N. 2002. Gender, dress and self-empowerment: Women and burial societies in Botswana. *African Sociological Review,* 6(2): 1-27.

Oduro, A.D. 2010. *Formal and informal social protection in Sub-Saharan Africa.* http://erd.eui.eu/media/2010/Oduro_Formal%20and%20Informal%20Social%20Protection%20in%20Africa.pdf [Accessed 11 September 2016].

Olivier, M.P.; Kaseke, E. & Mpedi, L.G. 2008. Informal social security in Southern Africa: Developing a framework for policy intervention. Paper presented at the International conference on Social Security, 10-14 March 2008, Cape Town.

Radipotsane, M.O. 2007. Determinants of household saving and borrowing in Botswana. *IFC Bulletin,* 25: 284-296.

Rankopo, M.J.; Osei-Hwedie, K. & Modie-Moroka, T. 2006. *Five-Country Study on Service and Volunteering in Southern Africa: Botswana Country Report.* http://www.vosesa.org.za/botswana.pdf [Accessed 10 September 2016].

Sekwati, L. 2010. Labour based public works in Botswana: Review of Ipelegeng. *AfricaGrowth Agenda,* Oct / Dec: 23-27.

Seleka, T.B.; Siphambe, H.; Ntseane, D.; Mbere, N.; Kerapeletswe, C. & Sharp, C. 2007. *Social Safety Nets in Botswana: Administration, Targeting and Sustainability.* Gaborone: Lightbooks.

Serema, B.C. 2002. Community information structures in Botswana: A challenge for librarians. Paper presented at the 68th IFLA Council and General Conference, August 18-24, 2002, Glasgow.

Sharma, K.C. 2010. Role of local Government in Botswana for effective service delivery: Challenges, prospects and lessons. *Commonwealth Journal of Local Governance.* Issue 6: 136-142.

Statistics Botswana. 2015. *Botswana Literacy Survey 2013: Stats Brief.* http://www.cso. gov.bw/images/literacy.pdf [Accessed 12 September 2016].

Testa, M.F. & Rolock, N. 1999. Professional foster care: a future worth pursuing. *Journal of Child Welfare,* 78(1):108-24.

The Patriot. 2014. *Khama's poverty projects fail.* http://www.thepatriot.co.bw/news/ item/202-khama-s-poverty-projects-fail.html [Accessed 10 September 2016].

Togarasei, L. 2011. Introduction. In: L. Togarasei, S.K. Mmolai & F. Nkomazana (eds.). *The Faith Sector and HIV/AIDS in Botswana: Responses and Challenges.* Newcastle upon Tyne: Cambridge Scholars Publishing: xi-xvi.

United Nations International Children's Fund (UNICEF). 2012. *Final report for the review of Ipelegeng programme.* http://www.unicef.org/evaluation/files/ Botswana_2012-004_Final_Ipelegeng.pdf [Accessed 11 September 2016].

World Bank. 2016. *Botswana overview.* http://www.worldbank.org/eng/country/ botswana [Accessed 10 September 2016].

World Bank. 2013. *Botswana Social protection Assessment.* http:// documents.worldbank.org/curated/en/421451468199469145/ Botswana-social-protection-assessment. [Accessed 10 September 2016].

World Health Organisation (WHO). 2016. *Botswana: Factsheets of Health Statistics 2016.* http://www.aho.afro.who.int/profiles_information/images/0/05/ Botswana-Statistical_Factsheet.pdf [Accessed 9 September 2016].

02

INDIGENOUS SOCIAL SECURITY SYSTEMS IN POST-COLONIAL NAMIBIA: A BASIS OF LEGITIMACY FOR TRADITIONAL AUTHORITIES

Laura Weidman

Introduction

> The public service... is an interesting example of the transformation involved in the formation of Namibia's new state and highlights to a degree the policy of reconciliation (Lindeke, 2014: 66).

The Namibian Government is driven by the need to reconcile the country and to build on the globally advertised values of modernisation and good governance (UNDP, 1997: 5). Among premises of democracy, transparency and equity, the central state is compelled to taking charge of social protection and security. In the spirit of reconciliation, the legislation is furthermore considerate of demands for cultural rights (Government of the Republic of Namibia, 1990) and includes the Traditional Authorities (henceforth referred to as TAs), as well as customary laws in the legal and administrative systems. In the process of this inclusion however, the TAs' position is undergoing thorough modification.

While the central Government continues to extend and improve on its welfare projects, this inclusion process has also allowed for TAs to substantiate their importance within the *market* of social services. Yet, a TA's status and legitimation depends not solely on formal recognition. Rather, it is grounded in a permanent exchange of legitimisation practices and aspirations in both the formal and informal realms of governance. This chapter thus aims to establish how the TAs' political power and legitimacy are intimately intertwined with protection and services, building on the promise that security is only legitimately offered by those who are assumed to have the power to threaten such security (Duffield, 2002: 161). The central claim of this chapter is that the local power negotiations implicate a TA's recognition – or legitimisation – with much more immediacy than their formal acknowledgment in the national governance system. This claim is not new, albeit contested by authors who perceive a general shift in governance systems which render "traditional institutions of checks and balances on power and accountability [...] obsolete, or at the very least less effective" (Van Kersbergen & Van Waarden, 2004: 155).

To shed light on this specific matter, it is important to ask the question: How do TAs adjust their offers in social security systems to new state projects and changing local interests, in order to support their own authority? This question is based on the assumption that in the present situation, all TAs (in this study those belonging to the traditional community of the *Oukwanyama*, encompassing Headmen and women who lead at the village and regional levels) aim to maintain or increase their power and pursue strategies that involve social services in any of their diverse forms. A legal anthropological perspective helps to understand these different strategies, of which each reflects certain understandings of fairness, entitlements and tradition. This provides a picture of how the different strategy patterns impact on local relations among state authorities, the TAs and the Namibian citizens.

In this chapter, the TAs are formally considered the embodiment of indigenous governance and social security patterns, as the Traditional Authorities Act (TAA) Section 3.1 states:

> [T]he functions of a traditional authority, [...] shall be to promote peace and welfare amongst the members of that community, supervise and ensure the observance of the customary law of that community by its members, [...] (TAA, 2000).

Paradoxically, however, this formalisation itself weakens many of its 'indigenous' aspects for instance, its formable nature (Bennett & Vermeulen, 1980: 210-211). This flexibility is inhibited by the formal documentation and delimitation of TAs' responsibilities and their resulting upward accountability. While a Village Head (wo) man may distribute bags of maize meal from the drought relief programme according to his/her personal estimation of each households' need for assistance (Interviews with a Headman, 22 and 26 November 2013), any villager who feels treated unfairly may lay a complaint with the local Government representative. Thus, while those indigenous social services, which conform to the Government's values are strengthened, others such as transfers of food or labour between Headmen and villagers are under the threat of disappearing from the TA's scope of action. This can either be due to a lack of time, money, sovereignty, or simply because the effort is not worthwhile. However, new ways are found to fill the gaps in statutory social service provisions, which TAs adopt as a substitute source of legitimation. The next section delves deeper into ISSS and allied issues in the Namibian context.

Traditional leaders and social services – a historical perspective

The opinion that social security and services play a vital role in the TAs' legitimisation is widely shared among scholars of African societies (Utas, 2012: 8-9; Hayes & Haipinge 1997; Dobler, 2008). TAs remain the anticipated providers of a sustainable setting for livelihoods, through ensuring that valid capitals and capabilities resiliently retain their values (Ingram, Ros-Tonen & Dietz, 2015: 3). The research that informs this chapter was based on the Oukwanyama TA. In this regard, this TA has a long history of knitting power and social services tightly together. The former also served as tools for promoting personal or collective legitimisation throughout the pre-colonial and colonial periods (Kyed & Buur, 2006: 11). For example, a local narrative of King Mandume, leader of the Oukwanyama at the beginning of the 20th century, presents him as a role model in terms of leadership. He had provided security as a means of effecting socio-economic stability and prosperity for the whole kingdom:

> These [naturally rich] people will help to save the nation during a serious period of hunger. [...] If people are being killed because of their property, then others will not have courage to work hard and accumulate property because they fear for their lives (Hayes & Haipinge, 1997: 50).

The foregoing argument mirrors the 'traditional' discourse of the time as it related to the protection of individuals and property among the Oukwanyama. Considering the limited access to Government services in the area, it only makes sense that material welfare and security – "output legitimacy" (van Kersbergen & van Waarden, 2004: 156), or "performance legitimacy" (Williams, 2010), still take priority over the integrity of political processes, or "input legitimacy" (van Kersbergen & van Waarden, 2004: 156).

Wealth, Cattle and Traditional Tenure

Devereux and Getu (2013a) explain that it is more difficult to provide social protection for pastoralists than it is for other groups, "because of low population density [...] limited road networks and telecommunications infrastructure" and "different sources of vulnerability." As a result, these groups are more likely to continue to rely on what the two authors refer to as 'informal mutual support systems' (Devereux & Getu, 2013a: 6). Because the former challenges prevent state services from reaching the rural areas in the former homelands, both in time and actual scope, TAs remain vital service providers for their community members' well-being. Thus, it can be argued that the TAs' advantage over the central Government hinges on their political and geographical vicinity to their communities (Thévenot, Moody & Lafaye, 2000: 249). Therefore, their understanding of the community's ideas regarding social needs and fairness is thus central to their legitimacy that the state cannot easily substitute.

Whilst scrutinising the history of power dynamics in Namibia's north-central kingdoms, where the Oukwanyama are located, Dobler (2008: 13) traces the circular influence of wealth (in the form of cattle) and political power back to a relation of patronage between a chief and his subjects. Furthermore, a foundation of a local Headman's legitimacy is the maintaining of social cohesion among the community members (Dobler, 2014: 191-192). Chabal (2011) deduces that the exercise of power and the basis of political legitimacy remain essentially patrimonial, which means that accountability is conceived in terms of what patrons can deliver to their clients (Chabal, 2011: 106). We are thus not dealing with a service-for-money-system, but with one that exchanges services for power. Hence, it is not a Headman's or Headwoman's mere wealth that defines his/her legitimacy, but rather his/her performance in sharing and facilitating benefits to his/her community. One Headman explains:

> [S]ometimes I help the old people in my village. I have to give them one bag of 15 kg [of Pearl Millet]. Ja, just to sustain themselves. But only to the old, old people. [...] I must know [...] that person (Interview with Headman, 16 February 2014).

Albeit this sponsorship, in cases of emergency this has not essentially changed, political participation and power narratives have diversified from the 1940s onwards. According to Dobler (2014) this shift coincided with a movement of the younger, economically stronger individuals calling for more attention to their political interests. They consequently take on positions in the national Government, notwithstanding them lacking traditional leadership assets (Dobler, 2014: 190). Despite this slow detraditionalisation in some political spheres, local land governance retains the typically traditional or indigenous marker of closely entangled economic transactions and social ties. Prominent evidence of this is the continued customary payments for land. According to descriptions by several TAs and communal farmers, land allocations never consist of an economic transaction alone, but implicate a process of intense social evaluation. The contract does not entail a property-versus-payment logic, but rather symbolises an applicant's dedication to the land and to the community membership. A comparable transaction is applied when a TA acquires a village or a district. This moment that public wealth demonstration provides the communities with a confidence that the TA is able and willing to render the services and protection, he 'owes' them as his subjects.

The central state and formal recognition of traditional actors and services

Logan (2011) and Lindeke (2014: 84) agree that in Namibia, no functioning alternative to the TAs has been established on a local scale of governance so far, either because local Government branches "have simply never been introduced, or have been established so recently that traditional leaders still remain virtually the only source of public authority in rural areas" (Logan, 2011: 3). Not least due to their knowledge of the local population and its needs, the traditional leaders have officially been included in several Government projects and initiatives. Nevertheless, they remain in an ambivalent realm between formal and informal, statutory and customary, public and private. It is a matter of continuing debate, whether the state's reliance on TAs stems from lack of resources (whether lacking or a reluctance to invest), or a deliberate calculation to capitalise the TAs' 'customary' role as providers of services and security. Instead of addressing this question, this chapter asks *how* the state and the TAs coexist by looking at their relationships' politics of inclusion and exclusion and how responsibilities are distributed or transferred between the two.

Tenure security: Who is to provide it?

An important aspect of indigenous social security is a provision of a legal framework to secure land tenure in communal areas, which were formerly demarcated as Homelands: Constitutionally, land is accessible to all (Constitution of Namibia, 1990), but in

33

communal areas, it is not to be privately owned. Instead, it is held in a trust, especially for the "traditional communities", in particular of "the landless" and for "the purpose of promoting the economic and social development" (Parliament of the Republic of Namibia, 2002). As a basis for agriculture, residence and business, land is substantial for many forms of livelihoods and their security. Its legal governance – especially the provision of fair access and protection of land rights – thus requires careful administration. In this matter, as mentioned earlier, the Government relies on the established position of traditional leaders. Their knowledge of people's yet undocumented identities, marital status and land rights are only few of the factors that render the TAs indispensable in the governance chain (Ingram *et al*, 2015). Building on this knowledge, their role within the social security network is not limited to the administration of land rights. They also vitally support the distribution of Government grants such as old-age pensions, grants for vulnerable and orphaned children, disabled people and the drought relief programme. Their support involves management and facilitation of the distribution itself, but also bookkeeping of beneficiaries and payments. On the other hand, they transmit the community's needs to the ministerial offices (Interview with Headwoman, 15 March 2014). The TAs thus literally embody the nexus between formal and Indigenous Social Security Systems.

Whether this reluctance of taking control is generally due to lack of motivation or because of *de facto* power, is often difficult to determine. Naturally, if an administrative duty carries more threat to their immediate legitimisation than potential gains, the interest of a TA in enforcing the Government's land policies is meagre. Apart from lack of economic reward for their governance support, the TAs' fundamental means for control are inhibited through rising state interference. The use of force as a means of coercion has become an exclusive privilege of the modern state, with its sovereign claims over the citizens' bodies (Foucault, 1994: 18-19). However, in communal areas the police force often only intervenes when violent conflicts occur; verbal disputes or threats are still referred to the traditional leaders (Informal discussion with a Villager, on 13 February 2013). A second traditional means of coercion, the social control within communities, is threatened by increasing social and spatial mobility, and absenteeism, which all weaken the controllability of more mobile members. With these two coercion mechanisms rendered illegal or ineffective respectively, positive incentives remain as the only means for TAs' legitimisation; either by fostering the 'common identity' to gain moral legitimisation, or by offering services to earn performance legitimisation.

During research, various stakeholders were asked about their sense and opinion of the tasks a TA should fulfil these days. One Clerk from the regional Ministry of Local and Regional Government and Housing (MLRGH) argued, as to why Headmen should not be paid by the Government in exchange for their role in the chain of outreach for state services, as follows:

> [The TA's] are used as committees, and the committees are not paid, in most cases [...] most of the committees they are there for the people because we want people to be involved, to decide [...]. [The G]overnment will definitely not at this stage [...] pay these committees. But as part of decentralisation they are saying it is you to take care of your resources! Manage it, but we are not paying you to manage your resources! Because it is working in your benefit (Interview with a Clerk at a regional Ministry of Local and Regional Government and Housing on 17 July 2014).

Leaders of an indigenous system, who build on traditional foundations of authority and coercion, are hence re-interpreted as volunteering citizens, however with immense responsibilities and accountability towards state institutions.

The responsibility to provide security

The discourse of good governance ascribes national Governments the responsibility to provide their citizens with a minimal living standard and protection. In this normativity, all informal mechanisms and 'institutions' are highly contested matters – especially if they are of such autonomous design as are traditional power systems in Namibia. Numerous authors (most of whom focus on African contexts) argue for a view that is more inclusive with indigenous social security mechanisms, stressing that those are locally rooted in the identities and common sense and thus closer to local realities than the globalising idea of a nation-state (Hebo, 2013: 9; Polack, Cotula & Côte, 2013: 3). Others argue for a complete nationalisation of social welfare and social protection, claiming that informal mechanisms are not designed to alleviate poverty and that their sustenance can thus only lead to more social inequality (Olivier, Kaseke & Mpedi, 2008: 17). A counter argument to any approach that monopolises the state's role in security matters, builds on the power-narrative that a discourse on security offers. By fostering a fear of chaos, a promise for security can achieve far-reaching powers (Bubandt, 2005), regardless whether the actor is the state, TA or an individual. This strategy takes effect particularly in plural legal societies where this fear is increased by "the assumed dissolution of centres of Government authority" (Von Benda-Beckmann, von Benda-Beckmann & Eckert, 2009: 7). This scenario can be an actual symptom of the Namibian context, in which services or protection are now offered and recognised by different and dynamic authorities.

The state intervenes

Devereux and Getu (2013a: 5) ask: "What if the state, instead of being a protector, is one of the threats that citizens need to be protected against?" In a plural legal system like Namibia, where the Government is visibly overwhelmed by the number and diversity of claims it must register, this question is valid. Every citizen assesses which authority provides better for their interests, namely for social services and protection. Devereux and Getu identify the two as mutual consequences and components: "[S] ocial protection interventions that stimulate the demand for social services without a corresponding increase in the availability and quality of the supply-side will not achieve the desired outcome" (Devereux & Getu, 2013b: 6-7). With two authorities competing for legitimisation, this double-service stands on unsteady grounds. Land registration through the Government for instance fails to ensure complete tenure security, despite this being its main goal and benefit. The Government remains the owner of the land and reserves its right to expropriate it in the public interest (CLRA, 2002). Toulmin views this arrangement in a critical light:

> Many Governments claim ownership of land, with customary use rights recognised only when land is not sought by other more powerful interests, including the state (2009: 11).

In this perspective, the 'security' provided by the Government appears nearly as ambivalent as the previous system which was governed by the TAs.

Case studies: Of priorities, capital forms and ways to serve the nation

One key features of 'bigmanity' in Africa is its relational character (Utas, 2012: 8-9). Also, its authority is not hierarchically fixed, but depends on its legitimisation within the community, as well as by the statutory control system. Legitimisation as a form of social interaction can either be formalised or spontaneous, depending on the different capitals (Bourdieu, 2012) that are employed. The basis of this approach is provided by Bourdieu's concept of how capital sets, and symbolic capital specifically, that which is engaged in strategic moves in the making of the "legitimation of the social world" (Bourdieu, 1989: 21) and in the pursuit of imposing "the scale of values most favourable to [one's] products." A reference to 'tradition' for instance, can be engaged as a "mobilising metaphor" to achieve legitimisation for a certain action (Kyed & Buur, 2006: 11). More short-term, individual means of negotiation can be categorised in three strategy types: Conservationist, Developmental and Social Advisor. They are by no means a complete list of all possible or existing strategies. However, they do not describe types of actors, but rather types of acting. One actor may combine several of these strategies simultaneously and transform from one to another over time, or switch between them in different socio-political contexts.

Conservationist approach

To maintain their authority as land managers, some TAs come up with innovative land use and land distribution plans. A conservationist strategy describes a proactive engagement in the conservation of the community's livelihood, or certain aspects of it. Because it cannot be supported by coercive mechanisms, consensus and co-operation among community members is needed to successfully implement a conservationist project. One example of such a project is the securing of a communal grazing area within the village. By keeping the cattle in the vicinity to the crop fields, soil fertility is preserved. In one observed case such a grazing project is merely based on the social agreement on a settlement-free zone (Interview with a senior Headman, 27 February 2014), in another, it is assured by the instalment of a fence around the common grazing area (Interview with a senior Headman, 14 March 2014), and in a third case, where the village contains no more space for grazing, the Headman organises the sharing of a cattle post (seasonal grazing areas, away from villages or towns) among his villagers (Interview with a senior Headman, 31 March 2014). A fourth example describes a much more personal strategy. This relates to where a Village Headman advised his villagers to extend their land parcels, in such a way that there were no empty spaces left to be registered (Informal group interview with Villagers, on 16 March 2013). Such advice clearly aims at the enclosure of the village against new settlers from *outside*. It may lead to preserving the community's grazing areas comparably to the other strategies.

This may mark confidence towards the villagers and their ability to self-govern the land and to build almost exclusively on social cohesion and consensus. In backing out of the land allocation *business*, which for many remains an important basis for legitimacy, this TA functionary avoids potential allegations of *clientelism* or favouritism, but arguably he merely evades his accountabilities. The sensitive aspect in these conservationist strategies lies in the volatility of the community's livelihood choices. If all members – or the most powerful among them – accept a grazing area (or any other land management plan) as legitimate, or at the very least, not as contradictory to their interests, a Headman (or woman) may gain a strong acceptance through such projects. The required *assets* are thus not strictly contained; economic or political capital can however, and often does, enhance the speed of implementation and the number of available projects. In any case, symbolic capital in the form of trust by the community is needed for the implementation and the persistence of the project. Legitimisation is gained through proving to be loyal to the community by presence, engagement and identifying with similar problems and priorities as the community members themselves.

Development approach

At times, a Headman/woman locates the needs of the community in modernisation rather than by conserving customary ways. This is what this author refers to as the Development approach. Taking on a Development approach is not a deliberate choice *per se*, but rather an effect of a Headman's professional identity and network. As gatekeepers to state offices or political parties, these individuals often hold exclusive information on state policies and laws. They preside over political and mobile capital, mostly through their profession or education, are therefore assumed to have knowledge of state services and – even more importantly – have practical ideas on how to implement them in their communities. In short, these Headmen do what is expected of them by all stakeholders: They operate as a link between the Ministries and their communities. One Headman explains his role like this:

> NamPower [the national electricity utility] does not feel the pain, but it is the community that feels a need. [Even if] there are now counsellors who are as a channel [it] is the community that must take a step through the Headman and then [the] counsellors will contact NamPower (Interview with a former Headman, 15 March 2014).

One Headman in a more densely populated and serviced area is even involved in applying for the village's declaration as town land. All reasons he states how this would benefit his community, are directly linked to services and protection. As land becomes a commodity, the community will consequently gain access to insurance, loans and compensations (Interview with Headman, 14 July 2014). This same Headman also advertises public participation in the development discourse and follows thus a 'modern' politics approach by having established a "developmental committee of the village." He states that it purposefully includes some younger people, "just to see whether we come up [with] some new ideas [on] how to develop our village." In a similar way he also shares his authority in land disputes with a committee consisting of village elders "who know the area." Such subdivision of authority benefits the TA in a way that is strengthening the community's involvement and co-responsibility and the trust in his intentions to serve the community's needs rises considerably.

To summarise the development strategy, the concepts of 'development' and 'participation' are actively engaged in the management of the village, whilst nursing a sense of complicity. Meanwhile, the Headman acts as a mouthpiece for the community by lobbying for protection and welfare. Interestingly, despite the modernist development-discourse, the customary cattle and/or crop farming sustains a high priority in the development strategy of all observed villages. A development strategy may of course also provoke protest, when TAs attempt to provide a material form of development through their own means. There is a thin line between what may be promoted as social services in the name of development and what is identified as a business effort for private gains. The following statement shows how delicate, yet manifest, it is to make personal profit in the name of *public interest* or of *development*:

> [In earlier] days, [a Headman] was seen as a son of [...] that village, so you have that thing, you know, to assist the people with goods! [...] Yah, but you see, it's not really fitting in a... in a [tradition – note from the author], [such] big thing [as the retail businesses of Mr. X]. You have to have a shebeen (unregulated beer business) with the commodities you know, [so that you] can satisfy the immediate needs of the people, yah, but sometimes you have all sort of things. As I said you know, traditionally... they have to be careful (Interview with a Journalist, 23 July 2014).

Particularly the last sentence underlines that TAs find themselves manoeuvring between material services that are perceived as a required service to their community and those that are considered illegitimate self-enrichment. To circumvent such moral conflictions, some TA's, retreat from economic projects to a strategy of exclusive and social leadership.

Social Advisor

If a village is assumed by a town authority, or if no more unallocated land remains within its realms, a Headman has no choice but to withdraw from land governance. In accordance with Duffield's equation (Duffield, 2002: 161), the TA's influence on land tenure then dissolves, because the Headman has neither the power to protect, nor to threaten a land right. One Headman of those encountered had experienced that transition (Interview of 4 April 2014). To maintain an authority status notwithstanding, he actively exerts himself for a subject-focused leadership, by aiming to offer arbitration services of high quality. Necessary assets are the disposal over time and presence in a village, diplomatic skills, historical and customary knowledge and an understanding of everyday troubles of the villagers.

In some of the observed cases, this role of a social advisor was outsourced to (or gradually taken over by) a Deputy Headman, committee, or secretary, while the Headman resided outside the village (Interview with Headman, 16 March 2014). As further example, the *Men and Women Network* (a semi-vigilante organisation acting as a village patrol where state police is understaffed or lack a mandate for active prevention), simultaneously helps the TAs in their representation and coercion and leads to a stronger social involvement and participation in village matters (Village Meeting, observation of 1 February 2014). This subdivision of authority at times earns the Headman legitimisation as promoter of decentralisation and community participation.

Clientelism, corruption and abuse of power

The three types of strategy outlined above share a common goal, namely, achieving or sustaining a lasting legitimation within the village community. Such a power basis relies however not merely on the actions or capitals of TAs or officially assigned authorities, but on all holders of any form of symbolic capital. There are two possible rational motivations for TAs to abuse their power status. If a leader esteems his/her status of authority to be particularly strong, he/she may act with less consideration for the agreement or legitimacy of his/her entire community. In a contrary situation, when a leader finds his/her authority basis melting away, he/she may engage in unacceptable practices in a strike of resignation. As wealth discrepancies increase within village communities, frictions between different sets of values rise and can ultimately deteriorate social cohesion (Hebo, 2013: 37).

Elderly people are especially interested in the continuity of traditional values and social services, because they lack resources in modern capitals, such as political and economic and this results in general an "insecurity of life" (Van Beek, 2011: 41), to which the well-connected, mobile and rich members of the community are more immune. Such insecurity provokes a need for a "powerful figure over one's head", which makes the former more vulnerable towards a TA's despotic practices:

> Clientelism in such conditions is a security arrangement, costly in individual pride, but efficient as a productive use of one's social capital (Van Beek, 2011: 41).

A term like clientelism and its moral condemnation offers an instrument to contest a TA's despotic behaviour. However, this discourse has become a tool for the politically and legally educated only, while the vulnerable members are restricted in employing national symbols and thus remain at the mercy of the traditional leaders, or other elites in the village:

> You cannot say anything against this [well-connected] person. Because if you lose this person, you will lose the wealth of the village. [...] This person is the one who is connected, and if this person withdraws, she will withdraw with her the developments and you will feel it, [...]. (Interview with a Clerk at the regional Ministry of Lands, 14 November 2013).

What this Ministry clerk describes is a commonly encountered perception among the rural population. It explains why corrupt or clientelistic practices *de facto* remain accepted to a considerable extent, despite being opposed by a strong normative narrative. And this acceptance is not only restricted to an informal common sense, but it is even legally prescribed that a traditional leader serves *his* community exclusively in promoting peace, welfare and affirmative action (TAA of 2000). The most problematic aspect of such particularising politics is to reconcile it with an equal or fair delivery of social services. As has been touched upon earlier, in rural areas – and especially among the less wealthy

– legitimacy can be extorted by advertising (the prospect of) service delivery through personal funds. In other words, output legitimacy can cause communities to turn a blind eye to the TA's corrupt or clientelistic practices. However, the community may be driven by multiple interests and often the wealth distribution turns TAs into clients of wealthier community members.

Conclusion

The case presented in this chapter illustrates how in north-central Namibia the indigenous social security and service systems are yet far from completely assumed by the state; offering room, instead, for the TAs to re-invent and renegotiate their individual power identity. If performance and 'development' are in demand in the Ohangwena region, performance legitimacy remains "a critical part of the overall legitimation process" (Williams, 2010: 29). The service of security is yet going to have a longer-lasting effect on local legitimacies. In either role – as provider of security or development – a TA's legitimacy is determined by its ability to negotiate potential threats or opportunities for its community. A TA thus requires strong links with the Government, legal and political knowledge, and mobile capital, to deal with non-state actors and a certain economic sufficiency, preventing clientelistic or corrupt practices. The increasing heterogeneity in capital sets, values, livelihood trajectories and accordingly diversifying expectations towards social services, alter relations of power and thus, the constellations of those who may potentially threaten and provide security (Duffield, 2002: 161). It will therefore not suffice for a TA to rely on one strategy without keeping track of its community's needs and especially those which are not consensual:

> The transformation of the chieftaincy [...] will ultimately depend upon whether traditional leaders will make decisions that are consistent with the existing moral order (Williams, 2010: 230).

As much as the TAs engage in different social service projects, their motivations and priorities will be diverse and volatile. And the choice of strategies is not to the least dependent on available capital forms of the TA and to a considerable extent to those of their village's elite. In general, all strategic types this chapter has described are easier to perform for those who hold "large amounts of symbolic capital" and "who are well-known and recognised" (Bourdieu, 1989: 21-22), but not all TAs fulfil these conditions to the same degree. Namibia's national security agenda relies considerably on indigenous mechanisms and services. The latter are generally quicker to perceive and respond to local needs and often dispose over more human resources in marginalised rural areas. This shows how, at this point in decentralisation, their inclusion appears to be the most efficient and impartial mode to provide social security to Namibian citizens. According to the United Nations discourse, their role ought however not to extend to a degree, in which the Government abdicates its responsibilities (UNECOSOC, 2001: 5). It is thus a matter of on-going negotiations to include the TAs in a way that supports the Government administratively, without undermining the public's trust in the state's intentions to achieve a democratic, modern form of national governance.

It is thus crucial for the Government to observe any shifts in effectiveness and acceptance of social security services – both by the state and by traditional leaders – and react promptly upon detection of a gap therein. After all, if the indigenous mechanisms fail, the responsibility of providing all services would fall on the Government. The TAs' co-operation is a fundamental complement for Namibia's welfare services, but they exist in an unsteady realm between the informal and the formal. A complete formalisation of traditional mechanisms may deprive the TAs of their sources of legitimisation, but increasing competition over capitals threatens their legitimacy within the informal realm. In the meantime, the Namibian security governance relies on both the formal and the *indigenous* institutions and mechanisms, constituting a constant tension between national normative discourse and legal and practical realities.

References

Bennett, T.W. & Vermeulen, T. 1980. Codification of Customary Law. *Journal of African Law*, 24 (2): 206-219. https://doi.org/10.1017/S0021855300009542

Bourdieu, P. 2012. *Die feinen Unterschiede. Kritik der gesellschaftlichen Urteilskraft. 22. Edition.* Frankfurt am Main: Suhrkamp.

Bourdieu, P. 1989. Social Space and Symbolic Power. *Sociological Theory*, 7(1): 14-25. https://doi.org/10.2307/202060

Bubandt, N. 2005. Vernacular Security. The Politics of Feeling Safe in Global, National and Local Worlds. *Security Dialogue*, 36(3): 275-296. https://doi.org/10.1177/0967010605057015

Chabal, P. 2011. How can Africa develop? Reflections on theories, concepts and realities. In: J. Abbnik & M. de Bruijn (eds.). *Land, law and politics in Africa: mediating conflict and reshaping the state.* Leiden: Brill: 99-116. https://doi.org/10.1163/9789004218062_007

Devereux, S. & Getu M. 2013. The conceptualisation and status of informal and formal social protection in Sub-Saharan frica. In: S. Devereux & M. Getu (eds.). *Informal and formal social protection systems in Sub-Saharan Africa.* Addis Ababa: Organisation for Social Science Research in Eastern and Southern Africa (OSSREA). 1-8.

Dobler, G. 2014. Traders and trade in colonial Ovamboland, 1925-1990. *Elite formation and the politics of consumption under indirect rule and apartheid.* Basel: Basler Afrika Bibliographien.

Dobler, G. 2008. Boundary-drawing and the notion of territoriality in pre-colonial and early colonial Ovamboland. *Journal of Namibian Studies*, 3: 7-30.

Duffield, M. 2002. War as a Network Enterprise: The New Security Terrain and its Implications. *Cultural Values*, 6 (1-2):153-165. https://doi.org/10.1080/1362517022019793

Foucault, M. 1994. *Überwachen und Strafen. Die Geburt des Gefängnisses. 1. Aufl.* Frankfurt am Main: Suhrkamp.

Government of the Republic of Namibia. 1990. *The Namibian Constitution.* 1990. http://www.namibweb.com/const.htm [Accessed 14 November 2012].

Hayes, P. & Haipinge, D. 1997. *'Healing the Land': Kaulinge's History of Kwanyama. Oral Tradition and History by the late Reverend Vilho Kaulinge of Ondobe as Told to Patricia Hayes and Natangwe Shapange.* Köln: Rüdiger Köppe.

Hebo, M. 2013. 'Giving is Saving': The Essence of Reciprocity as an Informal Social Protection System among the Arsii Oromo, Southern Ethiopia. In: S. Devereux & M. Getu (eds.). *Informal and formal social protection systems in Sub-Saharan Africa.* Addis Ababa: Organisation for Social Science Research in Eastern and Southern Africa (OSSREA): 9-42.

Ingram, V.; Ros-Tonen, M.A.F. & Dietz, T. 2015. A fine mess: bricolaged forest governance in Cameroon. *International Journal of the Commons*, 9 (1): 1-23. https://doi.org/10.18352/ijc.516

Kyed, H.M. & Buur, L. 2006. *Recognition and Democratisation: 'New Roles' for Traditional Leaders in Sub-Saharan Africa.* Danish Institute for International Studies Working Paper. 11: 1-25.

Lindeke B. 2014. Conflict resolution by institutional design: Democratic development and state formation in independent Namibia – public service and decentralisation experiences. *Journal of Namibian Studies*, 15: 63-93.

Logan, C. 2011. The Roots of Resilience: Exploring Popular Support for African Traditional Authorities. *Afrobarometer Working Papers*, 128.

Office of the President. 2004. *Namibia Vision 2030: Policy Framework for Long-term National Development.* Windhoek: Office of the President.

Olivier, M.P.; Kaseke, E. & Mpedi, L.G. 2008. Informal Social Security in Southern Africa: Developing a Framework for Policy Intervention. Paper prepared for presentation at the International Conference on Social Security organised by the National Department of Social Development, South Africa, 10-14 March, Cape Town.

Parliament of the Republic of Namibia. 2002. Communal Land Reform Act. Act No. 5, 2002. *Government Gazette of the Republic of Namibia,* 2787, August 2002. Windhoek: Parliament of the Republic of Namibia.

Parliament of the Republic of Namibia. 2000. Traditional Authorities Act. TAA No. 25, 2000. *Government Gazette of the Republic of Namibia 2456,* 22 December 2000. Windhoek: Parliament of the Republic of Namibia.

Polack, E.C.; Cotula, L. & Côte, M. 2013. *Accountability in Africa's land rush: What role for legal empowerment?* London: International Institute for Environment and Development (IED) and International Development Research Centre (IDRC).

Thévenot, L.; Moody, M. & Lafaye, C. 2000. Forms of valuing nature: Arguments and modes of justification in French and American environmental disputes. In: M. Lamont & L. Thévenot (eds.). *Rethinking comparative cultural sociology: Repertoires of evaluation in France and the United States.* Cambridge: Cambridge University Press: 229-272.

Toulmin, C. 2009. Securing land and property rights in Sub-Saharan Africa: the role of local institutions. *Land Use Policy,* 26 (1): 10-19. https://doi.org/ 10.1016/j. landusepol.2008.07.006

United Nations Development Programme (UNDP). 1997. *Governance for Sustainable Human Development.* New York: United Nations Development Programme.

United Nations Economic and Social Council (UNECOSOC). 2001. *Enhancing social protection and reducing vulnerability in a globalising world: Report of the Secretary-General on the World Summit for Social Development.* New York: United Nations.

Utas, M. 2012. Introduction: Bigmanity and network governance in African conflicts. In: M. Utas (ed.). *African conflicts and informal power: Big men and networks.* London: Zed Books. 1-34.

Van Beek, W. 2011. Cultural models of power in Africa. In: J. Abbnik & M. de Bruijn (eds.). *Land, law and politics in Africa: Mediating Conflict and Reshaping the State.* Leiden: Brill. 25-48.

Van Kersbergen, K. & van Waarden, F. 2004. 'Governance' as a bridge between disciplines: Cross-disciplinary inspiration regarding shifts in governance and problems of governability, accountability and legitimacy. *European Journal of Political Research*, 43: 143-171. https://doi.org/10.1111/j.1475-6765.2004.00149.x

Von Benda-Beckmann, F.; von Benda-Beckmann, K. & Eckert, J. 2009. Rules of Law and Laws of Ruling: Law and Governance between Past and Future. In: F. von Benda-Beckmann, K. von Benda-Beckmann & J. Eckert (eds.). *Rules of law and laws of ruling. On the governance of law.* Farnham: Ashgate: 1-32.

Williams, J.M. 2010. *Chieftaincy, the state and democracy: Political legitimacy in post-apartheid South Africa.* Bloomington: Indiana University Press.

03

INDIGENOUS SOCIAL SECURITY SYSTEMS IN SWAZILAND

Lungile Mabundza & Clement Dlamini

Introduction

This chapter examines Indigenous Social Security Systems (ISSS) in Swaziland and seeks to cast some light on the state of ISSS, currently in existence in the country. As a point of departure, the authors acknowledge the fact that globally, state-run social security systems emerged because of industrialisation and urbanisation, in the late 19th century, especially in Europe (Ruparanganda, Ruparanganda & Mupfanochiya, 2017: 214). These systems were geared towards the protection of employees from work related injuries, as well as provided pensions to individuals upon retirement (Marc, Graham, Schacter & Schmidt, 1995: 11). In this regard, these "concepts were originally applied to economies where the formal sector was predominant, that were culturally homogenous and where poverty was viewed as transitional. The African context is very different today" (Marc *et al*, 1995). Such a narrow focus of social security presents dilemmas for African countries where ISSS had been in existence for many centuries. For instance, the current problem with the state based social security system in Swaziland is its exclusionary nature as most people in Swaziland are without social security because they do not meet the eligibility criteria as stipulated by formal laws. Because of this exclusion, many of the vulnerable poor have had to rely on ISSS of mutual support, which have been the cornerstone of community life for many African communities and/or families. They have also guaranteed the former's protection from risks and crises (Iliffe, 1989: 58). Even though ISSS have not been recognised for their positive role in the lives of the poor and vulnerable populations, they nonetheless provide a lifeline for most of the vulnerable poor in Swaziland.

According to Ruparangada *et al.* (2017) social security is not new in Africa. Like other African societies, the Swazis had well-established mechanisms of protecting the welfare of their members throughout the lifecycle. They were interdependent and cared for each other and the extended family was the main conduit for kinship care. It is important to note that social security is not merely necessary to achieve social justice, but it is also an indispensable tool in the fight against poverty (Dekker, 2005). Therefore, social security schemes are important in dealing with vulnerability in developing countries such as Swaziland where there are extreme levels of poverty, HIV and AIDS, unemployment and lack of social protection (World Bank, 2012). The model of social security provision adopted by the Swaziland Government has not deviated much from that of the former colonial master – Britain – regardless of the diverse socio-economic and political conditions found in these different countries. Swaziland provides social assistance and social insurance, but these safety nets are not structured to effectively respond to the needs of poor and vulnerable populations. As a result, a significant number of the vulnerable fall through the cracks since the social safety nets (SSNs) are unable to provide comprehensive and/or universal coverage for the vulnerable groups. For instance, social assistance targets the poor and vulnerable members of the society using in-kind and cash transfer type of benefits, but they must meet the eligibility criteria since this is a means-tested programme (Pain, 2016: 10). It can be argued that myriad issues ranging from unpredictability, conditionality and occasional unavailability of resources have compounded the provision of social assistance in Swaziland. Furthermore, the poor are sometimes required to prove that they 'deserve' social assistance (Pain, 2016). Therefore, the different problems faced by vulnerable groups require a diverse portfolio of context-specific social security responses, not merely relying on cash transfers as a one-size-fits-all solution to problems of poor populations.

On the other hand, the social insurance component targets the working class who are in urban areas and it is based on contributions between the employer and employee so that on retirement the individual can earn an income via his/her pension (World Bank, 2012). The main issue with the current social security dispensation in Swaziland is that it excludes at least 70 per cent of the population residing in rural areas where poverty rates are extremely high (World Bank, 2012). Over and above the exclusionary nature of formal social security systems, vulnerable Swazis have had to find alternative survival mechanisms. Dekker (2005: 2) argues that formal social security systems and ISSS can be seen as traveling on parallel roads; one on a tarred road and the other on a dirt road, but they all lead to the same destination.

Unfortunately, as earlier mentioned, countries such as Swaziland have not acknowledged the critical role played by ISSS amidst increasing social insecurity in the country. The lack of recognition of ISSS has not been interrogated by most Governments in Africa as discussed by some authors (Von Benda-Beckman, von Benda-Beckmann, Casino, Hirtz, Woodman & Zacher, 1998; Midgley, 1994; Dekker 2005). Dekker (2005: 2) posits: "An interesting result of the exclusionary nature of the formal social security system is that, for the longest time, people who were excluded from formal social security had no alternative other than to devise social security mechanisms outside the state regulated system." According to the World Bank (2012), 63 per cent of the 1,2 million Swazi people live below the 2 USD (E 14,00 – equivalent currency of Swaziland) per day, suggesting that few people in formal employment and even fewer people in informal employment can afford to contribute towards their social security upon retirement. It also suggests that there is need to expand the social security base so that more people benefit from social welfare and social care services.

Furthermore, in the absence of universal or comprehensive state coverage it means that people are forced to find alternative arrangements to protect themselves against risks and vulnerabilities. These alternative sources of social security are not regulated by the Government, but are based on reciprocity and social networks found in communities and/or families (Apt, 2002). These are arrangements, which have been the foundation of social care within families and communities from time immemorial and which are referred to as ISSS in this book and chapter. Arguably, ISSS rarely feature in Government discussions, but their role cannot be overemphasised as more people are not being captured by formal systems and thus live without adequate protection or cushioning mechanisms. The definition of social security in Swaziland omits ISSS, as well as the individuals involved in informal employment and this issue needs to be considered when defining social security in the country. This chapter emanates from an empirical research, which was undertaken by the authors. It had sought to ascertain the extent and reach of ISSS in Swaziland. In addition, this research was informed by earlier collaborative efforts, involving Southern African and West African academics and researchers, of which these authors were part.

In March 2016, the University of Johannesburg hosted an International Workshop on Indigenous Social Security Systems, which had attempted to identify synergies between the former and Government policies in Southern and West Africa. The argument that was advanced by the Workshop was that Indigenous Social Security Systems could no longer be ignored because of the important role they played in protecting vulnerable groups in society. Also, it was prudent to investigate if Governments in the Southern and West African regions acknowledged ISSS and if they had created linkages between the formal social security systems and ISSS. Thereafter, the participants of the Workshop were challenged to undertake research that would establish whether ISSS existed in their various countries or not and determine whether such systems were incorporated into public policy-making.

Flowing from the foregoing, the research in Swaziland hinged on the following objectives:

1. To determine the existence of Indigenous Social Security Systems in Swaziland.
2. To explore the importance of Indigenous Social Security Systems to ordinary people in Swaziland.
3. To investigate and determine whether the Government of Swaziland incorporated Indigenous Social Security Systems into mainstream Government public policies and public policy responses.
4. To make recommendations on how Indigenous Social Security Systems could be incorporated in Swaziland's public policy-making processes.

State social security systems, policies and programmes in Swaziland

The Constitution of the Kingdom of Swaziland of 2005 makes social security provision a responsibility of the state – in satisfying its social contract to its citizenry. It can be argued that state-based social security has not digressed much from that of the colonial state where social protection was a 'privilege' for the selected few. However, this was not the case in the traditional set-up. Traditionally, the portfolios of the Queen Mother included ensuring the development of communities, and attending to welfare issues of children, women and older people. The Queen Mother's role also included safeguarding the emotional, spiritual and physical aspects of the nation. Nowadays, there is limited acknowledgement of this critical role played by the Queen Mother. The Queen Mother through *Philani MaSwati* (a charity organisation) has been instrumental in advocating for the needs of older people, as well as other vulnerable groups. She has been the "whisperer behind the stool". She has been a liaison between vulnerable populations and services. All her efforts eventually paid off when the King of Swaziland, His Majesty Mswati III, through a decree during the opening of Parliament in 2005, decried the levels of vulnerability ranging from old age poverty, orphaned and vulnerable children and rural-urban migration to the HIV pandemic in the country and how the former negatively impacted on the lives of the elderly. Consequently, the Government quickly established the Old Age Grant (OAG). This was an indirect way of supplementing while formalising the Queen Mother's informal methods used in meeting the needs of vulnerable groups. As a formal social security mechanism, the OAG lacks risk and needs identification, assessment and management – all of which have significantly undermined the effectiveness of the OAG. Due to the gaps that still exist, *Philani MaSwati* continues to provide food parcels, blankets and other essential items to older people

Since the turn of the 21ˢᵗ century, social security in Africa has taken precedence and most Governments on the continent want to be seen doing something in this area. As a result, the Government of Swaziland has ratified several international treaties, agreements and conventions, which advocate for better and universal or comprehensive social security provisions. To domesticate social security provisions, Swaziland hosted a social protection conference in 2011, where international experts presented papers on the different options that Swaziland could adopt in terms of a social protection floor. This was by far a giant step that demonstrated the commitment of the Government of Swaziland to find a social protection floor that effectively deals with the needs of the vulnerable poor in the country. In 2016, the Government of Swaziland welcomed a task team from the European Union (EU). Since then it has been reviewing the social security system in the country, with an emphasis on how Swaziland can improve the social security provision to the vulnerable and poor in Swaziland. Of significance, is the recognition of decentralised structures in the regions and communities, which can assist in making service delivery more efficient and sufficient.

The Swaziland National Pension Fund

At present there is a proposed draft law under consideration at the Ministry of Labour and Social Security (MoLSS), entitled "Swaziland National Pension Fund Bill, 2016," which has been prepared and submitted to the MoLSS for consideration. However, this has yet to be taken to consultation with all stakeholders. This draft law envisages the establishment of a new national pension fund that will ultimately replace the Swaziland National Provident Fund (SNPF) with a pension scheme that mirrors some schemes in other SADC countries. It envisages a new administration, new pension scheme, provision for the transition to the new fund, whilst maintaining present members' entitlements at the same level for those over 45 years of age, but with options to buy-in etc. and those who are younger having access to the new pension scheme (Pain, 2016). It envisages also a different level of contribution payable (arguably above the current ten per cent evenly split between employers and employees subject to fresh actuarial assessment), with a minimum and a ceiling being applied. This pension system will provide for indexation of pensions each year. Pensions provided include retirement, invalidity and survivors in addition to a funeral grant. It does *not* make any provision for short-term benefits such as illness, unemployment or maternity benefits. It is also expected to find ways of incorporating those who are in the informal sector and who are in dire need of social security coverage (Pain, 2016).

Furthermore, the EU Technical Task Team is proposing an integrated social security system, which would ensure that the most disadvantaged and marginalised households and individuals, whatever their location, would be able to access a basic package of health and education and income support to enable them to cope with chronic and sudden crises without having to overcome barriers of geography or multiple unconnected services. Currently, despite a national PIN system of personal identifiers, health and education records are not integrated and many Swazis who are born at home, especially in rural areas, lack birth registration – a basic identity that can ensure allocation of resources. Currently the Deputy Prime Minister's Office (DPMO) and other Ministries rely on chiefs to be gatekeepers in communities to help locate the most vulnerable children. An integrated social security system will require coherence between these ministries – meaning shared principles, information, support, co-operation and decision-making to maximise benefits from efforts being made and avoid wasting resources, effort and time (Pain, 2016). Such an approach will help reduce and eliminate the risk of families, adults and children of falling into extreme poverty or being excluded from services. In this regard, Government ministries must be seen to lead the way, guide others and thereby encourage all other stakeholders to lead by example in a concerted and coherent manner to the benefit of all concerned (Pain, 2016). According to Pain (2016) developing a single registry and coherent Management Information System (MIS), that is linked to the Local Government *Tinkhundla* structure is critical. *Tinkhundla* is an administrative subdivision that is smaller than a district, but larger than a chiefdom.

There are 55 *Tinkhundla* in Swaziland in total: 14 in the Hhohho District, 11 in the Lubombo District, 16 in the Manzini District and 14 in the Shiselweni District. This registry could ensure that every person has a record of access to health services, education and basic income grants or cash transfers and thus help in avoiding duplication or exclusion (Pain, 2016). The registry could be augmented with the proposed development of community-based monitoring of services and mechanisms for grievances and appeals against errors of exclusion from services. Orphans and Vulnerable Children (OVCs) and school dropouts, antenatal and early childhood care can be monitored when the different service providers communicate at community level without breach of confidentiality. People with disabilities do not have access to the same level of education services and to cash transfers, other than the former welfare grants that lacked unambiguous criteria for disbursement (Pain, 2016). The 2007 National Census projected 16,8 per cent of the population or 170,000 as people with disabilities. However, only just over 5,000 received disability grants (World Bank, 2012).

Taking the abovementioned issues into consideration, it is proposed here that an integrated social security system must be founded on technology levels that are inclusive of all efforts in the social sector. Technology is fundamental to many decisions made by the Government and it also impacts a high percentage of citizens – even though such technology is still being developed within the country (Pain, 2016). Equally important, it must be ensured that controls are in place, to minimise abuse of systems and to maximise confidence that the systems in use are meeting targets and efforts are not being wasted or duplicated and that people are not slipping through the cracks of the system (Pain, 2016). The 2012 Report of the Auditor General on the OAG identified E 1 million losses to the Government, through a range of false claims, although this is less than one per cent of the total disbursement. Therefore, technology would help to curb fraud in the system.

Decentralised structures

The current Government structures are linked to the four Regional Headquarters whereby the Regional Administrator, convening the chiefs and the *Tinkhundla* system, collaborates with the Regional Secretary, convening the Heads of Sector Ministries in the region. This helps to achieve a degree of integration at regional level. However, there are still tendencies for officials to have vertical 'silo' type of reporting to their line Ministries in Mbabane, the capital city, until they face problems in their immediate environment and then seek support from the structure under the Regional Administrator. Professional programme implementers tend to use the chiefs for information and communication and as access points to the community rather than as partners in a responsive service provision. At the household and community level in the rural areas, those in need seek support from their chief to access basic resources, with the respected Rural Health Motivators, chosen by the community and recognised by the Ministry of Health (MoH) through the payment of a small allowance and thus providing the only link with the formal health service system.

There are also 11,000 child protection volunteers trained by the national programme *Lihlombe Lekukhalela*, which provides a link with the police and more remotely with the social welfare system located at regional and urban levels, with limited resources, to meet those in need in their communities (Pain, 2016). Despite the chiefs' commitment to the well-being of their communities, they are not trained to identify beneficiaries and for either manual or electronic registry recording and for monitoring payments and referrals for social welfare interventions. Also, there are no accountability mechanisms in every *Inkhundla*, although the Department of Decentralisation is supporting the pilot use of scorecards (Pain, 2016).

Indigenous Social Security Systems (ISSS) in Swaziland

Indigenous Social Security Systems have been part of the way of life of the Swazi people for centuries. The ISSS are largely based on reciprocity, social care, trust, self-interest, equity, subsidiary and risk sharing. They have made it possible for the most vulnerable groups to have some form of social security. On the other hand, formal social security schemes in Swaziland, as in other developing countries, have an urban bias. They favour those in paid employment and ignore most of the people in the rural areas who are involved in the informal economy (most of whom are women). Even though not adequately defined, ISSS refer to social security as provided by the family, kin and/or community members (Dekker 2008: 119). Reciprocity and social cohesion were the pillars of ISSS... acts of reciprocity, altruism, social cohesion and personal intimacies were sufficient to guarantee social security in both good and bad times to all members of the family by ensuring equity and social justice (Ouma, 1995: 6). An outstanding feature of ISSS is one where the community or individuals conceptualise and define what constitutes ISSS based on the obtaining risks and fortunes. ISSS stands out because it is a way of life and it promotes social care for all kin membership and/or community.

The central pillar of ISSS has been its ability to respond to the corresponding needs of individuals – ranging from shelter, spiritual care, physical care, etc. For instance, in pre-colonial Swaziland, the King kept large storehouses for grain and maintaining food reserves was essential to guard against hunger and scarcity. The chief's granaries, in the community, were also another effective way to provide for the most vulnerable members of the society. Contemporary Swaziland has seen a slight change in the way ISSS are administered. Contemporary ISSS is overseen by the Queen Mother who is taking up the role of 'mothering the nation' and ensuring that people have sufficient food. This is not to suggest that the system of social care is perfect, but it shows the continued existence of the ISSS even in modern times. In most communities there exists fields such as *emasimu endlunkhulu* which are intended to feed the destitute, elderly, OVCs and people living with disabilities. Traditionally, there were mechanisms weaved into the institution of the family to ensure that there were no mendicants or vagabonds in society.

With the growing needs and demands of everyday life, ISSS are expanding compared to the formal social security systems – which exclude most of the poor and vulnerable populations. These days, more and more people need some form of protection, due to their inability to keep up with the high cost of living. Even though the extended family is under tremendous strain, social security support is still the most important source for most of the poor and vulnerable groups in Swaziland. When babies are born, families still celebrate their birth and initiation ceremonies are still practised to show acceptance and support to the new mother and her baby. The extended family continues to provide some form of support during marriages and deaths. Social support, at these critical times, adds credence to the notion that people are social animals who flourish in the company of others: "I am because we are." With the HIV pandemic, the extended family has been a source of security for most of the OVCs who are now being cared for by grandmothers. Also, internal adoptions are still being done, where extended family members take some of the children and support them after their parents die. In times of drought and famine, the family is also a source of security and support. Those members of the family who are well off make use of the cheap labour from relatives who in turn get some of the harvest or money. Those farmers with surplus offer gifts to create some network of obligation amongst the kinsmen or neighbours.

In old age, the extended family is a source of livelihood for the aged. It is also important to state that contemporary ISSS is seeing a shift in the roles within the family whereby grandmothers are caring for younger children without the necessary support they need to effectively care for the OVCs, as well as other family members. The significance of ISSS is seen in the form of demand and supply. In terms of demand, a lot of Swazis are unable to find employment due to an economy that performs badly, where there are high rates of unemployment and underemployment; as well as dependence on subsistence farming, other informal activities and exclusion from formal social security coverage (World Bank, 2012). Even though there are still gaps in terms of access to state-based social security systems, the community still deals with crises and risks, which the vulnerable poor face. The community is seen as an insurance institution since it enables its members to have access to protection throughout the lifecycle. Women in the informal sector are normally excluded and discriminated against by banks and other formal money lending institutions. As a result, ISSS rotational savings have emerged in the country. These money-lending schemes assist women to accumulate credit so that they can be able to achieve agricultural yields. Some women can expand livestock and operate small businesses in the communities. Other forms of these schemes focus on rotational food parcels. These schemes promote social solidarity and social cohesion. They also empower women and raise their self-worth and esteem within the family.

On the supply front, Indigenous Social Security Systems have become the new strand in the social security provision in Swaziland even though their role is yet to be acknowledged by the central Government, NGOs (local and international), as well as Local Governments. The reality is that the interventions by the state are not sufficiently reaching all the vulnerable and poor individuals. In Swaziland for instance, there are no policies, which are targeting vulnerable families whilst other public assistance programmes are too weak or small to respond to the needs of the poor in the communities. Poor households and families are being supported to effectively deal with contingencies and crises and as a result there is increased reliance on community schemes, which respond to their needs of food, shelter, clothing and health care. For instance, Neighbourhood Care Points (NCPs) are one example where school-going children can go and have at least one descent meal per day. Volunteers in the community are responsible for the upkeep of these NCPs. Often the volunteers sacrifice their time, food and energy in ensuring that destitute community members have something to eat. The church and religious organisations have emerged as other institutions that have managed to close the gap when it comes to the provision of social security in Swaziland. From the time of missionaries, to date, the church is there when there are problems faced by children, people with disabilities and the aged. The Church provides food, clothes and medical attention where possible. In principle the Church, as a form of ISSS, seeks to close the gap between the haves and have-nots.

Four characteristics of Indigenous Social Security Systems can be found in contemporary Swaziland. Firstly, individuals rely on their economic efforts (mostly informal) in deriving a livelihood. A lot of women find themselves having to play the dual role of breadwinner and nurturer because most men leave the family for the cities in search of employment. This is a colonial legacy, which ushered in poverty and dependence in families and left women to undertake new roles within the family.

Secondly, the family is an important conduit for ISSS for most people in the communities who derive their livelihood from the informal sector. Belonging to a family or clan automatically qualifies an individual to get assistance whenever he/she is faced with a crisis or any form of vulnerability. People in the urban areas still return to the rural areas when crises strike. Some urbanites have learnt to form new relationships in the urban areas so that they can get assistance with rent money, food, accommodation and support during sickness and/or death. Burial schemes are also emerging as a form of

ISSS for disadvantaged populations. As earlier noted, extended families still exist in contemporary Swaziland and the customary kinship ties are still relatively strong in rural communities. Even though the family is expected to step in and respond to the crises of its members, its ability is hampered by lack of resources to cushion vulnerable children, the elderly and people living with disabilities.

Thirdly, most individuals belong to some informal groups, such as money rotating schemes, burial schemes and other community organisations from which they can access some form of assistance whenever the need arises. Fourthly, NGOs and Churches play a significant role in the provision of social security to those individuals excluded by the formal social security system. The church has taken care of the homeless, aged, the sick, hungry and destitute and plays a significant role during the death of most members of communities.

ISSS in practice: protective, preventive, promotive, transformative and transitional functions

The following discussion focuses specifically on Swaziland in trying to determine the existence of ISSS. Based on the responses from a research which was conducted by the authors, this section focuses on how ISSS manifests itself in terms of: protective, preventive, promotive, transformative and transitional dimensions. The responses are based on in-depth interviews, which were conducted with three Government officials and three ordinary people to ascertain how they used ISSS in dealing with shocks and insecurities relating to lack of income, assets and overall vulnerability. In Swaziland, ISSS are still functioning, even though they might have slightly changed to accommodate the changes in society because of colonialism, urbanisation, migration, education, modernisation and globalisation. This is because 70 per cent of the people in Swaziland live in rural areas, while 63 per cent live below the two USD per day threshold (World Bank, 2012) and most of these individuals are engaged in informal employment, which is excluded from formal social security. Nonetheless, ISSS are on the decline in Swaziland due to the increasing incidents of poverty and high death rates. Respondents (Rs) made the following observations:

> We are getting to a place where you cannot adopt or allow a stranger into your home because you are struggling to feed yourself and your children. This is so

unSwazi, but what can we do? The heart is willing, but the realities for each family makes it hard to survive on a day-to-day basis (R1).

Another respondent shared in this way:

> Living in a community means that different people will cross paths at one point or another. We have rural health motivators who are keen to keep the community healthy. As a result, in those homesteads where there is need some rural health motivators bring their own food and other amenities in a quest to assist needy families... this is what community spirit does (R2).

Another respondent echoed similar sentiments:

> Daily we realise that I need others to survive umuntfu ngumuntfu ngebantfu... in case of emergency that when you realise that you need others (R3).

Thus, increasing vulnerability levels are quite high and the new types of families emerging due to the impact of HIV and AIDS need more support from indigenous structures in the community due to their proximity and urgency to problems. Grandmother Headed Households (GHHs) and Child Headed Households (CHHs) stand to benefit from the protective and preventive functions of community based social security systems. The inaccessible nature of the formal social security system and rising needs for social security amongst the poor and vulnerable population have resulted in such groups reverting to ISSS to try and address their needs. Respondents reported how such groups make use of ISSS:

> We come together once a month to contribute towards a scheme which helps us with small loans when we are in dire need. But if you do not borrow from the scheme the returns are quite high at the end of the year. We can get a bag of rice, meat, soap and other amenities, which are handy within the household. But you must wait until December to appreciate the effort of saving. It is hard to save when you are this poor and when needs arise we borrow the money to the point that in December most of us get absolutely nothing (R1).

Another respondent noted:

> People are forced to look for alternatives to formal social security because the Government is unable to care for all of us. Right now, the Government tries to give the elderly some money, but that money never comes on time. We are so poor and vulnerable; at times the children and I go for many days without eating... what can we do? We are poor. I am still 57 years and I do not qualify for the elderly grant. I try to use the women in the community to help me with some money. I mean I

ask them for employment. If it is ploughing time I go house-to-house asking to assist them and in return they give me whatever they have. The other day I needed mealie-meal, so I asked that as my repayment… they give me some so that I can be able to cook thin porridge for the children at home (R2).

Another respondent made the following observations:

The rural health motivators (bagcugcuteli), child protection volunteers programme (Lihlombe Lekukhalela) and the chieftaincy have become the avenue through which indigenous social security is transmitted. Within some communities the chief sets aside fields which are meant to cater for the elderly, disabled and child headed households. The rural health motivators are people who have in most cases been whistle blowers in terms of abuse and discrimination of certain groups in society. They sometimes feed the elderly using their own resources and they can identify the neediest households in the communities because of proximity. The Lihlombe Lekukhalela is also another initiative which has been an outlet for children who are being abused – these people have a way of reporting these cases to the police (R3).

Another initiative, which has been highlighted as supporting the ISSS, has been the Neighbourhood Care Points (NCPs), although the Ministry of *Tinkhundla* has set these up, while supported by development partners. In these centres children from disadvantaged backgrounds are fed at least one good meal per day and they are also given the most basic preschool level education. Another important role played by these NCPs is that health personnel can access children who they would otherwise not be able to encounter. Then they can be immunised especially if there is an outbreak of childhood diseases. Another respondent shared these sentiments:

People bring their own food, material for teaching and sometimes clothes to give to the children and older people at NCPs. You know the people running NCPs are from the community, they are not paid and they devote themselves to bettering the lives of others… that is the essence of the Swazi culture and way of caring for one another (R1).

It is still true that individuals, families and communities in Swaziland have to rely on ISSS due to circumstances beyond their control such as exclusion and marginalisation by the formal system (Gsanger, 1993). It is also true that ISSS cannot provide for all the social security needs of the society and they cannot be ignored because they are still playing a pivotal role in the lives of the poor and vulnerable in the African context as confirmed by this respondent:

> Some of the families in the community are headed by children and so some of the women in the community take turns in caring for the children. By caring I mean they visit the home and assist the children with cooking... in fact imparting skills rather than creating dependencies... we try to teach them how to do most activities in the home... if there is a garden we teach them how to plough and all so that they can have food... this assists the children to navigate and transition this new path they are taking (R2).

Communities in Swaziland are still a very important source of social security and welfare for those families that are unable to maintain and sustain their livelihoods. Swaziland has the highest level of HIV globally and this has undermined the strength of ISSS as so many households are affected. A family exists within a community and that is one of the reasons why communities need to be explored as possible sources of sustenance, resilience and development.

> Chiefs are still expected to ensure that the livelihoods of all members of the community are within acceptable standards, but that is more easily said than done. Despite their commitment to the well-being of community members, they face challenges in distributing the necessary material needed in each household within the communities. The population is much higher than in the past, such that some of the commodities cannot satisfy all the needy people within the community (R4).

Ubuntu (an African principle of mutual support and reciprocity) and social care have been demonstrated in the communities especially when a crisis unfolds. People still come together for the benefit of needy and vulnerable members of the community. It can be argued that there is more emphasis on community efforts in furthering the values of ISSS. This is partly because the mortality rate is very high. Now the community, as opposed to the family, must safeguard the welfare of fellow members. This is not to suggest that the family structure is no longer carrying out this role, but other actors within the community are coming together for the greater good.

> In some communities the Chief will assign people to go and plough for orphaned and vulnerable children who might be living alone or with an elderly person. Sometimes when there are storms and people lose their houses, the Chief commissions the community to assist the families in crisis (R5).

Even though colonialism and urbanisation disrupted the African support systems there have been examples of social security that is provided to members of the family who are HIV positive. In most cases people migrate to the urban areas in search of paid employment. But as the individual falls ill she/he returns to the rural areas to be cared for by her/his family members:

> I am raising my grandchildren whom my daughter left in my care when she died from HIV related illnesses. It is always amazing that certain people have their livelihood in the urban areas, but as soon as they are unwell they want familial care. Here we do not have adequate finances to care for the sick person, but no one is turned back because everyone belongs to the family. That is why in the past they used to say a person has two homes: the father's side and mother's side. In this case no one could be isolated because they can always run to the other family members for care and support (R6).

Another respondent noted:

> When someone new comes into the community there is a lot of gossip and harsh tones about the individual. This shows that the community is still interested in knowing what is happening in the different households... this is a positive thing because it shows that we still care about each other. News of someone being sick still spreads like wild fire; a birth is known and celebrated and in death we still come together to offer support to the remaining members whilst we celebrate the fallen hero. That is what we used to do to show we cared and we are a community (R7).

Furthermore, it should be acknowledged and appreciated that ISSS are to a lot of African individuals, communities and families a way of life (Kasente, 2002). They bring out one's humaneness and provide one the opportunity to belong, participate and share. This is typically African (Kasente, 2002). Africans, by their very nature, approach life as a unit. Africans and their values are inseparable. This is evident from the strong sense of pride of many Africans – more especially those who live in rural settings – who will resist anything that may threaten their sense of identity and togetherness.

Mechanisms to integrate indigenous and formal social security systems

Currently, indigenous and formal social security systems exist as two separate social networks in Swaziland. As presented above, the formal security focuses on individuals who are in paid employment. There are no formal linkages being made to come up with a complementary structure of ISSS and the formal social security system, although the NCPs could become integrated in this way if they were reformulated as support for ISSS in the community:

> Indigenous and formal social security can be described as traveling on parallel roads. The formal social security system is on a single, tarred carriageway. This road is in the process of being transformed into a dual carriageway. Indigenous Social Security Systems are travelling on a road and to the same destination, but its road is only a small dirt road with potholes. Since both roads lead to the same destination and run along more or less on the same course, it is time to consider whether they should not both form part of the greater road-planning project for the area (Dekker, 2005: 2).

Given the exclusionary nature of the current formal social security system in Swaziland, there is a need for the Government to acknowledge the existence and role of ISSS. The Government needs to take a lead in making ISSS an integral part of the overall social security mechanism in Swaziland. In fact, ISSS can be utilised as the foundation of an integrative and comprehensive social security scheme for the country. In addition, ISSS can assist in the identification and locating of the vulnerable members of society. For instance, psychosocial support staff working as Auxiliary Social Welfare Officers in the communities could be used to identify the families in dire need of protection and become the first point of referral in a social welfare case management system. Also, the *Lihlombe Lekukhalela* can be used in this decentralised process of ensuring that the vulnerable are reached by the integrated and/or comprehensive state social security. This can be important as Swaziland is slowly moving towards a national social protection system and these are some of the considerations that can be considered.

Furthermore, the involvement of multiple actors is essential to ensure that social security is inclusive and comprehensive. The recognition of the existing ISSS in the country is key in the establishment of a comprehensive structure of social security. Recognising the role of the ISSS by the state can assist in the formalisation of some community-based regulatory and monitoring mechanism to ensure that people who have been previously excluded do not continue to suffer from the same fate. The Government should not control or subsume the ISSS under the formal system, but the former can be a resource and act as building blocks for more responsive social security coverage in Swaziland. It is recommended in this chapter that the decentralised auxiliary staff could be the ones used in the identification of those individuals who do not qualify for assistance on the current system – either because they do not know the existence of social security benefits they are entitled to as citizens of the country or they do not have the required documentation such as PIN or identification documents. So far, there are still individuals who are not benefiting from the current system because they are illiterate and therefore cannot complete the required forms or even sign them. So, using decentralised structures can assist in the identification of these vulnerable people.

In terms of a comprehensive social security system, Swaziland needs to be able to implement one that can meet the most basic needs of the vulnerable populations. Social security interventions must be strengthened and/or build on the ISSS as provided by the family and community so that these units can be able to cover the risks and shocks that the vulnerable are exposed to. For instance, there is need to promote informal investment activities among beneficiary groups and the community so that during times of serious need or crisis, they can be able to have something to fall back on. Good social security interventions equally promote the aspect of social capital, which is an indigenous support system that exists within communities where those in need could be assisted and supported by those whose situation has improved because of, for example, cash transfers such as old age grants. This indigenous support mechanism at the local level could be promoted through community sensitisation, formation of informal savings or lending groups. It can also happen through village or community banking, asset creation through livestock development and support for market access.

It is also recommended by the authors that Swaziland needs to have a definition of social security that encompasses both the indigenous and formal social security systems. Suruma (2000: 3-4) argues that, "social security is comprehensively defined as that idea where there is security of income for every citizen of Swaziland. Under this ideal, every citizen is assured of access to the basic requirements of life namely, food, shelter, clothing, education and health care. The right of access to these basic needs is essentially unconditional... as such, civilised society is obligated to make arrangements for the protection of all categories of society." Such a comprehensive approach is needed so that indigenous and formal social security are complementary, rather than viewing them as separate and/or competing entities. The first president of Tanzania, Julius Kambarage Nyerere, once remarked: "While some nations aim at the moon, we are aiming at the village." This is a position that Swaziland needs to look at closely, especially because the

Government is seemingly looking to the family to continue caring for its members. The current situation is that most of the Swazis in communities are receiving assistance from fellow community members. The disadvantaged, widowed, infirm, aged or disabled that are part of the community are cushioned against all social and economic contingencies by having a much larger community around them.

Thus, even when they become less able to carry on working, the wider community is normally there to support them. This has created an important social security guarantee (Mugada, 2013: 31). Thus, empowering families and communities is key. Finally, the state can ensure that interventions such as social grants are sufficient in terms of ensuring that the people have food until the next disbursement of grants. Current proposals to raise the OAG, from E 240 per month to E 400 per month, will result in a large injection of liquid assets into poor rural communities which should result in increased community-level economic activity and demand for suppliers to supply affordable services as happened in Namibia, where a Basic Income Grant (BIG) was piloted (UNDP, 2015; Haarman *et al*, 2009). As the merger between the indigenous and formal systems takes place, the important thing to focus on is to invest in the people's way of living. For instance, the state can be the main purchaser of the produce or products from the poor, because the poor are always encouraged to start small businesses. This can ensure that they will have some money to keep businesses going and it guarantees food security.

The state can also provide certain meals a day at certain care points (NCPs) in various chiefdoms since not everyone is eligible for the grant money. This could strengthen links between ISSS and formal social security systems. Empowerment is also another component needed so that people are not always waiting for handouts. Some of these initiatives are possible if the Government creates a partnership with other role players in the provision of social security. For instance, an emerging social enterprise in Swaziland, "Jesus Projects", provides low-cost, basic foods in areas where drought grants are being distributed so that beneficiaries can purchase food at prices significantly below local market prices. Furthermore, Public Private Partnerships (PPPs) should be an option that the Government and the private sector could investigate to ensure that all citizens receive sufficient coverage by the social security mechanisms in the country. People must inform the process so that what the Government comes up with is responsive to the needs of the poor and vulnerable people.

Conclusion

This chapter had set out to discuss Indigenous Social Security Systems (ISSS) in the context of Swaziland. It first started by examining the formal systems, which exist in the country. This chapter also extracted responses from respondents who had participated in the research study that had informed the discussions to support its arguments. The key issue that was gleaned from the responses, among others, is that ISSS have been in existence in Swaziland for centuries. Due to this, many Swazis still rely on them in times of crises and socio-economic distress. Furthermore, it was mentioned that not all citizens could access the formal systems of social security. It was also gleaned from the responses that despite this, the Government had not made efforts to integrate the indigenous mechanisms into formal systems. Drawing from its discussions and the responses of the people who were interviewed, the chapter put forward several recommendations. It was also argued that Indigenous Social Security Systems possess protective, preventive, promotive, transitional and transformative functions in society. It is the hope of the authors that the discussions in this chapter and the responses from the research study can serve as a guide for future research in the foregoing areas.

References

Adesina, J. 2007. In search of Inclusive Development: Introduction. In: J. Adesina (ed.). *Social Policy in Sub-Saharan African Context*. New York: Palgrave/UNRISD: 1-53.

Apt, N.A. 2002. Aging and the changing role of the family and the community: An African Perspective. *International Social Security Review*, 55 (1): 39-47.

Burgess, R. & Stern, N. 1991. Social Security in Developed Countries: What, Why, Who and How? In: E. Ahmad, J. Drèze, J. Hills & A. Sen (eds.). *Social Security in Developing Countries*. Oxford: Clarendon: 41-80.

Dekker, A.H. 2008. *Can Informal Social Security assist Government to Guarantee Everyone a Right of Access to Social Security?* LLD thesis. Pretoria: University of South Africa (UNISA).

Dekker, A.H. 2005. Informal Social Security: A Legal Analysis. University of South Africa. Unpublished thesis.

Dhemba, J.; Gumbo, P. and Nyamusara, J. 2002. Zimbabwe. *Journal of Social Development in Africa, Special Issue: Social Security*, 17(2): 111-156.

Drèze, J. & Sen, A. 1991. Public Action for social Security: Foundations and Strategy. In: E. Ahmad, J. Drèze, J. Hills & A. Sen (eds.). *Social Security in Developing Countries.* Oxford: Clarendon: 1-40.

Gsanger, H. 1993. *Linking informal and formal social security systems.* Berlin: German Foundation for International Development (DSE).

Haarmann, C.; Haarmann, D.; Jauch, H.; Shindondola, H.; Nattrass, N.; Niekerk, I. & Samson, M. 2009. *Making the difference! The BIG in Namibia - Basic Income Grant Pilot Project Assessment Report,* April 2009, Windhoek, Namibia: Desk for Social Development.

His Majesty's Government. 2012. *Auditor-General's Report on the Swaziland's Old Age Grant.* Mbabane: His Majesty's Government.

Jutting, J. 1999. *Social Security Schemes In Low Income Countries: An Overview from an International Perspective.* https://www.zef.de/fileadmin/webfiles/downloads/articles/juetting-issr.pdf [Accessed 23 January 2017].

Kahf, M. 2006. *Introduction to the Study of Economics of Zakāh.* http://monzer.kahf.com/papers/english/introduction_to_the_study_of_the_econ_of_zakah.pdf [Accessed 24 January 2017].

Kahf, M. & Yafai, S.A. 2015. Social Security and Zakat in theory and practice. *International Journal of Economics, Management and Accounting,* 23(2): 189-215.

Kasente, D.; Asingwire, N.; Banugire, F. & Kyomuhendo, S. 2002. Social security systems in Uganda. *Journal of Social Development in Africa,* 17(2): 159-180.

Korpi, W. 1985. Economic Growth and the Welfare State: Leaky Bucket or Irrigation System? *European Sociological Review,* 1(2): 97-118.

Illiffe, J. 1989. *The African Poor: A history.* Cambridge: Cambridge University Press.

Magada, E.S. 2013. *An investigation into the influence of socio-cultural factors on HIV prevention strategies: A case study of HIV sero-discordant couple in Harare-Zimbabwe.* Masters Thesis. Pretoria: University of South Africa (UNISA).

Marc. A.; Graham, C.; Schacter, M. & Schmidt A. 1995. *Social action programmes and social funds: a review of design and implementation in Sub-Saharan Africa.* World Bank Discussion Paper 274. Washington DC: World Bank.

Midgley, J. 1999. *Has Social Security Become Irrelevant?* New York: John Wiley and Sons Limited.

Midgley, J. 1984. *Social Security-Inequality and Third World.* New York: John Wiley and Sons Limited.

Mouton, P. 1975. *Social security in Africa.* Geneva: International Labour Office.

Ouma, S. 1995. The Role of Social Protection in the Socio-economic Development of Uganda. *Journal of Social Development in Africa*, 10 (2): 5-12. http://sanweb.lib.msu.edu/DMC/African%20journals/

Pain, D. 2016. *Inception Report: Technical assistance for the development of social protection system in Swaziland.* Mbabane: Hulla & Co, Human Dynamics, PWC and ITC.

Platteau, J.P. 1991. Traditional Systems of Social Security and Hunger Insurance: Past Achievements and Modern Challenges. In: E. Ahmad, J. Drèze, J. Hills & A. Sen (eds.). *Social Security in Developing Countries.* Oxford: Clarendon: 112-170.

Rattray, Capt R.S. 1929. *Ashanti law and constitution.* Oxford: Clarendon Press.

Ruparanganda, L.; Ruparanganda, B. & Mupfanochiya, A.T. 2017. Traditional Social Security in the face of Urbanization: Lessons from a rural community in Buhera District of Zimbabwe. *International Journal of Humanities and Social Science*, 7(3).

Sen, A. 1981. *Poverty and Families: An essay on entitlement and deprivation.* Oxford: Claredon Press.

Shepherd, A.; Marcus, R. & Barrientos, A. 2005. Policy Paper on Social Protection. Paper presented at CPRC-IIPA Seminar on Chronic Poverty: *Emerging Policy Options and Issues.* New Delhi: Indian Institute of Public Administration.

Suruma, F. 2000. *A contribution towards a comprehensive view of social security reform in Uganda, PEC paper.* Kampala: Presidential Economic Council.

Töstensen, A. 2004. Towards Feasible Social Security Systems in Sub-Saharan Africa. Working Paper 2004 No. 5. Bergen: Chr. Michelsen Institute.

UNDP. 2015. The Impact of Cash Transfers on Local Economies. *Policy in Focus*, 11: 1.

Van Ginneken, W. 2007. Extending social security coverage: concepts, global trends and policy issues. *International Social Security Review*, 60(2-3): 39-57.

Von Benda-Beckman, F.; von Benda-Beckmann, K.; Casino, E.; Hirtz, F.; Woodman, G.R. & Zacher, H.F. (1998). *Between kinship and the State: Social security and law in developing countries.* Dordrecht: Foris Publications.

Von Braun, J. 1991. *Social Security in Sub-Saharan Africa: Reflections on Policy Challenges.* Oxford: Oxford University.

World Bank. 2012. *Global Economic Prospects: Uncertainties and Vulnerabilities.* Washington, DC: World Bank.

04

INDIGENOUS SOCIAL SECURITY SYSTEMS: A SOUTH AFRICAN PERSPECTIVE

Boitumelo Seepamore

Introduction

The purpose of this chapter is to discuss Indigenous Social Security Systems (ISSS) in the South African context. The chapter focuses on a particular ISSS known as *Letsema* for its analysis and expositions. *Letsema* is one of the enduring ISSS in the African communities of South Africa. In a climate of high unemployment and poverty, communities rely on each other through their mutual aid associations which are referred to in South Africa as *stokvels*. These are also used in conjunction with formal social security systems such as social grants for the benefit of communities. Based on the traditional African system of communal living, *stokvels* have a protective, ameliorative and transformative function and they have been adapted to meet the needs of individuals and communities and stave off their risks in urban settings. However, these ISSS still exist on the periphery of South Africa's formal social protection system. This chapter is based on a research study that had endeavoured to ascertain how domestic workers from eThekwini, in the province of KwaZulu-Natal of South Africa, used social grants and *stokvels* – which are also called *umjikelezo* – to survive the harsh effects of poverty.

The relevance of Indigenous Social Security Systems in modern-day South Africa

Developing countries are faced with a myriad of developmental challenges, among them, limited access to basic services such as water, sanitation, housing (Pawar, 2014), low quality employment (Chitonge, 2012) and increased levels of HIV/AIDS, particularly in Sub-Saharan Africa (Mupedziswa & Ntseane, 2013). Because of historical segregation and discrimination, poverty in South Africa affects 23 per cent of the population according to Statistics South Africa (Stats SA) (2014). The poorest sections of society are mainly children, the youth, elderly, African women and people with disabilities (Patel, 2012; Sewpaul, 2014). Although social assistance is available to 16 million South Africans, the remaining seven million people who are poor do not receive state social assistance. It begs the question: Where do they get support and how do they survive? Despite having a well-developed social security system in South Africa, the application process for social security is still cumbersome. The required documentation such as birth certificates and identity documents, clinic cards or proof of disability are not always readily available. Communities then tend to rely on systems that they know best, to meet their needs, which are indigenous in nature.

This chapter discusses ISSS in South Africa which are also known as *stokvels*. These ISSS are used by women in an urban community to meet their immediate needs and help them to cushion the harsh conditions in times of economic crises. It must be noted that the flexibility of *stokvels* makes them suitable for adaptation in a variety of settings. In this case, the chapter will show how a group of women in a low income community, employed and continue to use the *stokvel* together with social grants, to survive poverty. To contextualise the chapter, the discussion begins with a brief outline of poverty and unemployment in South Africa, followed by a theoretical discussion of both the formal and ISSS that exist in the country. The findings are discussed in relation to how both social grants and *stokvels* benefitted a group of women in a low-income community. Finally, the chapter advocates for the revival of *Letsema* to amplify social security to benefit communities.

To begin with, it can be observed that lack of consensus on the nomenclature around ISSS leads to confusion and people working at cross-purposes. Patel, Kaseke and Midgley (2012: 14) point out that while on the one hand ISSS is referred to as "traditional, informal or non-formal", on the other hand, formal social security is referred to as "social assistance, social insurance and social welfare." Researchers, development workers and policy makers also refer to economic security, income security, income protection, income transfers, cash transfers, transfer payment, welfare, etc. (Midgley, 2013). This lack of clarity regarding the basic definitions and terminologies used in this field, leads to each individual scholar interpreting his/her work differently. Thus, this increases the possibilities of responding to the same issue in a rather fragmented and duplicated fashion. Furthermore, social security is usually associated with income protection and cash transfers and this narrowly focuses on income, however non-traditional forms such as "commodity subsidies, food for work, minimum wages, or other provisions provided by Non-Governmental Organisations (NGOs) are normally disregarded (Midgley, 2012; Devereux, 2002). It is Standing (2007) who cautions against summing up any form of social assistance as social protection as these terms are not mutually inclusive, rather a distinction is made about the different dimensions of social security and social protection.

Widespread poverty in South African communities

Despite being a middle-income country, which is "widely praised for the coverage, generosity and efficiency of its social protection system" (Devereux, 2011), structural poverty is endemic in South Africa with a human development index of 0,683 in 2013. By 2015, over 23 million people or 45,5 per cent of the population lived in poverty in the country. High levels of unemployment exist, partly because of economic globalisation, historical racism and sexism under apartheid laws, coupled with low levels of education for a majority of the population. The most vulnerable groups are Africans living in rural areas and informal settlements – and generally it is more women than men. Despite having adopted a neo-liberal economic policy in post-apartheid South Africa, the economy has grown, albeit, without creating jobs. In 1996, the Growth, Employment and Redistribution (GEAR) policy was adopted and it was supposed to have generated massive economic spin-offs, with over 1,3 million jobs created per annum and exponential economic growth was forecast. However, these have not materialised. Instead, foreign debt seems to be serviced at the expense of citizens' welfare (Padayachee, 2005; Ferguson, 2007) and the trickledown effect that was envisaged to spread to all communities because of a growing economy seems to have not done so, as over 5,2 million people are unemployed and this figure keeps rising. By adopting a neoliberal economic strategy, South Africa has also experienced what other countries in the developing world are witnessing – casual labour and a divided and weakened workforce (Sewpaul, 2014; Triegaardt, 2009).

Women are generally dominant in both the informal sector and low paying jobs such as domestic work, street trading and farm work. The lack of monitoring of the conditions of employment and procedures of dismissal in domestic and farm work exacerbates exploitation. However, this power imbalance has shifted from being a race-based one to a class-based phenomenon, which keeps these employees underemployed and poor (Patel, 2012). Nevertheless, numerous efforts have been put in place by the Government to deal with unemployment, however there does not seem to be much success. For instance, the Expanded Public Works Programme (EPWP), which was introduced in 2004 and makes work opportunities available, particularly to the youth, through Government Departments (Jacobs, Ngcobo, Hart & Baipheti, 2010) has not been very successful in reducing unemployment. However, reporting on unemployment and job creation seems to have its own controversies, as the trend of reporting on the number of job opportunities is rather misleading. Job opportunities are not equivalent to sustainable employment. The use of terminology particularly in Government reporting on the creation of job opportunities implies employment, when in fact, people are given the opportunity to work for short-term, part-time and temporary projects (Triegaardt, 2009), not in permanent and meaningful employment. The 'beneficiaries' of EPWP projects usually perform unskilled work such as cleaning the streets and participating in home-based care work which does not provide skills. It does not also enable them to work in the formal sector or operate their own businesses. Therefore, if the Government continues reporting on work opportunities and not real employment, unemployment and poverty will remain high in the country.

State social assistance

There is non-contributory social assistance in South Africa and other Southern African Development Community (SADC) countries like Botswana, Swaziland, Namibia and Lesotho (Chitonge, 2012), albeit these are means-tested and targeted social assistance programmes, for example, the older people grant. In South Africa various social grants exist which cover children, people with disabilities, older people, war veterans and those undergoing crises such as fire or floods. Largely because of political will and a vibrant civic culture, the provision of non-contributory social assistance to millions of South Africans, continues (Devereux, 2011) together with a prioritisation of budget toward social assistance. From R 118 billion (8,7 billion USD) or ten per cent of the national budget in 2014, the social assistance budget increased to R 129 billion (9,6 billion USD) in 2015/16 and is projected to be R165 billion (12,2 billion USD) in 2018/19 (The Mail & Guardian, 2016). This calculation is based on an exchange rate of 1 USD to R 13,42. Holzmann, Sherburne-Bez and Tesliuc (2003), make a compelling point and state that social security is not a luxury that only rich countries can afford or regarded as a drain on a country's resources, but should rather be a Government-led investment in its people, whilst focussing on social transformation and societal inclusion (Midgley, 2012; Standing, 2007). The foregoing assertion resonates with arguments for a Basic Income Grant (BIG) (Taylor, 2002), a social protection floor (Mpedi, 2008) for a country and indeed have merit in developing countries, particularity where social inclusion is missing. Political will, and the view that social security is an opportunity for people to become active participants in their well-being and can become self-reliant, is also critical (Devereux, 2011). The 2002 Taylor Commission of Inquiry, recommends comprehensive social security, encompassing more than just the traditional concept of social security in the form of social grants, but also development strategies and programmes designed to ensure, collectively – a minimum acceptable living standard for all citizens (Devereux, 2011).

In addition to formally recognised social security systems, there are also Indigenous Social Security Systems which have been operational since pre-colonial times which include community support networks from neighbours and Chiefs and mutual aid associations (Mupedziswa & Ntseane, 2013; Patel et al, 2012; Buijs, 1998; Biggart, 2001). There are multiple goals to social security and Chitonge (2012) explains these in turn are based on principles of prevention (pre-emptive), mitigation (palliative), coping (preservative) and promotion (transformative). Prevention aims to safeguard people from becoming vulnerable, that is, to reduce the occurrence of shocks and therefore putting proactive measures in place, so that risks and shocks are reduced, and not severely felt. Social relief of distress and other social assistance measures which are put in place when disasters or crises occur, have a mitigating function – in South Africa this is often used in cases of floods or fires (Triegaardt, 2009) and recently when there were xenophobic violent attacks on foreign nationals. Because of their short-term nature, social relief measures act as a safety net for a limited period only. Both social grants and mutual aid associations have a longer-term preservative function.

Contributory social assistance is usually available to a selected few who can afford it, whether private or state-administered. The Unemployment Insurance Fund (UIF) benefits workers in the event of incapacity: such as maternity, unemployment, injury or illness, or any reason leading to an inability to work. Standing (2007: 513) refers to it as 'a model of privilege' mainly applicable to employed people. It is not accessible to most people in Sub-Saharan Africa in general, and South Africans in particular, because of pervasive unemployment and high numbers of unregistered workers and casual employees. Social insurance seems more realistic in developed countries with a vibrant economies and high levels of permanent, stable and well-paying jobs. Many of the unemployed do not qualify for social insurance because of its contributory nature and they depend on state-funded and administered non-contributory social assistance which, in many instances, is inadequate to meet their needs on a long-term basis. With a loss of income, families are likely to be immediately rendered indigent should they not have social insurance (Midgley, 2012).

A non-traditional form of social security which is normally overlooked, is the minimum wage which is "one way of investing in people and transforming the lives of the poor without much Government spending" (Midgley, 2012: 11). It has a transformative function (Devereux, 2011; Chitonge, 2012) which can, in the long-term, respond effectively to chronic poverty. Domestic workers and farm workers in commercial farms became formally employed people under the Basic Conditions of Employment Act (1997) – Sectoral Determination 7 promulgated in 2002. The Department of Labour regulates and annually reviews minimum wage, leave entitlements, employment contracts and dismissal procedures of all workers. Formally employed people are entitled to maternity benefits and social insurance through the Unemployment Insurance Fund (UIF) which is managed by the Department of Labour. This makes it possible for employees in sectors which previously did not have access to services and benefits such as maternity leave or the compensation for injury on duty, be able to open bank accounts and have access to credit. However, despite civic society activism and mobilisation, there is a lack of monitoring in this sector.

Indigenous Social Security Systems in African communities

Indigenous Social Security Systems depend on locally arranged measures based on people's cultural beliefs and norms and are self-organised and self-regulating systems of both obligation and entitlement offering not only financial aid, but also psychological and emotional support (Olivier, Kaseke & Mpedi, 2008; Mupedziswa & Ntseane, 2013; Mpedi, 2008). Unlike Olivier and Dekker (2003) who argue that non-formal social security is the counterpart of formal initiatives, this author concurs with Patel *et al*, (2012), whilst citing von Breda-Beckman and von Breda-Beckman (1994). By simply placing formal and non-formal or traditional and modern categorisation of social networks in binary opposites is an oversimplification of the complex culturally institutionalised practices that characterise social welfare and social security in many African countries. These systems have been put in place to support and care for the vulnerable and may vary according to situations of chronic or transient vulnerability. In addition to family and kin, mutual aid associations are recognised and are widely used forms of social security.

Family and kin as forms of social protection

Family and kin support is based on a system of obligation and reciprocity between family and kin to help one another in times of need (Patel *et al*, 2012). This assumes that those closely related by blood or marriage will assist each other socially, financially, economically and psychologically in times of crisis or vulnerability (Siqwana-Ndulo, 1998; Mupedziswa & Ntseane, 2013). The extended family has an obligation to assist and similarly members are entitled to offer support regardless of age or gender. Although family and kin support are the first port of call in emergencies, urbanisation, migration and HIV/AIDS have weakened this form of social protection. Spatial distance has also led to families living far from one another or only seeing each other at certain intervals, affecting the speed and willingness to offer support in times of need. Oduro (2010: 18) argues: "The social network based on the family can straddle more than one location." The composition of family may change according to resources and needs. Other cultural arrangements such as "strengthening family ties" where children live with other relatives to strengthen family ties, reciprocity and obligation still exist (Oduro, 2010). The distance between family members, their size and composition and their willingness or capacity to assist, may be limited. Despite oscillating migration between places of employment in urban areas and family homes in the rural areas (Posel, 2010), weakening the ties between individuals, families and communities, culturally institutionalised norms of obligation and reciprocity and the necessity to survive new and changing environments, indigenous welfare practices continue to operate (Patel *et al*, 2012).

Community support networks

Having been in existence from pre-colonial times, community support networks have changed form, but continue to play a vital role in meeting community needs, particularly in times of crises. Mupedziswa and Ntseane (2013) and Olivier *et al*. (2008) expand on these concepts and refer to the practices of communal grazing, chief's granary or lending cattle to the poor, as community support systems that have helped to sustain the vulnerable in many communities. One of the most enduring community support systems is that of mutual aid societies and in particular *stokvels*.

Mutual aid groups and associations – *stokvels*

Various names are used to refer to savings and credit co-operative societies depending on where one comes from, but in South African communities they are called *stokvels*, *gooi gooi* or *diswaeti umgalelo, umjikelezo* (Ngwenya, 2003; Smets & Wels, 1999) or *susu* in West African countries (Boon, 2007) or *tontines* in francophone Africa. Membership is based on periodic contribution which may be weekly or monthly and these *stokvels* may be burial societies, funeral association or benefit associations that have evolved mainly from burial societies (Mupedziswa & Ntseane, 2013; Patel *et al*, 2012). *Stokvels* are an existing type of indigenous peer lending arrangement (Biggart, 2001; Buijs, 1998) which is different from microcredit however they operate along similar lines, to make interest-free and collateral-free credit available to people who do not usually qualify for credit in formal financial institutions. Because they are contributory in nature, but not so prohibitive, that they exclude the very poor who are meant to benefit from them, these systems provide a safety net for those in informal employment.

Members save and have periodic access to relatively substantial amounts of capital, which are used for various purposes, including business or consumption (Biggart, 2001). Although *stokvels* operate mainly in the informal sector, they have also been commercialised in Southern Africa and are still dominated by women (Mupedziswa & Ntseane, 2013; Ngwenya, 2003; Smets & Wels, 1999). In the eThekwini municipality, the urban area where the sample research was sourced, *stokvels* were based on communal area of origin and area of employment in Durban. Ngwenya (2003) shows that *diswaeti* may be based on work, ethnicity or cut across social and physical lines. Membership may also vary from a few people in the informal associations to thousands of members. Biggart (2001) explains that generally, the organiser of a *mjikelezo* may be a trusted person, with good social standing and credentials in the community. This person may also invite membership to trusted people so that others may be comfortable and assured of payment when it is their turn. *Stokvels* mainly exist in communities with strong communal ties, similar social status where obligations are collective, and it is a requirement that individuals have socio-economic and geographic stability (Smets & Wels, 1999; Biggart, 2001).

Although these women are employed, they do not always have access to social insurance or other forms of formal social protection mainly because they are not registered employees. The predicament of women in low income jobs is that some earn more than the minimum to qualify for a social grant which is means tested and others earn very little to qualify for the social grant despite being employed. They are often locked into poverty because on the one hand, they depend on their jobs and cannot leave, and on the other hand, they do not get the social support which may help them escape poverty. These women have had to bank on each other (Biggart 2001) to survive poverty through the creative use of rotating savings clubs, by using a system of *letsema/ilima*.

Letsema/Ilima

In Setswana (one of the indigenous languages of South Africa), *Letsema* or *ilima*, means 'to voluntarily work together'(Lebeloane & Quan-Baffour, 2008). This is where a group of people work towards a common goal (Ramagoshi, 2013). This form of volunteering is not a new concept. *Letsema* has always been an important indigenous practice where communities would work in teams in farming: First to prepare the field, sow and harvest the communal land, which was usually allocated by the Chief (Ramagoshi, 2013) and then divide themselves into teams that would work on their own farms on a rotational basis until all the community members had been assisted. This voluntary work extended to the construction of houses, barns, pens and kraals (Lebeloane & Quan-Baffour, 2008). Therefore, communities combined their human power for maximum benefit of all. Because there was no payment for services, community members would be given food and beer as a sign of appreciation, not as a form of payment (Ramagoshi, 2013). Rankopo, Osei-Hwedie and Modie-Moroka (2006) emphasise the socialisation of all community members into collective participation and mutual aid. Other forms of community volunteering include *mephato*, where age graded regiments would be involved in the development of infrastructure or *letsholo* where people would donate time and other resources for the benefit of the community (Rankopo *et al*, 2006). For example, the community would come out as *letsholo* to look for a child who had strayed or to track a domestic or wild animal. Other forms of mutual aid included what Mupedziswa and Ntseane (2013: 89) refer to as *mafisa* – the donation or lending of livestock to underprivileged members of the community – or *majako* where poorer members of the community would work in the fields of those who are not well to do so themselves, in return for a share of the harvest.

Another type of ISSS is known as *Go tshwara teu*, where able-bodied young men would look after the cattle of others and in return, be given a cow each year to start their own herd. There are also different words meant to describe similar practises, for instance, the allocation of communal land either by the Chief or the *kgotla* (village council) for all to benefit. Particularly the vulnerable such as: Orphans, widows and people with disabilities are referred to as *Zunde raMambo* or chief's granaries in Zimbabwe (Patel *et al*, 2012), or *difalana* in Botswana (Mupedziswa & Ntseane, 2013) with massive urbanisation and the development of new communities. These practices have been brought to the urban setting where mutual aid continues, albeit in a different form. The idea of *stokvels* and *megodisano* or *masakhane* reflects how mutual aid societies work in different settings. This type of *Letsema* is "a mechanism for them to try to cope with the struggles and hardships of urbanisation that have been acculturated" (Ramagoshi, 2013: 54). This ability to respond to the immediate and future risk of communities makes these *stokvels* relevant and popular. Mutual aid associations in the form of *umjikelezo* are discussed in relation to how they have been adapted in the form of *Letsema* to meet the immediate needs of women in low income employment.

Methodology

This study made use of three individual interviews and one focus group discussion to solicit responses from respondents regarding ISSS related issues. The respondents were invited to participate in the study based on the criteria of them belonging to a mutual aid society, working either as domestic workers or in low income employment. Their ages ranged from 32-40 and each was a breadwinner supporting her own children and other members of the extended family. Their highest level of education was Grade 12. Their wages ranged between R1,700 (127 USD) and R2,500 (186 USD) per month. Although not an inclusion criterion, all the participants received the Child Support Grant (CSG). Despite being employed, the meagre salaries of the participants necessitated that they supplemented their income. One participant worked piece jobs when she was off from work and another sold wood blocks from her house. Others wished to change their jobs or engage in small businesses to augment their wages. The focus group comprised of five women who worked in the suburb of Glenwood in Durban as live-in domestic workers and lived in the community of Inanda, also in the city of Durban. Three women who were individually interviewed lived at Inanda, but worked in different parts of Durban. Inanda is characterised by high rates of poverty, unemployment and crime. It is a low-income settlement. Of these three, two were sleep-out domestic workers and one was a tea-lady working at a car dealership. Convenience sampling was used for the focus group discussion and this was when the women were at their monthly *stokvel* meeting. For the individual interviews, snowballing was used with the first respondent being identified incidentally through her maid's uniform. The purpose of the study was explained to the members and further clarification was made to members at the focus group discussion which lasted for about an hour and a half. Data were analysed thematically through content analysis.

Results and discussion

Similar to other mutual aid associations, *umjikelezos* work on a rotation system with each member having a turn to get support and is obligated to give support when another person asks for assistance. The participants stay in Inanda and live in mud houses or shacks which they plan to convert into brick structures. Although this *mjikelezo* started in 2013, the women feel that they have accomplished much since their first meeting. Their *mjikelezo* is called *bafazi sukumani* which loosely translates into 'rise women'. They invest their social grant money into the *mjikelezo* and use the collective kitty to buy building materials for each other and a small amount goes towards food and toiletries. For a group of ten women it means that with an investment of R 650 (48 USD) per month, each member receives R 5,850 (442 USD) worth of building materials, they buy supermarket stamps to purchase groceries of their own choice and with a further amount of R 100 per month (7,45 USD) each member receives R 900 (67 USD) when it is her turn to host the *mjikelezo*, once a year (the currency conversion is based on rates when the study was undertaken).

The transformative nature of *stokvels*

One of the approaches to social protection is its promotional or transformative nature which is long term and whose objective is to build assets to manage chronic risks (Chitonge, 2012). Mutual aid societies fulfil this role. The participants in this group decided to build their own homes using the financial and human resources from this group. The initial contribution of R 650 (48 USD) per month is multiplied so that each member receives R 5,850 (3,609 USD) worth of building materials and free physical labour to build her home. This process is expedited by their *Letsema* approach where the entire group works together to build each person a home. One of the women, explained that the group has no experience in bricklaying, but acquired the skills through trial and error and usually consulted neighbours who had the skills and experience in building – should the need arise. They see the backbreaking work of making their own bricks as a labour of love. When the bricks have hardened and are ready for use, the women come together to build the structure. This is done in turns, therefore if one's bricks are not ready, they miss a turn until the *mjikelezo* rotates back to them, nine months later. Building physical assets protects these women from future risks. It puts them in better stead to have their own homes as a form of social security should the need arise.

Stokvels are a source of social protection

Not only do these women benefit financially and materially from their *stokvel*, they also have psychosocial support. The sense of unity and love for one another was summed up by one participant when she said:

> We are a family, I take everyone here as my sister. I know that I will never go to bed hungry while they are around.

The participants gave a sense of mutual dependence and relied on one another for emotional support and motivation. It was also established that some of them met regularly on a social basis. However, one of the obligations of the *umjikelezo* is to support one another when they have special occasions such as weddings, birthdays or in times of bereavement and funerals. Ramagoshi (2013) explains that neighbours and community members normally circulate a book where they record condolences and collect cash which is given to the family for expenses related to the funeral. The members of this *mjikelezo* are obliged to make a sizeable contribution and the member is entitled to their support in cash or in kind, or both. They make use of *umjikelezo* to pool their available resources in a climate of high levels of poverty. Although it is sometimes referred to as a strategy, belonging to a *mjikelezo*, it is also a way of life for these women. It is an old age practice from their rural areas and has been adapted to their urban environment. They found *stokvels* to be relevant and able to meet their immediate needs, such as food and to building a house. Ramagoshi (2013) asserts that women are mostly concerned with household and care issues, therefore their *stokvels* are mainly meant for the provision of food, paying school fees and providing financial and other assistance at social functions.

Social grants complement mutual aid support

Spreading social grants to meet the diverse needs of the household is a common practice in South Africa (Hölscher, Kasiram & Sathiparsad, 2009). Although sometimes perceived as mismanagement, or a diversion of funds to meet other immediate needs of the household, this enables the women to have access to resources and services they would not otherwise have had if they have not been recipients of social grants. Pooling resources and making productive use of the grant creates resilience and enhances the coping capacity of these women. It was vociferously stated:

> Without the child support grant, I would not have been able to join this mjikelezo.
> I do not know how my life would have been, honestly.

All the participants received the Child Support Grant, despite some not being primary caregivers residing with their children due to the nature of their work as domestic workers. This social grant is paid out to the primary caregiver who may not necessarily be the child's mother, to meet the child's needs. Despite the participants being employed, they rely on the social grant as a means of regular income and this money is used for the benefit of the entire household. At present the value of the child support grant is R 360 (27 USD) per month, having increased from R 350 (26 USD) on 1 April 2017 and is available to all children under 18 years of age. To qualify, the child must be a South African citizen, permanent resident or refugee, not living in a state institution and with the parent earning less than R 3,300 (246 USD) per month or a joint income of not more than R 6,600 (492 USD) per month for both parents. Although the grant is payable to the primary caregiver of the child, some of the women do not live with their children, but received the grant on behalf of the caregivers. They claimed not to know that this was incorrect and illegal. One of the participants explained:

> Yes, I receive the social grant for Sphelele because I am his mother. Because he is the father he must maintain his child, more so because he stays with him. What can you do with R360 when children have so many needs?

Social grants have a preservative function (Chitonge, 2012) and when used together with mutual aid societies, the benefits are exponential. Formal and Indigenous Social Security Systems are not only intertwined, but also reinforce each other in this way. The receipt of social grants enables the participants to take some risks such as joining a *stokvel*, which they may not have had access to had they not received the social grant: "Because I am sure that I will get this money (social grant) every month, I am able to join a *stokvel* and also a funeral policy... people know that I will pay them back when I make a loan, otherwise when you do not have a grant, they will not lend you any money. You are on your own."

It can be seen from the foregoing account that the reliable monthly income made it possible for individuals to take a risk and invest in a *stokvel*, which enabled them to access a lump sum at least once a year and cushion them against risk or help them to manage it better.

Conclusion

The use of *Letsema* as adapted to the urban environment shows how indigenous forms of social security are still relevant in present day South African communities and can be used to benefit recipients. This system is socially acceptable and meets the immediate needs of members in any setting, however with high levels of poverty it would not have worked had members not received a state social grant. In joining a *stokvel*, participants were able to have some respect and dignity in that they were perceived as socially reliable in that they had stable monthly income. This income also helped them to prevent and manage social risk, as well as cushion them in times of crises. The discussions in this chapter point to the fact that Indigenous Social Security Systems and formal social security systems are already being integrated by individuals in poor communities across South Africa, such as Inanda, in Durban. Through their initiatives, poor people can reinforce the two forms of protection in a very innovative way whilst academics, policy-makers and politicians are still debating whether such a feat is feasible or not.

References

Biggart, N.W. 2001. Banking on Each Other: The Situational Logic of Rotating Savings and Credit Associations. *Advances in Qualitative Organisation Research*, 3: 129-153.

Boon, E.K. 2007. Knowledge Systems and Social Security Systems in Africa: A Case Study on Ghana. In: E.K. Boon & L. Hens (eds.). *Indigenous Knowledge Systems and Sustainable Development: Relevance for Africa*. New Delhi: Kamla-Raj Enterprises: 63-76.

Buijs, G. 1998. Savings and Loan Clubs: Risky Ventures or Good Business Practice? A Study of the Importance of Rotating Savings and Credit Associations for Poor Women. *Development Southern Africa*, 15(1): 55-65.

Chitonge, H. 2012. Social Protection Challenges in Sub-Saharan Africa: Rethinking Regimes and Commitments. *African Studies*, 71(3): 323-345.

Devereux, S. 2011. Social Protection in South Africa: Exceptional or Exceptionalism? *Canadian Journal of Development Studies*, 32(4): 414-425.

Devereux, S. 2002. Can Social Safety Nets Reduce Chronic Poverty? *Development Policy Review*, 20(5): 657-675.

Ferguson, J. 2007. Formalities of Poverty: Thinking About Social Assistance in Neoliberal South Africa. *African Studies Review*, 50(2): 71-86.

Hölscher, D.; Kasiram, M. & Sathiparsad, R. 2009. "Deserving" Children, "Undeserving" Mothers? Multiple Perspectives on the Child Support Grant. *Social Work/Maatskaplike Werk*, 45(1): 11-26.

Holzmann, R.; Sherburne-Bez, L. & Tesliuc, E. 2003. Social Risk Management: The World Bank's Approach to Social Protection in a Globalising World. www.worldbank.org [Accessed 13 March 2016].

Jacobs, P.; Ngcobo, N.; Hart, T. & Baipheti, M. 2010. Developmental Social Policies for the Poor in South Africa: Exploring Options to Enhance Impacts? Conference Paper – Overcoming Inequality And Structural Poverty In South Africa: Towards Inclusive Growth And Development. 20-22 September, Johannesburg.

Lebeloane, L.D.M. & Quan-Baffour, K.P. 2008. 'Letsema': A Way of Inculcating and Preserving African Indigenous Knowledge in the Youth through Formal Education in the 21st Century. *Journal of Educational Studies*, 7(2): 43-49.

Midgley, J. 2013. Social Development and Social Protection: New Opportunities and Challenges. *Development Southern Africa*, 30(1): 2-12.

Midgley, J. 2012. Social Protection and Social Policy Key Issues and Debates. *Journal of Policy Practice*, 11(1-2): 8-24.

Mpedi, L.G. 2008. *Pertinent Social Security Issues in South Africa*. Community Law Centre: University of the Western Cape.

Mupedziswa, R. & Ntseane, D. 2013. The Contribution of Non-Formal Social Protection to Social Development in Botswana. *Development Southern Africa*, 30(1): 84-97.

Ngwenya, B.N. 2003. Redefining Kin and Family Social Relations: Burial Societies and Emergency Relief in Botswana. *Journal of Social Development in Africa*, 18(1): 85-111.

Oduro, A.D. 2010. Formal and informal social protection in Sub-Saharan Africa. Paper prepared for the ERD 2010. Final report.

Olivier, M. & Dekker, A.H. 2003. Informal Social Security. In: M. Olivier (ed.). *Social Security: A Legal Analysis*. Durban: LexisNexis Butterworths: 559-593.

Olivier, M.; Kaseke, E. & Mpedi, L.G. 2008. Informal Social Security in Africa: Developing a Framework for Policy Interventions. Paper Presented at the International Conference on Social Security, 10-14 March, Cape Town.

Padayachee, V. 2005. The South African Economy. *Social Research*, 72(3): 549-580.

Patel, L. 2012. Poverty, Gender and Social Protection: Child Support Grants in Soweto, South Africa. *Journal of Policy Practice*, 11(1-2): 106-120.

Patel, L.; Kaseke, E. & Midgley, J. 2012. Indigenous Welfare and Community-Based Social Development: Lessons from African Innovations. *Journal of Community Practice*, 20(1): 12-31.

Pawar, M. 2014. Social Work Practice with Local Communities in Developing Countries: Imperatives for Political Engagement. *Sage Open*, 2014: 1-11.

Posel, D. 2010. Households and Labour Migration in Post-Apartheid South Africa. *Journal for Studies in Economics and Econometrics*, 34(3): 129-141.

Ramagoshi, R.M. 2013. The Role of Letsema in Community Struggles: Past and Present. In: C. Landman (ed.). *Oral History: Representing the Hidden, the Untold and the Veiled*. Proceedings of the Fifth (Cape Town, 2008) and Sixth (Cape Town, 2009) Annual National Oral History Conference. Western Cape.

Rankopo, M.J, Osei-Hwedie, K. & Modie-Moroka, T. 2006. *Five-Country Study on Service and Volunteering in Southern Africa*. Vosesa: Volunteer and Service Enquiry Southern Africa. Republic of South Africa.

Sewpaul, V. 2014. Community Work and the Challenges of Neo-liberalism and New Managerialism: Resistance, the Occupy Movement and the Arab Spring. In: A.K. Larsen, V. Sewpaul & G.O. Hole (eds.). *Participation in Community Work: International Perspectives*. London: Routledge Taylor and Francis Group: 217-229.

Siqwana-Ndulo, N. 1998. Rural African Family Structure in the Eastern Cape Province: South Africa. *Journal of Comparative Family Studies*, 9(2): 407-417.

Smets, P. & Wels, H. 1999. *Trust & Co-Operation: Symbolic Exchange and Moral Economies in an Age of Cultural Differentiation*. Het Spinhuis: Amsterdam.

Standing, G. 2007. Social Protection. *Development in Practice*, 17(4-5): 511-522.

Statistics South Africa. 2014. *Poverty Trends in South Africa: An examination of absolute poverty between 2006 and 2011*. Pretoria: Statistics South Africa.

Taylor Committee. 2002. *Transforming the Present-Protecting the Future: Report of the Committee of Inquiry into a Comprehensive System of Social Security for South Africa*. Pretoria: Department of Social Development.

The Mail and Guardian. 24 February 2016. *Pravin Gordhan's full 2016 budget speech*.

Triegaardt, J. 2009. Pursuing a Social Development Agenda in the Context of Globalisation: A South African Perspective. *Social Work/ Maatskaplike Werk*, 45(1): 1-10.

05

INDIGENOUS SOCIAL SECURITY SYSTEMS IN ZAMBIA: ADVANCING A PUBLIC POLICY AGENDA?

Ndangwa Noyoo & Beatrice Mutale Sakala

Introduction

This chapter disscusses Indigenous Social Security Systems (ISSS) in Zambia. The main objective of the chapter is to ascertain whether ISSS are considered by policy-makers when they develop public policies for the country. The chapter also discusses the notion of ISSS in the context of Zambia, by firstly casting some light on the pre-colonial period where ISSS were the main forms of protection against want, deprivation and other social ills, before the coming of the Europeans to this part of Africa. Thereafter, the chapter examines the colonial era when the Europeans introduced the formal social security system in the country. As it will be shown later, the forgoing system was part of the formal social welfare system that was introduced in colonial Zambia and which was almost a replica of the British system. This was due to the fact that Zambia was a British colony. The discussion then focuses on the post-colonial era and attempts to show how the colonial experience was inherited or not even altered much in some respect by the Zambian Government, especially when it comes to the country's formal social security system. This chapter's insights are informed by findings from an empirical research which was undertaken by the authors. The research had sought to find out if ISSS were referred to when public policies were developed in Zambia. This research was part of a larger study that focused on ISSS in the two regions of Southern and West Africa. It was initially conceptualised in 2014 and had comprised country-specific studies which were led by researchers and academics from Southern and West Africa. To understand the chapter's main points, it is important to revisit its conceptual anchoring.

Conceptual definitions and theoretical underpinnings

Historically, social protection has formed the core of social policy. It comprises *social insurance, social assistance* and the central element of *family care and solidarity*. Based on contributions, social insurance is a tool for mitigating lifecycle risks and covers such risks as illness, unemployment, old age and injury. Social assistance, which is usually seen as a tool for poverty alleviation, is generally financed from the public budget and may take the form of financial assistance to people in need or subsidies (Economic & Social Commission for Western Asia, 2009). In this discussion, Indigenous Social Security Systems are derivatives of Indigenous Knowledge Systems (IKS). The latter underpin the former. By way of definition, the word *indigenous* refers to the root, natural or innate to something (Odora-Hoppers, 2002). Indigenous knowledge is an integral part of culture. Thus, IKS refer to the combination of knowledge systems encompassing technology, social, economic and philosophical learning, or educational, legal and governance systems.

Furthermore, IKS is knowledge relating to the technological, social, institutional, scientific and developmental aspects of life (Odora-Hoppers, 2002). Indigenous knowledge is associated with the term 'local knowledge' or 'ethnoscience', indicating knowledge systems that are specific to cultures or groups in social or historical contexts (Seleti, 2013). Regarding the above-mentioned, it can be seen that ISSS and IKS are also cultural specific. When considering how much a given agent, such as the state, ought to aid those targeted by social protection, it is natural to think that it should do so to the maximum degree (subject to available resources). Thus, an agent's intentions in this issue matter especially from a moral stand-point. Indeed, under certain conditions, this means that it could be appropriate to trade off some degree to which others are aided (Metz, 2016).

The Zambian research study

For the authors who wrote this chapter to embark on the research which informed this chapter, they needed to pose a research question which, in turn, had to guide the research process. The research question of the study was the following: Does public policy-making in Zambia incorporate ISSS? The main assumption of the research was that indigenous knowledge or ISSS were not considered by the main driver of the public policy agenda of Zambia – the Government – when it was formulating public policies. The research was guided by the following objectives:

1. To determine the existence of Indigenous Social Security Systems (ISSS) in Zambia.
2. To find out how ISSS were being utilised by ordinary people in Zambia.
3. To investigate and determine whether the Zambian Government incorporated ISSS into mainstream Government public policies and public policy responses.
4. To make recommendations on how ISSS could be incorporated into Zambia's public policies.

Methodology

This study had employed a qualitative research approach and then utilised an exploratory research design. This is because the research had endeavoured to answer questions which would eventually assist in ascertaining the extent to which the Zambian Government mainstreamed ISSS in public policy formulation or not (Babbie & Mouton, 2001). The researchers had used this kind of design because of the nature of the data which was qualitative in nature. The study focused on two different population groups at: (a) provincial and (b) district levels.

Population sample and sampling

The individuals who had participated in this research were sampled from the city of Lusaka and the rural town of Katete. Lusaka is the capital city of Zambia and had served as the provincial sample for the research study. The second population was sampled from Katete district which is a rural set-up with an estimated population of 268 852 in 2010 (Central Statistical Office, 2011). The research had sampled participants using the purposive sampling technique because the researchers were interested in gathering information from people who had a certain level of understanding or knowledge of ISSS. Hence, these individuals were split into two categories (De Vos, Strydom & Delport, 2011). The first category comprised Government officials, whilst the second group was made up of ordinary citizens who were mainly semi-professionals or worked in the non-governmental sector. This selection criterion was followed to have richer information and also to ensure that the objectives of the study were met. The total number of the sample was 12 participants. In this regard, six individuals were drawn from the Government sector whilst the other six were sampled from the non-governmental sector. There were also six individuals from Lusaka and six people from Katete district who had participated in the study. The participants were recruited by the researchers after they were each asked to participate in the study and after they had volunteered to be part of the research. Prior to interviewing the selected participants, the researchers had made appointments with them and explained to them, in detail, the purpose of the study. After the participants had pointed out that they understood what the purpose of the study was, the research got underway.

Data collection

Being a qualitative study, data was collected through a semi-structured interview schedule which had structured questions. The choice of the data collection tool was influenced by the need to develop themes from the data (Creswell, 2003). The interview schedule had a list of questions which were derived from the aim and objectives of the study. These questions had also included some demographic questions, which among others, referred to the gender and the place of residence of the participants – whether they were from rural or urban areas. There was also a section that solicited information pertaining to the positions of the respondents in specific organisations and whether they were employed or not. The respondents were also asked what their ages were. It was important to have included this section in the research tool to ascertain the experience and knowledge of a respondent. After all the information was collected, the researchers had to then analyse and interpret the data.

Data analysis

Since this was a qualitative research, data was collected via a semi-structured interview and it was then analysed manually through what is known as a thematic approach (Ritchie, Jane & Lewis, 2003). Data was analysed through themes which were derived from the aim and objectives of the study. This is because the interview schedule used for collecting data already comprised structured questions. Despite already having a set of themes, it is worth noting that there were other themes that emerged during the data analysis. Thereafter, both emerging and set themes were coded and after being coded a process of thematic analysis was undertaken. This is a method of data analysis mostly used for qualitative studies (Fereday & Muir-Cochrane, 2006). For each theme, similar responses were grouped together. For instance, under theme one, which was concerned with the need to establish the level of knowledge/awareness of participants regarding ISSS, all the responses that had expressed some awareness/knowledge, were grouped together. The rest of the themes were analysed in a similar manner.

Ethical considerations

This research, just like other qualitative researches of the social sciences, followed ethical standards. Thus, social science research ethics were adhered to. One important indication regarding the foregoing issue was that the researchers had not only sought permission from the research participants, but also from relevant authorities where the individuals worked. For instance, permission was sought and obtained from Government Departments so that individuals could be given permission to participate in the study. A letter of introduction which had clearly stipulated the purpose of the study and the need for the participant to take part in it, was furnished to the heads of Government Departments. Also, the participants were not forced to take part in the study, but were instead asked to volunteer to participate in the research. Another crucial issue relates to the confidentiality and anonymity of the research participants. These two aspects were stressed throughout the research process by the researchers. Another way this issue was expressed was to make sure that the interview schedule had a section which did not require the participant's name.

After looking at the research process and its methodological considerations, the following section contextualises the chapter's discussions.

The context and background

Zambia is a landlocked country which is situated in south-central Africa, with a landmass area of 752 614 km². Its neighbours are Angola in the west, Botswana in the south, Namibia to the southwest, the Democratic Republic of the Congo (DRC) to the north, Malawi in the east, Mozambique to the southeast, Tanzania in the northeast, while Zimbabwe is to the south of the country. According to Zambia's 2010 census results, the country's population stands at 13 046 508, with 49 per cent males and 51 per cent females. Regional distribution of the population shows that 7 978 274 people (61 per cent) reside in rural areas and 5 068 234 (39 per cent) live in urban areas. At the provincial level, Lusaka, the capital city, has the largest population of 2 198 996, followed by the Copperbelt at 1 958 623. The Northern Province (which was split into Muchinga and Northern provinces in 2012) is the third largest with a population of 1 759 600, followed by the Eastern and Southern provinces at 1 707 731 and 1 606 793 respectively. Exhibiting the lowest population numbers are Luapula Province, Western Province (Barotseland) and the North-Western Province with 958 976; 881 524 and 706 462 people in that order (Central Statistical Office, 2011). Zambia became independent on 24 October 1964 and had adhered to a multi-party political system until 1973, when it became a one-party state dictatorship. Zambia only reverted to the multi-party system when the founding president of Zambia, Kenneth Kaunda and his United National Independence Party (UNIP), were overwhelmingly defeated at the polls by the Movement for Multi-Party Democracy (MMD) in 1991. When the MMD came to power, Zambia's economy had virtually collapsed due to Kaunda's and UNIP's imprudent policies and political actions.

According to the Central Statistical Office (CSO) (2012) the Living Conditions Monitoring Surveys, conducted from 1991 to 2006, have shown that the incidence of poverty has reduced over the years. The results show that poverty declined from 70 per cent in 1991 to 64 per cent in 2006. The gains of this reduction can be noticed in rural areas, where poverty reduced from 88 per cent in 1991 to 78 per cent in 2006. In contrast, poverty in urban areas increased from 49 per cent in 1991 to 53 per cent in 2006. After growth in the Zambian economy, from around 2000 to 2007, the Zambian economy has been contracting, especially after the Patriotic Front (PF) came to power in 2011. The PF was voted by the citizens due to its populist rhetoric of "putting more money in the pockets" of Zambians.

The late president and PF leader, Michael Sata (2011-2014) and now the new president and PF leader, Edgar Lungu, followed and continue to follow policies that have led to the contraction of the Zambian economy and increasing poverty trends. One of the major shortcomings of their approach to governance has been the heavy borrowing that the PF Government has pursued and that has led Zambia back into the debt hole it emerged from in 2005. According to a report by the African Development Bank (AfDB), Organisation for Economic Co-operation and Development (OECD) and the United Nations Development Programme (UNDP) (2016) in 2015, the Zambian economy faced economic headwinds initially due to fast rising expenditures and a fiscal deficit that more than doubled in 2013. Slowing demand from China had reduced copper prices to their lowest level in more than seven years. The situation was exacerbated by low agriculture output and a growing electricity crisis. Real economic growth fell to its lowest in 15 years, with Gross Domestic Product (GDP) growth estimated to have slowed to 3,7 per cent from 5,0 per cent in 2014. Due to this and as in the past when Zambia's economy was not performing well, many Zambians have once more resorted to using ISSS.

It can be asserted that ISSS have existed in Zambia for centuries, even prior to colonial rule. Most of them derive their meaning from the traditional systems of the country's more than 72 ethnic groups. In the pre-colonial era, different societies (of present-day Zambia) had various ways of meeting the needs of their members. All these pre-colonial societies had mechanisms to look after those who were disadvantaged or could not fend for themselves. Over the centuries, it can be argued that almost all pre-colonial societies had devised means, to safeguard people's well-being. Thus, ISSS that responded to human needs and predominated in the pre-colonial period was exemplified by communal existence. For example, those who were considered vulnerable or in need, were initially looked after by their families in such societies. During this period, the extended family system met the needs of individuals through strong bonds of solidarity and networks of reciprocity (Noyoo, 2015). The extended African family was the first form of defence against want and deprivation, as it provided for the emotional, material and spiritual support of its members. Mutual-help reinforced family solidarity, as adults provided for the needs of children, whilst the elderly socialised them. Children supplied labour and companionship to parents and grandparents (Boon, 2007). Therefore, in pre-colonial Zambia people were, in many cases, attached to each other through reciprocal relations of social support that were embedded in cultural norms and practices. In these times, it was considered taboo to ridicule the infirm, elderly and people with disabilities. Also, vagrants were quite rare in the village environment since families were obliged to look after their less fortunate members. In such circumstances, widows, orphans and the aged were cared for by their relatives.

It is safe to say that the formal social security system was introduced in Zambia by the colonialists. Colonial rule in Zambia was facilitated in the late 1880s by the British South Africa Company (BSAC) which was headed by Cecil John Rhodes, an ardent agent of British imperialism in Southern Africa. The BSAC was a commercial entity whose prime objective was the exploitation of natural resources for the benefit of Britain. Hence it was not concerned with the development of the territory and only built basic infrastructure during its rule. Its sole purpose was to export the territory's natural resources to Britain. During the rule of the BSAC, Zambia was administered as two separate territories, namely, North-Western Rhodesia and North-Eastern Rhodesia. In 1911, the two areas were amalgamated to form Northern Rhodesia which came under formal British colonial rule in 1924. What is important to note here is that formal social security systems were created by the British to respond to the needs of the few Europeans in the colony. This system was also a derivative of the social welfare system which was created in colonial Zambia by the British. The development of welfare systems in the British colonies was dependent on certain global developments at the time. Significantly, the Great Depression of the 1920s and 1930s and the Second World War, stand out as main events that made the British to create these systems in Africa.

These two dislocating forces inadvertently triggered positive reactions from European countries which had colonies to firstly put in place comprehensive and high quality social welfare systems for their citizens resident in the colonies. Secondly, they were compelled by changing global circumstances, to respond humanely to their colonial subjects. This change in attitude was tempered by economic and security realities. The Great Depression had led to a fall of prices of many commodities of the colonies on European markets. This resulted in dwindling revenues which were critical to both the imperial countries' fortunes and of the colonies. In addition, social problems were also increasing in the colonies and burdening their already politically volatile urban environment.

Colonial subjects were getting disgruntled and beginning to demand for better living conditions. Therefore, the provision of social welfare services was beginning to be crucial to securing the livelihoods of colonial subjects by the colonial authorities. On the other hand, the Second World War had fundamentally transformed imperialism and led to a rethink of the European countries' imperial desires. Against Nazi and fascist threats, Western Europe had galvanised its colonial subjects towards the war effort under the banner of justice and freedom. This had the unintended consequence of raising African people's desire for self-rule as earlier intimated. It is therefore not coincidental that most African nationalist movements that emerged to fight colonial domination were formed during or after the Second World War. In some cases, as in colonial Zambia, the nationalist movements had Welfare Associations as their precursors. The African Welfare Associations in colonial Zambia had been formed by the locals to press for better living conditions for Africans in the urban settings:

> The African Welfare Societies were anxious about the social disorder in the towns. With the help of missionaries and social workers they organised football matches, started small libraries and run small clubs (Hall, 1965: 130).

In May 1946 Dauti Yamba, who was the founder of the Luanshya Welfare Association, together with representatives from 13 other Welfare Associations scattered across the colonial territory (both in the urban and rural areas) called for the uniting of all welfare organisations under one body. In attendance at this meeting in the town of Kabwe were several delegates such as Godwin Mbikusita Lewanika of the Kitwe African Society, Nelson Nalumango of the Livingstone Welfare Society, N.S. Liyanda of the Mongu Welfare Society, Sykes Ndilila of the Broken Hill (Kabwe) Welfare Society, Joseph Y. Mumba of Lusaka Welfare Society and George W.C. Kaluwa of Mazabuka Welfare Society. All these formations were amalgamated into the Federation of African Welfare Societies with Yamba as President, Mumba as Assistant Secretary and Kaluwa, the Organising Secretary (Rotberg, 1965).

The federation of these formations aimed to create co-operation and mutual understanding between constituent societies of Northern Rhodesia in both the rural and urban areas. Two years later, in 1948, this movement was reconstituted into a nationalist political organisation known as the Northern Rhodesia Congress (NRC) under the leadership of Godwin Mbikusita Lewanika. Other office bearers were the two Vice Presidents of Congress: L. Mufana Lipalile and Robinson M. Nabulyato. Mateyo Kakumbi was the Treasurer whilst John Richmond was Assistant Secretary and George Kaluwa was the Assistant Treasurer. According to the Constitution that it adopted, this formation wanted to "promote the educational, political, economic and social advancement of Africans" and be the Africans' mouthpiece. It would "only do its best to interpret truly and faithfully the real African opinion in building up a satisfied, peaceful and progressive Northern Rhodesia" (Rotberg, 1965: 212).

After independence, on 24 October 1964, Zambia, like most of post-colonial Africa, used the colonial frameworks as building-blocks to create a new social welfare dispensation. Naturally, Zambia's formal social welfare system in general and its social security system in particular, had British roots due to again, colonialism. Kenneth Kaunda was the first president of an independent Zambia and he headed the United National Independence Party (UNIP)-led Government. Kaunda and UNIP espoused socialist ideals and principles which would also shape and define social welfare and social security interventions in post-colonial Zambia for three decades. Due to this, an interventionist approach to social welfare and social security was followed after independence:

> In addition, there were substantial social service expenditures aimed at alleviating poverty. These included subsidised education, health-care and other social service delivery. The social service expenditure comprised roughly a third of the total Government budget. Although many of the social programmes had well-meaning objectives, they generated adverse side effects and did little to solve the structural causes of poverty (Kalinda & Floro, 1992: 7).

Nevertheless, in the early years of independence, former colonial officials and other expatriates reinforced the colonial legacy through Eurocentric social welfare models and intervention strategies. Also, since social welfare services in the colonial era were geared towards safeguarding the needs of the colonisers and not of the local people, ill-informed interventions that were mostly not attuned to local conditions were adhered to, especially in the first decade after independence. Nonetheless, formal social security measures were strengthened after independence when the Zambia National Provident Fund (ZNPF) was founded in 1966 and the Workmen's Compensation Board was established in 1969. The ZNPF aimed, among other things, to enable aged people to enjoy some measure of financial independence based on contributions made during their working days (Department of Social Welfare, 1966). Although well intended, the ZNPF confined itself to only Zambians who were in formal employment and did not cater for those in self-employment or the informal sector. At the outset, there was more focus on social security and social insurance measures as opposed to social assistance in Zambia.

According to Siamwiza, Sikwebele and Makonne (1993: 8), when Zambia faced an economic downturn in the late 1970s, the social security system continued to be restrictive, as all its programmes were geared towards the protection of employed people. Social security was supposed to guard against economic and social distress caused by reduced earnings, unemployment, injury, old age, medical needs and death. Benefits were provided only to those in gainful employment who contributed to a pension, retirement, or gratuity programme, and where employers also made contributions to employees' contributions. This system, therefore, did not provide medical assistance or other benefits to the unemployed. Thus, Zambians who were not covered by formal social security arrangements relied on Indigenous Social Security Systems to survive the harsh economic conditions. Mukuka, Kalikiti and Musenge (2002) echo the foregoing views and note that Zambia has two social security systems existing side-by-side. The first is offered by the state while the second is the traditional system, which we refer to in this chapter as the indigenous one. For the traditional social security, the extended family and semi-formal schemes such as reciprocal urban networks, the Church, *chilimba* (indigenous banking systems) and market associations are pivotal in providing social protection to poor and vulnerable Zambians. The former authors also point out that traditional social security arrangements were destroyed by a series of Governments, starting with the colonial authorities and continuing through to the late 1990s under different post-colonial Governments.

What can be deciphered from the foregoing account is that the actions of the post-colonial Government were at times detrimental to the standing of the ISSS in Zambia:

> The burial societies and market associations that had existed in the Copperbelt during the colonial days were discontinued after independence. The philosophy of Humanism, entailing an elaborate system of the free provision of social services, combined with policies directing all employers to provide their employees with loans and funeral grants combined to discourage the continuation of the pre-independence burial societies. These also undermined other non-formal schemes, such as the chilimba scheme and market associations (Mukuka *et al*, 2002: 95).

Furthermore, there is a variation in content when it comes to urban and rural ISSS in Zambia. Urban social networks have been used to cover many contingencies including job losses, funerals, sickness, political support and disputes. While in rural areas the ISSS have been sustained by and depend on the extended family system, in urban areas indigenous social security schemes are largely sustained by and depend on non-kin reciprocal social networks (Mukuka *et al*, 2002: 93). Despite the differences in the urban setting, the extended family system remains the cornerstone of ISSS in Zambia. What is also instructive about ISSS is that they were instrumental in reducing the adverse effects of the country's economic auterity measures in the 1990s, when Zambia was strictly adhering to the Structural Adjustment Programme (SAP) of the International Monetary Fund (IMF) and the World Bank. When the MMD Government (which replaced the UNIP Government in 1991) started to implement the SAP, it adopted a strategy of 'disengagement' in regard to social welfare and social security matters. This was manifested in such measures as cost-sharing (user fees), reduction in budgetary allocation to social services in real terms, cash budget system of public finance and decontrolled pricing regime (Masiye, Tembo, Chisanga & Mwanza, 1998).

Hence, the strategy of the MMD (especially during the presidency of Frederick Chiluba, from 1991 to 2001) was predicated on the principle that the welfare of the public was primarily the responsibility of the individual, families and communities. The role of the Government was limited to the formulation of policies and programmes aimed at creating an enabling environment for economic growth. The assumption was that economic growth would generate job opportunities which would enable individuals and families to become economically and socially self-sufficient and reduce poverty (Masiye *et al*, 1998). At best, during this period, the formal social security systems had either collpased or were severely compromised by the SAP. Presently, Zambia's social security system rests on the formal pillar which was not so pronounced in the 1970s and '80s and this is social assistance. Social cash transfers are now being touted as the Government's major anti-poverty measure in Zambia. After they were initially piloted in 2003, in Kalomo District of the Southern Province by an international donor organisation, they have now been rolled out to several parts of the country.

Nevertheless, despite their importance, ISSS still exist on the peripheries of Zambia's public policy-making process. Therefore, it can be argued that there is a disconnect between public policies in Zambia and ISSS – which are currently meeting the needs of marginalised and poor Zambians especially, during economic downturns. In the next section the findings of the research which informed this chapter are presented and discussed.

Presentation of findings of Government officials' responses

To arrive at the findings of the research, data had to be analysed and then interpreted after it was collected. Data collection had been undertaken in order to ascertain the extent of the use of indigenous knowledge in the development of public policies in Zambia. The findings of the research were analysed thematically based on the research question, aim and objectives and the research methodology. The first part of the research had focused on Government officials who worked at both the National Government and Local Government levels. The first theme that had guided the analysis and interpretation of data dealt with the issue of knowledge/awareness of Indigenous Social Security Systems in the country. From the findings of the research, it was discovered that most Government officials who were interviewed for the study (at both national and local levels) were aware of the existence of ISSS in Zambia. About 75 per cent of the Government officials even provided detailed explanations as to what ISSS were. This clearly shows that Government officials are not ignorant about ISSS. They also seem to know what they are and stand for. For instance, one respondent referred to ISSS as:

> Social security by local initiatives or community groups and most of them are economic in nature. Some of them are supported by Non-Governmental Organisations and Civil Society Organisations. They include chilimba, economic initiatives by community members and community savings.

In addition, the responses from Local Government stakeholders, were well-articulated regarding the concept of ISSS, in contrast to those at the national level. This understanding flowed from the practical examples that were provided by the respondents which included village savings and Savings and Internal Lending Communities (SILCs). Even more striking, those officials at the national level had expressed interest in the formal social security systems such as national pension schemes which are currently being provided by the state. It can thus be speculated that this evidence showed that ISSS were probably not seriously considered at that level. The second theme that guided the analysis of data and its interpretation was the incorporation of ISSS into policy-making. The findings also revealed that only one respondent (from all those who had been interviewed) agreed that ISSS were currently incorporated into policy formulation in Zambia. The rest of the respondents noted that ISSS were not incorporated into policy-making. These findings confirm that the Zambian Government does not prioritise ISSS in public policy development.

Ordinary Zambians' responses

To get richer information on ISSS in Zambia the researchers interviewed ordinary Zambians who did not have a vested interest in the area under examination. This was done to have a different perspective from that of policy-makers and Government actors. This approach was also meant to determine the extent of knowledge/awareness and the incorporation of ISSS into policy development, from the perspective of ordinary Zambians. Most respondents who were sampled, at both local and national levels, acknowledged being fully aware of the existence of various ISSS in the country. Like the responses of Government officials, most participants were able to provide various explanations relating to what ISSS signified. Some explanations worth highlighting include the following:

1. Indigenous Social Security Systems are groups within the communities with locally defined procedures, and terms on how to invest or save money which can be used later by individuals/ participants of that particular group.

2. These are systems set up to help in times of need when one may not have the resources ready.

3. When groups of people come together and put money together to help one another, in business or for basic home needs.

From the foregoing explanations which were provided by respondents, it can be discerned that some Zambians do have some knowledge about ISSS. More importantly, it is interesting that respondents were able to acknowledge the usefulness of ISSS, especially in times when an individual was in dire need of resources. In terms of the theme relating to the incorporation of ISSS into public policy-making, generally all the respondents noted that ISSS were not incorporated into this process. The ordinary citizens' responses were also analysed by referring to another theme, namely: The utilisation of indigenous knowledge to deal with shocks and insecurities. When it came to the former issue, the respondents were of the view that Indigenous Social Security Systems were vital and played a key role in circumstances where people's needs were not met by formal social security systems. The implication of this response is that people can deal with financial shocks and insecurities by making use of the ISSS. The respondents also mentioned the fact that in the absence of ISSS it was very difficult for people to cope, particularly those who are mainly located in the informal sector. However, the respondents observed that even for people in the formal sector, when the formal social security systems were not available, the ISSS were very helpful in providing support to such Zambians.

The last section of the research tool endeavoured to elicit responses from the research participants in relation to the last objective of the study that sought to: Make recommendations on how ISSS could be incorporated into Zambia's public policies. There were various recommendations that were provided by the respondents. Some of the recommendations were the following:

- The Government of Zambia is implementing the Social Cash Transfer Programme which is like ISSS, though not the same. The Government is also supporting women's groups under the Department of Community Development. The Government could provide a framework or (policy) guidelines on ISSS by aligning social cash transfers with ISSS. The indigenous ones should be adopted by Government by providing policy guidelines.

- The ISSS are making great impacts in the households of people especially 'marketeers' (referring to market traders) and rural communities. They would result into bigger or greater impact if supported or guided by Government policy.

- Policy makers should first dialogue with people at the grass roots level and get their views before incorporating ISSS into policy-making.

- Government should first come up with a law to regulate the ISSS.

- The Government should put up deliberate policies to support ISSS, especially considering that in developing countries such as Zambia, the informal sector is larger than the formal sector.

- The village saving and loan associations under the social welfare programme should be incorporated into policy formulation because it is something that people are practising as a form of social security.

- The Government should generate policies that will be flexible and easier for ISSS to be mainstreamed into public policies.

- The Government should collect data related to how best the community feels or would like ISSS to operate.

The abovementioned recommendations were made by ordinary Zambians and this chapter duly notes them.

Conclusion

Based on the discussions in the preceding sections of the chapter, it can be argued that after 53 years of independence, Zambian policy-makers seem to be still giving more preference to Western forms of social security than to indigenous ones. The purpose of this chapter was to investigate the extent to which ISSS have been mainstreamed into Zambia's public policy-making processes. Some of the questions it posed are the following: Does public policy-making incorporate Indigenous Social Security Systems or not? If not, why? Also, a normative position was taken which asked whether there was even a need to incorporate ISSS into Zambia's public policies. This chapter's findings show that there is a need to bridge the divide between formal social security systems and ISSS in Zambia. Even though the latter have existed parallel to the former, they have safeguarded the livelihoods of Zambians when the country experienced economic hardship. For instance, during the implementation of the IMF's and World Bank's SAP, ISSS were relied upon by many Zambians to cushion the harsh effects of the economic austerity measures, that were implemented by the Zambian Government and that were inspired by the IMF and World Bank. The research study on which this chapter is based was also able to decipher that even though Government officials and policy-makers were aware of the existence of the Indigenous Social Security Systems they have not made any concerted efforts to mainstream them into the public policy-making endeavours of Zambia.

Although the research that informs this chapter was able to provide some new insights relating to ISSS in Zambia and their non-inclusion in public policy-making efforts, more work still needs to be undertaken in this area. In concluding this chapter, we reiterate the observations which were made by Mukuka *et al*, (2002:73):

> It had been widely recognised that the formal social security system in Zambia is inadequate in terms of its capacity and coverage and that many people rely on non-formal social security systems and schemes. However, there are still gaps in available knowledge, especially about non-formal social security systems and schemes because no previous comprehensive study on social security has analysed and documented them. These gaps include an understanding of their structures, capacity, functions, contingencies covered, viability and conceptualisation of social security itself.

Finally, it must be stated that what ordinary Zambians pointed out in the findings, which are presented in this chapter, should not be taken lightly or even dismissed. Indeed,

Zambian politicians and policy-makers should reflect on them. It can be seen that a significant number of the respondents are in favour of the idea of incorporating ISSS or indigenous knowledge into formal public policy-making processes. This is a very important point and hopefully soon the Government will heed the citizens' advice on this matter.

References

African Development Bank (AfDB), Organisation for Economic Co-operation and Development (OECD) & the United Nations Development Programme (UNDP). 2016. Zambia. www.africaneconomicoutlook.org/sites/default/files/2016-05/Zambia_BG-2016%20WEB.pdf [Accessed 13 December 2016].

Babbie, E. & Mouton, J. 2001. *The practice of social research*. Oxford: Oxford University Press.

Boon, E.K. 2007. Knowledge Systems and Social Security in Africa: A Case Study on Ghana. In: E.K. Boon & L. Hens (eds.). *Indigenous Knowledge Systems and Sustainable Development: Relevance for Africa*. Delhi: Kamla-Raj Enterprises. 63-76.

Central Statistical Office (CSO). 2012. *Living Conditions: Poverty in Zambia – 1991-2006*. www.zamstats.gov.zm/lcm.php [Accessed 12 June 2012].

Central Statistical Office (CSO). 2011. *2010 Census of Population and Housing of Zambia: Preliminary Report*. Lusaka: Central Statistical Office.

Creswell, J.W. 2003. *Research Design Qualitative, Quantitative and Mixed Methods Approaches*. (2nd Edition). Thousand Oaks, CA: Sage Publications.

Department of Social Welfare. 1966. *Annual Report*. Lusaka: Government Printers.

De Vos, A.S.; Strydom, S.; Fouche, C.B. & Delport, C.S.L. 2011. Sampling and pilot study in qualitative research. In: A.S. de Vos, S. Strydom, C.B. Fouche & C.S.L. Delport (eds.). *Research at grass roots for the social sciences and human service professions*. 4th Edition. Pretoria: Van Schaik: 392.

Economic and Social Commission for Western Asia, (ESCW). 2009. *Social Policy and Social Protection*. www.escwa.un.org/information/publications/edit/upload/sdd-09-TP10.pdf [Accessed on 27 July 2011].

Fereday, J. & Muir-Cochrane, E. 2006. *Demonstrating rigour using thematic analysis: A hybrid approach of inductive and deductive coding and theme development*. www.ualberta.ca/~iiqm/backissues/5_1/html/fereday.htm [Accessed 12 June 2013].

Hall, R. 1965. *Zambia*. London: Pall Mall Press.

Kalinda, B. & Floro, M. 1992. *Zambia in the 1980s: A Review of National and Urban level Economic Reforms.* Washington, D.C: The World Bank.

Masiye, G.P.C.; Tembo, R.; Chisanga, B. & Mwanza, A. 1998. Social Policy and Research Environment in Zambia. *Journal of Social Development in Africa,* 13(12): 34-43.

Metz, T. 2016. Recent philosophical approaches to social protection: From capability to *Ubuntu. Global Social Policy,* 16 (3): 1-19. https://doi.org/10.1177/1468018116633575

Mukuka, L.; Kalikiti, W. & Musenge, D.K. 2002. Social Security in Zambia: Phase One Overview of Social Security in Zambia. *African Journal of Social Work,* 17(2): 65-96.

Noyoo, N. 2015. Social Development in Southern Africa. In: L. Calvelo, R. Lutz & F. Ross (eds.). *Development and Social Work: Social Work of the South, Volume VI.* Oldenburg: Paulo Freire Verlag. 167-185.

Odora-Hoppers, C.A. 2002. Indigenous Knowledge and the Integration of Knowledge Systems: Towards a conceptual and methodological framework. In: C.A. Odora-Hoppers (ed.). *Indigenous Knowledge and the integration of knowledge systems: Towards a philosophy of articulation.* Claremont: New Africa Books (Pty) Ltd. 1-21.

Ritchie, J.; Lewis, J. & Elam, G. 2003. Designing and selecting samples. In: J. Ritchie & J. Lewis (eds.). *Qualitative research practice. A guide for social science students and researchers.* Thousand Oaks, CA: Sage Publications. 1-21.

Rotberg, R.I. 1965. *The Rise of Nationalism in Central Africa: The Making of Malawi and Zambia, 1873-1964.* Cambridge, MA: Harvard University Press.

Seleti, Y. 2013. The value of Indigenous Knowledge Systems in the 21st Century. In: J.K. Gilbert & S. Stocklmayer (eds.). *Communication and engagement with science and technology: Issues and dilemmas.* New York, NY: Routledge. 261-272

Siamwiza, R.; Sikwebele, A. & Makonnen, A. 1993. A Historical Review of Social Policy and Urban Interventions. Washington, D.C: The World Bank.

06

INDIGENOUS SOCIAL SECURITY SYSTEMS IN ZIMBABWE: STRENGTHS, CHALLENGES AND PROSPECTS

Mildred T. Mushunje & Edwell Kaseke

Introduction

Based on a review of secondary data, this chapter discusses Indigenous Social Security Systems (ISSS) in Zimbabwe. The chapter explores how ISSS have been incorporated into mainstream public policies of Zimbabwe and provides recommendations on how this process can be further strengthened. A discussion of the social security system in Zimbabwe would be incomplete without reference to the colonial past as this also had a bearing on ISSS. The chapter is also premised on the notion that social security is a basic human right as enshrined in the Universal Declaration of Human Rights (1948) and the International Covenant on Economic, Social and Cultural Rights (1966) and because of this, all people are eligible for social security coverage, whether formal or informal.

Background to formal social security in Zimbabwe

There are various definitions of social security and in this instance, we define it as "all cash and in-kind social transfers that are organised by state or parastatal organisations or are agreed upon through collective bargaining processes. Benefits arising from this arrangement include: Cash transfers such as pensions, employment injury benefits, short-term cash benefits (sickness and maternity benefits, unemployment benefits), as well as benefits in kind such as health services" (Cichon, Scholz, van de Meerendonk, Hagemejer, Bertranou & Plamondon, 2004: 261). Social security is concerned with addressing risks and according to Holzmann and Jorgensen (2001), it consists of public interventions that seek to assist individuals, households and communities and the poor to address risk. In our case we define ISSS as traditional support systems that meet human needs at the individual, family and community levels. Olivier, Kaseke and Mpedi (2008: 3) note that the former are of two forms, namely: Those that are family or kinship based and those that are anchored in mutual aid arrangements and are community or neighbourhood-based and are driven by the principle of solidarity.

It is contended by the authors that formal social security in colonial Zimbabwe was a privilege of the whites as it was expected that the indigenous people would draw on structures like the extended family to mitigate against risks and disasters (Kaseke, 2003). From the period of colonialism until the attainment of independence in 1980, there was virtually no formal social security that was extended to the indigenous African and black majority. The understanding was that the blacks were in the urban areas on temporary basis and only there to work and would go back to their rural homes upon retirement where the Indigenous Social Security Systems would be catering for them. Because of this, the blacks created mechanisms to cope with retirement and economic hardships. As such, the notion of Indigenous Social Security Systems is not new in Zimbabwe. These systems have always been important for blacks because of the systematic marginalisation from mainstream social security and other systems.

Colonial laws in existence at the time included the Old Age Pensions Act of 1936. This Act provided old age pensions to non-Africans over 60 years and who only had been resident in the country for 15 years or more. Coverage was later extended to African workers although this was mainly concentrated in urban areas and formal sector workers to the exclusion of most of the informal workers. Although a pension scheme for agricultural workers was introduced by the Rhodesia National Farmers' Union (RNFU) in 1975, it had very limited beneficiaries. This is because the eligibility age was set at 60 when life expectancy during the time was only about 50 and consequently, not many indigenous black workers reached the retirement threshold (Dhemba, Gumbo & Nyamusara, 2002: 132-153).

Nonetheless, there were also several private occupational pensions during the colonial era. According to the Whitsun Foundation study (1979), less than 50 per cent of the Africans in formal employment in 1976 were beneficiaries. The white settler Government was also supposedly motivated by a desire to attract and retain white immigrants by providing conditions and services comparable to those obtainable in Great Britain. Incidences of discrimination, because of gender, were also rampant regarding African women, resulting in their marginalisation. Hawkins and Hawkins (1981), cite Riddell (1981: 172), who observed that the "demand for male workers in the wage sector, coupled with the belief that a woman's role lies in childbearing, has led to the extreme imbalance in access to schooling for African men and women." As a result, many women could not be members of occupational pension schemes and were discriminated against with regards to accessing social security. Even after independence, women remained marginalised in formal employment on which much of the formal social security is based.

At independence in 1980, the Zimbabwe African National Union – Patriotic Front (ZANU-PF) led Government sought to redress the colonial imbalances and introduced several social security provisions which would be more inclusive. These include:

▷ The NSSA Act of 1989, (Chapter 17: 04) which constituted and established the National Social Security Authority (NSSA), a parastatal tasked with implementing and administering social security services. NSSA administers every scheme and fund established in terms of this Act. Schemes under NSSA include the National Pensions Scheme (NPS), which is a compulsory employee/employer contributory scheme and the Workers' Compensation Insurance Scheme (WCIS). The Workers' compensation Insurance Scheme (WCIS), established and administered in terms of Statutory Instrument 68 of 1990, seeks to provide financial relief to employees and their families when an employee is injured or killed in a work-related accident or suffers from a work-related disease or dies thereof (Government of Zimbabwe, 1989).

▷ The NSSA schemes unfortunately only cover those employed in the formal sector leaving most of the labour force subsisting in the informal economy and unprotected.

Other schemes are:

▷ The Pension and Provident Funds Act (Chapter 24: 09), which was passed in 1976 and has been revised many times since then. The Act provides for the registration, administration and regulation of private pension funds in Zimbabwe.

▷ The Public Service Pensions Scheme which is governed by the State Services (Pensions) Act (Chapter 16: 06). This is a contributory pension scheme which provides for the payment of pensions, gratuities and other benefits to people employed by the State on retirement, discharge, resignation, death or other termination of service. An employee contributes 7,5 per cent of pensionable emoluments towards the Public Service Pension Scheme while the Government contributes 15 per cent.

▷ State Service Disability Benefits Act (Chapter 16: 05) which provides for compensation because of death or injury to people employed by the State.

▷ The War Pensions Scheme which is governed by the War Pensions Act (Chapter 11: 14) whereby compensation is provided to those injured while providing military service during the Second World War.

▷ The 1998 Social Welfare Assistance Act which provides limited public assistance to destitute people incapable of work and to people aged 65 or older or with a disability.

In January 2001, with technical support from the World Bank, the Government embarked on the Enhanced Social Protection Project (ESPP) which sought to support children whose parents and guardians failed to pay school fees through the Basic Education Assistance Module (BEAM). Other components of the ESPP included the Children in Especially Difficult Circumstances (CEDC), which was designed to identify and assist children in difficult circumstances (Mushunje & Mafico, 2010); the Public Works Component (PWC), which seeks to put in place labour-intensive public works that offer employment to the poor; Emergency Drugs and Medical Supplies component; Social Protection Strategy (SPS), which studies, analyses, consults and provides technical assistance aimed at improving strategic planning, monitoring and implementing programmes in the Ministry (Chikova, 2013). The programme was premised on Government's payment of arrears to the World Bank and as a result of failure to do so, the programme was suspended (Chikova, 2013). The following are also central to formal social security:

▷ The Disabled Persons Act (Chapter 17: 01) enacted in 1991 and revised in 1996, provides for the welfare and rehabilitation of disabled people, as well as for the establishment and functions of a National Disability Board.

▷ The War Veterans Pensions Scheme is another non-contributory scheme covering war veterans who took part in the liberation war from 1962-1980. This scheme also provides pension benefits to dependants of deceased war veterans. This scheme is governed by the War Veterans Act (Chapter 11: 15).

Whilst the social security programmes appear to be comprehensive on paper, the extent of coverage remains limited, especially with the economic hardships that the country is currently experiencing and because the programmes are underfunded (Gandure, 2009). Qualifying beneficiaries have often been turned away from social services offices for lack of funding. Anecdotal evidence also shows that a number of workers who are supposed to be covered by the Pensions and Other Benefits Scheme are not being covered because of non-compliance by their employers (Chikova, 2013).

Previous discussions suggested informal social security thrived because of the discriminatory provisions in colonial polices, but clearly, even after independence, the state is failing to provide comprehensive coverage for the workforce. For instance, the National Social Security Authority Act has had a long-standing objective of covering domestic workers and workers in the informal sector and self-employed people, against contingencies of retirement, invalidity and death. To date, this has not happened. The failure on the part of the Government to provide for the social security of all citizens has resulted in the necessity for individuals and communities to draw on the strengths of the informal social security systems. Indeed, the colonial era provisions were discriminatory, but, post-independence, the Government also failed the nation in terms of comprehensive social security. Since independence, there has been an increase in cases of vulnerability and the state machinery is overwhelmed. Some of the reasons for the increase in vulnerability after independence and the impetus for ISSS utilisation include the following:

Impacts of HIV and AIDS

HIV and AIDS is one of the most expensive illnesses ever recorded in the history of health in many countries. Moreover, Zimbabwe has been at the epicentre of the pandemic. HIV and AIDS has made many rich families experience extreme poverty and lack of resources to purchase the basics of life. The African kinship care system that would have absorbed orphaned children has also been affected by HIV and AIDS to the extent that extended families are no longer able to adequately carry additional responsibilities of caring for orphans, the aged, sick and destitute members. The blitz of AIDS has greatly transformed families into child-headed ones with children raising children – a phenomenon which is quite alien to Africans as it was believed that orphans were a community's responsibility (Mushunje, 2014). Pennington and Kanabus (2005: 2) note that "almost throughout Sub-Saharan Africa, there have been traditional systems in place to take care of children who lose parents for various reasons. The onslaught of HIV has slowly eroded this good traditional practice by simply overloading its caring capacity by the sheer numbers of orphaned children needing support and care." Because of increased HIV induced poverty, some traditional roles of the extended family have been disbanded. For instance, there is increased individualism which has been noted to be a result of economic hardships rather than selfishness on the part of households (Mushunje, 2014).

Less of the extended family and increasing individualism

The current urban lifestyle and tendency to emulate the Western nuclear family are also playing a role in eroding the concept of the extended family support system. Funeral rituals and expenses which were once an affair of the whole community are becoming a household burden. Children are no longer the collective responsibility of communities, a legacy that has been historically associated with child rearing in Africa (Pennington & Kanabus, 2005). Whilst the extended family has been known to be a form of Indigenous Social Security System, negative impacts such as those caused by HIV and economic hardships have undermined the extended family's resilience. According to Olivier *et al* (2008), Africans are, in their day-to-day existence, joined together by what may be termed 'African traditional values'. It is because of these values of solidarity, collective responsibility, compassion, equality, unity, self-determination, human respect and human dignity that individuals subsist as families and that families become closely interlaced communities which form a large society. However, protracted economic crises and others such as HIV/AIDS have weakened and undermined traditional coping systems (UNICEF, UNAIDS & USAID, 2004). Extended families no longer feel obliged to welcome orphans, or care for the needy when they are not even sure of the future for their own families. For instance, in a study by Foster, Makufa, Drew and Kralovec (1997: 155-168) it was found that in 88 per cent of the households studied, relatives did not want to care for orphans, not because of a lack of benevolence, but for sheer incapacity to provide any support. Devotion and attachment are slowly fading away as each family fends for its own survival and becomes more individualistic.

Increasing poverty

Soon after independence, Zimbabwe sought to create an egalitarian society through actions such as the provision of subsidised education, health and other social amenities. However, this became very expensive to maintain and the beneficiary base was very large. As the tide turned, the decade of the 1990s witnessed a downward turn as economic decline set in and poverty and inequalities increasingly became evident. Explanations for this melt down have been attributed to several factors including recurrent droughts, HIV and the non-realisation of the objectives of the Economic Structural Adjustment Programme, popularly known as ESAP and a much-contested land reform programme. The advent of Structural Adjustment Programmes (SAP) in the early 1980s in Africa, which was presented as the panacea for all economic ills, contributed to a marked increase in rural poverty and vulnerability to external shocks. As a result, the country was compelled to reduce its interventions in the economy – a move that included ceasing the subsidisation of agricultural inputs, such as fertiliser and privatising the commodity boards, that fixed producer prices and bought farmers' produce and an introduction of user fees for social services. Extreme chronic poverty set in and an estimated 35 per cent of households lived below the poverty line in 1995, compared to 26 per cent in 1990. There has also been a rise in unemployment rates which reached 63 per cent during this period and 94 per cent in 2008 (Mupedziswa & Ushamba, 2008). Due to this, a large part of the unemployed population joined the informal sector with its associated precarious working conditions.

Loss of or limited formal employment opportunities

Zimbabwe has suffered chronic economic melt-down for over a decade, which has resulted in the loss of jobs and therefore increased unemployment levels. The Zimbabwe National Statistical Agency (ZIMSTAT) carried out a Labour Force and Child Labour Survey in 2011, which showed that the currently employed population aged 15 years and above was estimated to be 5,4 million. Of this, 4,6 million (84 per cent) were in informal employment. Because formal social security is tied to formal employment, this means that the bulk of Zimbabweans must resort to indigenous forms of social security. Nearly eight out of ten in informal employment were workers in the agricultural sector (communal, resettlement and peri-urban farming). Ten per cent worked in other sectors and the remainder were either casual, temporary, contract or seasonal workers. The workforce landscape is also highly feminised, with females constituting 53 per cent of the population in informal employment. The formal systems are contributory-based and therefore only those who contribute are covered and this translates into less than 20 per cent of the population.

The impetus for the increasing requisite for informal social security

As Olivier *et al*, (2008) note, most of the poor in the SADC are side-lined and marginalised by the formal social security system which, in most instances, and as is the case in Zimbabwe, is state operated and urban biased. Since the bulk of Zimbabweans are agricultural farmers in rural areas, this bias is a major barrier for them to access formal social security. Chikova (2013) argues that the country does not have the financial capacity to provide social security to those in the informal sector. To deal with the various challenges brought on by the deterioration of the economy in the absence of comprehensive social security, households have been forced to look beyond the state for support and engage in other forms of coping mechanisms. According to Patel, Kaseke and Midgley (2012: 12-31) these informal systems have also evolved and changed into new systems of mutual aid and they now play a greater role in the community welfare system. As a result, ISSS is becoming more relevant as households have become more vulnerable. The most common forms of indigenous social security in Zimbabwe are discussed below.

Forms of Indigenous Social Security Systems

As Kaseke (2003: 43) asserts: "The problem of social exclusion in formal social security forces excluded groupings to turn to non-formal social security systems. Whilst these are more inclusive than formal social security systems, they offer only the most rudimentary social protection" but they are also considered to be more adaptive and responsive to the need at hand. According to Chirisa (2013), informal [indigenous] social security is depicted by social insurance which includes support from friends, relatives, voluntary schemes, kinship networks and rotating schemes, as well as people's own resources such as use of savings, working children and sale of assets. Informal social security schemes, although ideal have been known to have low coverage and the mobility of those in the informal sector, also poses a problem in terms of collecting contributions hence a high default rate is likely to be experienced (Chirisa, 2013).

Extended family – Kinship based indigenous systems

In the typical African context, the family, usually considered a backbone of Africa includes extended networks which are pivotal in the maintenance and sustenance of the entity (Sloth-Nielsen, 2003). The extended family, which is defined by Haralambos and Holborn (2004: 24) as that which "combines different generations and different branches of the family e.g. grandparents, parents, cousins, uncles and aunts" remains a relevant institution for providing an informal social safety net. For Zimbabweans, it represents a safe space for those facing social and economic challenges. Extended family members usually support each other through hard times with cash, food, housing and care for the sick or dependent relatives. They are also involved in the provision of material relief, labour and emotional support to destitute or bereaved families (World Bank, 2009). Whilst they have always existed, extended families became more visible after the emergence of HIV/AIDS – when households had to provide care for their sick relatives, especially in the absence of formal social security.

Although we mentioned earlier that the extended family's roles seem to be diminishing as result of economic hardships, there remains a semblance of *ubuntu* (an African principle of caring for each other's well-being through a spirit of mutual support) (Olivier *et al*, 2008). The spirit of community support drives even those who cannot afford to support other family members. Those without financial means tend to support

113

other extended family members with moral support such as looking after the infirm and providing nursing services, whilst those with financial means may provide money to the household where the infirm are being looked after. A web of care is thus established with one extended family member providing required financial provisions and another, the physical care. This also confirms earlier writings such as those by Bourdillon (1991) who saw the extended family as giving security and support, with family members sharing assets and sharing a sense of belonging to a larger family rather than an individual family arrangement.

Community based indigenous systems – *Zunde raMambo*:

Zunde raMambo or the 'Chief's granary' is a pre-colonial practice to promote food security, particularly among vulnerable members of society. The *Zunde* is a common field designated by a Chief for cultivating food crops by the community. The harvest was stored in a common granary under the direction of the Chief. The primary aim of the *Zunde* was to ensure that a community had food reserves which could be used in times of food shortage (Mararike, 2001; Mushunje, 2006; Patel *et al*, 2012). The system was suppressed during colonial rule by corroding the authority of the traditional Chiefs. There are now efforts to revive it, especially in the context of HIV and AIDS (Patel *et al*, 2012). Historically, *Zunde raMambo* was used not only to produce communal crops for food security, but also as a social, economic and political rallying-point for the community. It embodied the traditional values that promote togetherness and a sense of belonging (Mararike, 2001). It was also meant to provide social protection during periods of drought and famine and provided for orphans, widows, the infirm and the marginalised (Mushunje, 2006; Chirisa, 2013). Food security was therefore guaranteed. Proceeds were also used to sponsor funerals and other community functions and it was regarded an efficient mechanism for the protection of the welfare of the community.

Though widely acclaimed, the *Zunde raMambo* has been affected in many ways by developments in Zimbabwe. For instance, the land reform programme resettled people by bringing people from different areas to a communal area. This meant that people with different values were brought together under a Chief whom they had to select and this often led to conflicts and misunderstandings of the operations of the *Zunde*. Dhemba *et al* (2002) also note that several problems have adversely affected the concept, including a shortage of land, the lack of agricultural inputs and the Chiefs' lack of control of assets such as land, knowledge and organisation. Despite these challenges, the *Zunde raMambo* is still a viable means of community support for food security. It still has the capacity to bring together communities in the wake of hardships, but it needs to be strengthened.

Burial Societies

According to Chirisa (2013) Burial Societies are a form of ISSS that target those in the informal economy and they have existed as far back as 1919. They involve pooling resources together to provide financial assistance to members in the event of death or illness. They are generally seen to offer a measure of financial security in the event of bereavement and cater for some of the other social needs of members. Burial societies basically provide the following services: Advising members when a death occurs, meeting the cost of burial (coffin, providing food and transport for mourners), assist the bereaved family financially, visiting members who fell ill, paying hospital fees, assisting the unemployed and organising social gatherings for members. The advantage of burial societies according to Dhemba *et al,* (2002) is that they provide immediate assistance to the bereaved in the form of cash and other benefits such as coffin, depending on the way the society is constituted. With economic hardships, the viability of burial societies may be under threat as members may find it difficult to maintain contributions, which given the functions burial societies serve, require their strengthening.

Rotating/Income Savings and lending schemes

These are another form of ISSS that exist in Zimbabwe. Under this arrangement a group of people come together and contribute a certain amount of money every month and each one of them in turn accesses this money for their use. While this arrangement exists mainly amongst those in the informal sector, those who are formally employed can also participate in it. They are mainly meant to cushion members, financially and socially, so that they do not experience financial and economic duress. These schemes are a source of capital injection to embark on small business projects. Members of these schemes assist each other during times of death and weddings, with members coming together to provide catering services at the funerals/weddings of members and their immediate families.

Prospects for Indigenous Social Security Systems in Zimbabwe

Indigenous Social Security Systems are firmly established especially for those in the informal sector and who are poor. In the absence of comprehensive social security, the ISSS will continue to exist. They are the Zimbabwean's way of life. In view of this, we provide recommendations for future prospects.

Recommendations

Link community support systems with formal systems

Evidence exists which suggests that indigenous and formal social security systems can co-exist. For instance, Burial Societies may benefit from establishing linkages with formal burial insurance companies. Dhemba *et al*, (2002) note that one of the shortcomings of Burial Societies was that they lacked capacity in administration. Strong linkages can be established with formal institutions such as established funeral organisations. Firstly, most Burial Societies maintain a funeral parlour insurance policy (group policy) on behalf of their members. Secondly, some individuals take, in addition to their membership to a burial society, a funeral insurance policy with commercial insurers (Patel *et al*, 2012).

ECONET, a wireless service provider in Zimbabwe runs a funeral policy of a minimum contribution value of 0,50 USD per month. From this contribution of each member, the pay out on death is 500 USD. Burial societies have tapped into this. Linkages would need to incorporate the provision of services such as basic administration skills and financial literacy for burial society members. Rotating savings, credit clubs and burial societies are now linking with microfinance institutions by using their pooled resources as leverage to access formal financial services. This is mostly on an *ad hoc* basis. Therefore, Government should support such efforts and provide the rules which will protect the clubs so that they are not exploited. The popularly acclaimed *Zunde raMambo* should be linked to other formal support mechanisms where the communities can access inputs from the state programmes (Dhemba *et al*, 2002).

Income generation enterprises in the community

Households and the communities at large need to become owners of their social security provisions by generating community funds. This can be through activities such as Income Savings and Lending schemes (ISALs). These could also lead to the creation of community funds and even the establishment of community banks. ISALs, as means of income generation, seem to have become very popular, but their activities remain unregulated. It could be argued that the dynamics associated with non-regulation are perhaps what makes these schemes vibrant. According to a ZIMSTAT (2013) report, a total of 53 per cent households were members of agricultural extension groups, whilst 28 per cent were ISALs members and 17 per cent were participating in commodities associations. Such ISALs could link with microfinance institutions to access loans and finance services for their members in a systematic way which does not prejudice them. Such linkages should also be accompanied by capacity building in finance management if these funds grow. Chigova (2013) also notes that loans to Small to Medium Enterprises (SMEs) through umbrella organisations, like the Small Enterprises Development Co-operation (SEDCO), have been advanced to small businesses in the informal sector which sets the launch pad for strengthening the linkages.

Budgetary support to community safety net programmes

Linked to the above recommendations, the Government should consider providing predictable support to the communities to run local social safety net programmes. As part of its broader social protection strategy, the Government should also consider funding community-based programmes such as subsidised agricultural input schemes especially for programmes such as the *Zunde raMambo*. The suggestions which were made by Olivier *et al,* (2008) are also emphasised here. Government could engage in training to improve the managerial skills and investment abilities of members of indigenous social security schemes and provide subsidies to enhance the financial base of informal social security schemes, as well as technical assistance to help indigenous social security schemes manage risks associated with their enterprises.

Areas for further research

Literature on Indigenous Social Security Systems is limited. However, with the current challenges of HIV and AIDS, increasing levels of unemployment and general economic hardships, it is reasonable to assume that communities have developed adaptive coping mechanisms against such hardships. What needs to be clearly understood, in the context of changing environments and the way in which the indigenous mechanisms have been affected, is what adaptations have been made by households and communities to cope against risks and vulnerabilities. As Olivier *et al*, (2008) also note, there is increasing evidence that in the SADC region informal arrangements are not merely an expression of African cultural values, but, for the reasons advanced above, serve as gap fillers for the formal arrangements. Hence, there is need for in-depth research which would create enough evidence to influence policy.

Conclusion

Given the above discussion, it is evident that Indigenous Social Security Systems remain limited in their scope of coverage. All the discussed social security systems have certain characteristics in common. They all promote solidarity and require commitment on the part of those participating. They are also based on the benevolence of the people and on pooling of resources, which may not always be present. Though they are very progressive and respond to the needs of the vulnerable, the Indigenous Social Security Systems are also affected in a negative way by external factors related to the economy. Given the increasing economic hardships, there is growing pressure on these systems and they are not always able to provide predictable support. As Patel *et al*, (2012) conclude, Indigenous Social Security Systems do not have the capacity to provide the same level of protection provided by formal social security. On the other hand, the non-comprehensiveness of the formal social security system in Zimbabwe means that the poor, the unemployed and those in the informal sector employment will always be caught in the middle. Thus, Indigenous Social Security Systems will continue to co-exist alongside formal social security systems.

What is critical, is to identify and strengthen ways in which the formal and Indigenous Social Security Systems can co-exist and leverage on the strengths of each. Oduro (2010), had a concern that scaling up of formal social protection would displace informal social protection and have an adverse impact on the welfare of the poor and vulnerable, but given the context of Zimbabwe, this is highly unlikely. Criticisms have also been raised against the formal social security. For instance, Dominelli (2004), whilst talking of the family, cautions on the way public institutions have 'usurped' many of the family's earlier functions and in so doing undermining the coherence provided by the family as a means of social security. Glick (2000) and Goldstein and Warren (2000) also acknowledge that Government services have made extended family life less important for the care of the elderly. These views however need to be balanced in the context of Zimbabwe where the Government's social security is highly limited. Regardless of one's preferred view, social security remains a requirement in one's life, whether it is fulfilled from the indigenous or formal systems. In this vein, there is need to consider how ISSS can serve better those without access to other means of formal social security. What is important is to take heed of Olivier *et al's* (2008) caution, which points to the fact that there is need for a proper understanding of informal social security arrangements before these can be expressly linked to the formal ones. They also note that there is a need to understand and appreciate the reasons for the existence of indigenous social security arrangements, the different kinds of informal social security arrangements and the role, and importance of informal social security arrangements.

References

Bourdillon, M.F.C. 1991. *The Shona Peoples*. Gweru: Mambo Press.

Central Statistical Office Zimbabwe. 2000. *Quarterly Digest of Statistics*. Harare: Central Statistical Office Zimbabwe.

Chikova, H. 2013. *Social Protection in Zimbabwe: Country Paper*. International Conference on Social and Income (In) Security in the Informal Economy, 16-17 September, Birchwood Hotel Johannesburg.

Chinake, H. 2000. *Savings Clubs as a Strategy for Enhancing Women: Socio-economic Status: A Study of Club Members in Nyameni-Marondera*. BSW dissertation. Harare: University of Zimbabwe.

Chirisa, I. 2013. Social protection and instability in Zimbabwe: Scope, institutions and policy options in Informal and formal social protection systems in Sub-Saharan Africa. In: S. Devereux & M. Getu (eds.). *Informal and formal social protection systems in Sub-Saharan Africa*. Addis Ababa: Organisation of for Social Science Research in Eastern and Southern Africa (OSSREA): 121-158.

Cichon, M.; Scholz, W.; van de Meerendonk, A.; Hagemejer, K.; Bertranou, F. & Plamondon, P. 2004. *Financing social protection Quantitative Methods in Social Protection Series.* Geneva: International Labour Office.

Clarke, D. 1977. *The Economics of Old Age Subsistence in Rhodesia.* Gweru: Mambo Press.

Cormack, I.R.N. 1983. *Towards Self-Reliance: Urban Social Development in Zimbabwe.* Gweru: Mambo Press.

Dhemba, J.; Gumbo, P. & Nyamusara, J. 2002. Social Security Systems in Zimbabwe. *Journal of Social Development in Africa,* 17(2): 132-153.

Dominelli, L. 2004. *Social Work, Theory and Practice for a changing profession.* Malden: Polity Press.

Foster, G.; Makufa, C.; Drew, R. & Kralovec, E. 1997. Factors leading to the establishment of child-headed households: The case of Zimbabwe, *Health Transition Review,* supplement 2 to volume 7, 155-168, Family AIDS Caring Trust, Mutare, Zimbabwe.

Gandure, S. 2009. Baseline Study of Social Protection in Zimbabwe: A Report Prepared for the Social Protection Technical Review Group (SPTRG) of the Multi-Donor Trust Fund. Unpublished report.

Glick, J.E. 2000. Nativity, Duration of Residence and the Life Course Pattern of Extended Family Living in the USA. *Population Research and Policy Review,* 19(2000): 179-198.

Goldstein, J.R. & Warren, J.R. 2000. Socio-economic Research and Heterogeneity in the Extended Family: Contours and Consequences. *Social Science Research,* 29: 382-404.

Government of Zimbabwe. 2011. *Labour Force and Child Labour Survey.* Harare: Government of Zimbabwe.

Government of Zimbabwe. 2006. *Zimbabwe Demographic and Health Survey.* Harare: Government of Zimbabwe.

Government of Zimbabwe. 1996. *Workmen's Compensation Act Chapter 269.* Harare: Government of Zimbabwe.

Government of Zimbabwe. 1989. *National Social Security Authority (NSSA) Act.* Harare: Government Printer.

Government of Zimbabwe. 1984. *Registrar of Pensions Annual Report.* Harare: Government of Zimbabwe.

Government of Zimbabwe. 1980. *War Victims Compensation Act.* Harare: Government of Zimbabwe.

Haralambos, M. & Holborn, M. 2004. *Sociology: Themes and Perspectives.* 6th Edition. London: Harper Collin Publishers Limited.

Hawkins, R. & Hawkins, T. 1981. Two Views on the Riddell Commission. *Journal of Opinion*, 11 (3/4): 54-57.

Holzmann, R. & Jorgensen, S. 2001. Social Risk Management: A New Conceptual Framework for Social Protection and Beyond. *International Tax and Public Finance*, 8(4): 529-556.

International Labour Organisation (ILO). 2012. *Recommendation 202 of 2012 on Social Protection Floors*. Recommendation concerning National Floors of Social Protection Adoption: Geneva, 101st ILC session (14 Jun2012). file:///C:/Users/mushunje/Downloads/ILO%20(Social%20Protection%20Floors%20Recommendation,%202012%20(No.%20202).pdf [Accessed 17 May 2017].

Kaseke, E. 2003. Social exclusion and social security: The case of Zimbabwe. *Journal of Social Development in Africa*, 18(1): 33-48.

Kaseke, E. 1993. *Rural Social Security Needs: The Case of Zimbabwe*. Harare: School of Social Work.

Mararike, C. 2001. Revival of indigenous food security strategies at the village level: The human factor implications. *Zambezia*, 27(1): 53-65.

Mupedziswa, R., & Ushamba, A. 2008. A generation at the edge of a precipice: AIDS and child headed households in Zimbabwe. In: M. Tapologo, L. Levers & G. Jacques (eds.). *Changing family systems: a global perspective*. Gaborone: Bay Publishing: 312- 327.

Mushunje, M.T. 2014. Interrogating the relevance of the extended family as a social safety net for vulnerable children in Zimbabwe. *African Journal of Social Work*, 4(2): 78-110.

Mushunje, M.T. 2006. Child Protection in Zimbabwe: Past, Present and Future. *Journal of Social Development in Africa*, 21(1): 12-34.

Mushunje, M.T. & Mafico, M. 2010. Social protection for orphans and vulnerable children in Zimbabwe: The case of cash transfers. *International Social Work*, 53(2): 261-275.

Oduro, A.D. 2010. Formal and informal social protection in Sub-Saharan Africa. Paper prepared for the Workshop "Promoting Resilience through Social Protection in Sub-Saharan Africa" organised by the European Report on Development in Dakar, 28-30 June.

Olivier, M.P.; Kaseke, E. & Mpedi, L.G. 2008. Informal Social Security in Southern Africa: Developing a Framework for Policy Intervention. Paper prepared for presentation at the International Conference on Social Security organised by the National Department of Social Development, Cape Town 10-14 March.

Patel, L.; Kaseke, E. & Midgley, J. 2012. Indigenous Welfare and Community-Based Social Development: Lessons from African Innovations. *Journal of Community Practice*, 20(1): 12-31.

Pennigton, B. & Kanabus, A. 2005. *AIDS Orphans: The facts.* www.avert.org/aidsorphans [Accessed 20 September 2016].

Sloth-Nielsen, J. 2003. *'Too Little? Too Late?* The Implications of Grootboom for State Responses to Child-headed Households' Law Democracy and Development 113: Nelson Mandela Children's Fund Study into the Situation and Special Needs of Children in Child headed Households. http://www.saflii.org/za/journals/LDD/2003/6.pdf [Accessed 3 April 2017].

United Nations. 2015. *Universal Declaration of Human Rights.* http://www.un.org/en/udhrbook/pdf/udhr_booklet_en_web.pdf [Accessed 20 September 2016].

UNAIDS. 2004. *Report on the global AIDS Epidemic.* Geneva: UNAIDS.

UNICEF, UNAIDS & USAID. 2004. *Children on the Brink 2004: A Joint Report of New Orphan Estimates and a Framework for Action.* www.unicef.org [Accessed 20 September 2016].

United Nations Human Rights Office. 1966. *International Covenant on Economic, Social and Cultural Rights.* New York: United Nations Human Rights Office.

Von Benda-Beckmann, F., & Kirsch, R. 1999. Informal social security systems in Souther Africa and approaches to strengthen them through policy measures. *Journal of Social Development in Africa*, 14: 221-238.

Whitsun Foundation. 1979. Finance for Low income housing in Zimbabwe. Project 4. 06. https://books.google.co.za/books?id=bVBDAQAAIAAJ&dq=editions:STANFORD36105120511501 [Accessed 17 May 2017].

World Bank. 2009. *Social safety nets: lessons from rich and poor countries.* http://newsletters.worldbank.org/newsletters/listarticle. [Accessed 17 August 2017].

II
THE WEST AFRICAN SEGMENT

07

INDIGENOUS SOCIAL SECURITY SYSTEMS IN GHANA: PROSPECTS AND CHALLENGES

Albert Ahenkan

Introduction

This chapter presents the indigenous social protection systems in Ghana. The chapter is the outcome of an extensive review of the indigenous and formal social protection programmes in Ghana. The concept of social protection and the evolution of the indigenous and formal social protection systems in the country were reviewed. The chapter also discusses the various forms of indigenous and formal social security systems in Ghana, as well their prospects, challenges and sustainability.

Social Protection: Definition and Concepts

All over the world social protection has been used to safeguard the poor and the vulnerable by ensuring and guaranteeing a certain kind of living standard and the reduction of poverty. Social protection systems consist of a set of benefits provided by the individuals, community or state, to individuals or households to mitigate possible hardships resulting from shocks, reduction or loss in income due to sickness, maternity, employment, injury, invalidity, old age or death. Social protection is primarily concerned with the prevention of poverty among different population groups that experience reduction or loss of incomes in their life-cycle. The social protection coverage and benefits continue to expand especially in the developing countries. Kalusopa, Dicks, & Osei-Boateng (2012) have noted that the provision of social protection has become more relevant with the sharp manifestations of globalisation. Social protection systems play a key role in reducing poverty and inequality. The growing recognition of the potential impact of social protection systems has led to their ascendancy on the agenda of policymakers in the international development community. In recent years, increased social protection coverage in developing countries has been achieved through the expansion of a combination of programmes (Bastagli, 2013). The persistent inequalities in economic and human development, increasing volatility at the macro and household level, the threats posed to sustainable development by climate change and changing demographic trends have contributed to the increased relevance of social protection in developing countries (UNICEF, 2012). Some major international agencies, such as the World Food Programme (WFP), European Commission (EC), the World Bank (WB) and UNICEF have launched social protection strategies aimed at providing safety nets for both the poor and the vulnerable.

Various agencies and institutions have attempted to define social protection in varying ways – reflecting different objectives and approaches. To the International Labour Organisation (ILO), social protection comprises all measures providing benefits, whether in cash or in kind, to secure protection, due to insufficient income caused by sickness, disability, maternity, employment injury, unemployment, old age or death of a family member; the lack of access or unaffordable access to health care; insufficient family support, particularly for children and adult dependants; general poverty and social exclusion (ILO, 2010). According to the World Bank (2001), social protection consists of policies and programmes designed to reduce poverty and vulnerability by promoting an efficient labour market, diminishing people's exposure to risks and enhancing their capacity to manage economic and social risks, such as unemployment, exclusion, sickness, disability and old age. The United Nations Research Institute for Social Development (UNRISD, 2010) also defined social protection as the prevention, managing and overcoming situations that adversely affect people's well-being. It is an important mechanism for the pursuit of at least six out of the eight Millennium Development Goals (MDGs) by ensuring universal access to key essentials services in quality basic and maternal health care, education, nutrition and environmental health.

Social protection is a human right which must be enjoyed by all people, children and adults; men and women and the sick and the healthy.

The United Nations' task team on the post 2015 development agenda described social protection as a programme that tackles multiple dimensions of poverty and deprivation and can therefore be a powerful tool in the battle against poverty and inequality (UN, 2012). The team estimated that 80 percent of the global population has no access to comprehensive social protection. The gap between the haves and the have-nots has always been within the confines of the availability of respectable work, proper health care, quality education and good security in terms of food and income. As this gap widens it creates avenues for social unrest and political instability. The objective of social protection is therefore to bridge this gap to an acceptable level in society. The UN has therefore advocated and assisted in developing pragmatic social protection policies and programmes that will ensure an equitable distribution of wealth and to ensure both the disadvantaged and the vulnerable benefit from relevant social services such as healthcare, education, water, food security, decent work, etc. Social protection has been categorised into three areas: social assistance, market interventions and social insurance.

Social protection programmes are means by which the public collectively assist the poor and vulnerable through interventions that are financed by governments and donor communities. Social protection is relevant in ensuring sustainable development, especially in the developing world. The level of poverty in the developing world has always demanded that the Government intervenes in ensuring that the less privileged in society are catered for from the public purse. It is a fact that the developed world continues to support their citizenry with well-structured social protection programmes. According to the International Labour Organisation (ILO) (2015), social protection policies play a critical role in realising the human right to social security for all, reducing poverty and inequality and supporting inclusive growth – by boosting human capital and productivity, supporting domestic demand and facilitating structural transformation of national economies.

Social Protection Framework

The social protection framework (SPF) makes the case for investing in social protection for children and the vulnerable (UNICEF, 2012). SPF calls for action by relevant stakeholders, including governments, civil society and development partners. It demonstrates the cross-cutting nature of social protection and as a potential tool for complementing investments across sectors to achieve more equitable outcomes. Social protection helps to increase households' capacity, to take care of their families and overcome barriers to accessing social services. While social protection is important for societies in general, it should also reach the most vulnerable children and families, for whom barriers persist even when social services and national human development indicators improve.

Evolution of Social Protection in Ghana

Social protection in Ghana dates to the pre-independence era where community members were each other's keeper. Even though not documented, Ghanaians had a way of protecting each other and planning for the future as pertained in the modern day social security and pension schemes. Parental roles were not limited to one's biological parents, but to any adult in the society. People saw every child as their own and hence could provide any form of assistance. The aged were catered for by the friends, relatives, well-endowed or strong people in society. Grand children from either a nucleur family or an extended family were always assigned to older people to run errand services for them, while the aged imparted knowledge or provided training services to the children. Also, people secured their future by acquiring tangible assets such as land and houses and provided training for their children who were required to take care of their parents during old age. People also willingly shared their wealth with family members such as children, siblings, nephews and nieces. The poor and the vulnerable in society were supported by the rich and the chiefs of their communities. However, over time, modernity led to break down of the informal social security system and the emergence of alternative means of social protection. The subsequent sections discuss the forms of Indigenous Social Security Systems in Ghana.

Indigenous Social Security Systems (ISSS) in Ghana

Before the institution of a formal social security system in Ghana, the Ghanaians had their own traditional forms of social protection. These systems had been developed over the years to provide safety nets and support mechanisms to individuals in times of shocks, loss or reduction in income resulting from unemployment, sickness, old age and disability. These Indigenous Social Security Systems include kinship, the extended family system, voluntary savings associations, social network and associations, landed properties, etc.

Kinship System

Kinship plays a significant role in social protection in Ghana. Prior to formalised social welfare schemes, Ghanaians relied on the extended family and kinship networks. Kinship as a form of social protection refers to the support people obtain from the generation of their grandparents for their children. This ties individual members of the extended family system to an implicit contract between successive generations as a source of practical, emotional and financial support for the children and dependent elderly. Kinship serves as insurance for crisis situations like illness, unemployment, divorce and bereavement in Ghana. However, the level of commitment to these roles seems to vary both in culture and context, with the ability to sustain them also being constrained by demographic and social change. Ghanaians possess a collectivistic orientation which underscores a strong concern for the fate and well-being of one's kin and the need for family members, young and old, to support each other and to assist in the nurturing and supporting role of the family. This kinship support can also be in the form of care. This responsibility generally continues throughout the child-rearing years and enhances parents' participation in income generating and socially enhancing activities, thus contributing to social and economic empowerment.

The Extended Family System

The extended family system is one of the most popular and important socio-cultural and ethical institutions of the Ghanaian traditional society. It played an important role in the development of the individual. Before the advent of the formal social protection systems, certain traditional social security arrangements existed in Ghana which mainly focused on addressing challenges or problems of vulnerable members of society like the aged, widows, the sick and orphans among others. For example, Boon (2007) observes that the extended family system which continues to exist in most collectivist economies are traditionally responsible for catering for needs of this group grounded on "the principle of solidarity and reciprocity" (Boon, 2007; Akor, 2013). This practice promotes the idea that the extended family is responsible for members in times of need. Traditionally, the extended family has always been a social security system (SSS) that provides protection to its members. It involves obligations on members to support each other in times of need. The elderly people were respected and revered for their knowledge and wisdom and their role in interceding between the living and the dead. To a considerable extent, this guaranteed social protection for the elderly.

The traditional extended family was very much concerned about problems of the aged, the disabled, the sick, dependent widows, children and even with the victims of natural disasters. Chike (2012) stated that in time of crisis, the extended family serves as a place of refuge and a safe haven for its members. Any member who finds himself in a crisis runs to his or her mother's home to take refuge. In such a place, the individual is culturally and customarily protected and safe. Often, such an individual remained there until reconciliation and settlement of the problem was concluded, at the end of which he could return home to his father's own house or village. In times of death or when any member of the extended family is bereaved, all the other members would rally around bereaved members to console, help and assist them in the burial of the deceased. They would jointly participate in the raising of the funds and materials required for the burial, as well as take an active part in the various burial activities. The role played by members of the extended family at such occasions helps to reduce the level of psychological trauma of the bereaved member. However, the extended family social system in recent times has witnessed changes in varying respects and degrees in Ghana in the face of globalisation, misplaced modernisation and rapid urbanisation.

Voluntary Savings and Loans Association (*Susu*)

Another indigenous social protection mechanism in Ghana is the voluntary savings associations, popularly referred to as 'susu'. It is used by Ghanaians to save towards raising capital for starting small businesses, trading, credit for domestic expenditure and lifelong savings against contingencies as old age, invalidity and death

(Steel & Andah, 2003; Boon, 2007). *Susu* is an alternative financial institution, necessitated as a result of commercial banks' neglect of the microfinance sectors. The institution which is mostly informal, offers savings products to help clients in the informal sector to accrue their own savings over a period, normally ranging from one month to two years. Aside the last receiver, all members can receive their lump sum earlier than if they had saved in the bank or on their own (Steel & Andah, 2003). Best contributor or customers may also secure advances by requesting for their lump sum or even a short-term loan facility to cater for their urgent business needs. Although collectors are challenged by capital to offer such advances, some negotiate with savings and loan companies to achieve this. Considering their flexibility and micro nature in meeting the financial needs of the informal sector, this institution serves as a social security system by supporting local business owners who cannot meet the demands of the formal financial sector with savings packages and short-term loans. This promotes local economic development by stimulating the *susu* contributors to acquire capital and/or save towards expanding their businesses (Owusu, 1993; Steel & Andah, 2003).

Social Networks and Associations

Another significant indigenous social security scheme is the social networks and associations. This system involves the relationship between people of common interests. These groups include alumni groups, religious groups and citizens' associations in urban areas. Through these social networks and associations, people can share information and resources toward promoting their personal developments, human capacities, faith, or academic excellence and businesses. In recent times, there have been applications of social media, such as WhatsApp platforms, to facilitate social networks and support to members in times of crises.

Landed Property

These are fixed assets that are owned by individual members of the society. From these assets, individuals gain income without necessarily having to do any particular work on the assets. This may include estates and businesses owned by individuals. Most often, owners of these estates or businesses use them to acquire loans or capital from financial institutions as collateral to be used to repay debts in case of default. Individual members of society, may also use it as guarantee for other relations or friends to secure several varieties of benefits including their financial needs from other members of the society who have them. This is often used in instances of emergencies to attend to business or family needs. However, improper acquisition and titling processes often makes it challenging for financial institutions to provide financial assistance using landed properties as collateral. In Ghana, for stance, Decardi *et al*, (2012) argue that the banks find it difficult to provide collateralised mortgage finance considering the unsafe land titling systems.

The Formal Social Security Systems in Ghana

Formal social security in Ghana started in the early 1960s as means of reducing poverty and the protection of the vulnerable. The establishment of a national social security system (SSS) by Act 279 of 1965 saw the beginning of a formal social security scheme in Ghana. In fulfilling the human rights of the citizens of Ghana, the establishment of a social protection programme has been anchored on a rights based approach (RBA) and considered as an expression of Governments' commitment towards reducing inequality and poverty in Ghanaian society. The Government therefore subsidised the provision of basic social services such as education, health, water and sanitation. For instance, in the early part of the post-independence era, the Government of Ghana was responsible for providing free health care for the citizenry until it became unsustainable because of the need to provide more support to sectors such as education and agriculture (Abebrese, 2012). Subsidies were gradually reduced and the situation was substituted by the introduction of nominal fees and the popular 'Cash and Carry' system where patients were taken care of after they had made financial commitments to a health facility.

As a signatory to several UN and Africa Union (AU) conventions, treaties, policies, resolutions on human rights and social protection, it has become necessary for Ghana to come up with pragmatic policies and programmes on social protection. The Universal Declaration of Human Rights, to which Ghana is a signatory, states that Social Protection should be a fundamental human right for all citizens. The Commission for the AU has also identified social transfers (social protection) as a key tool for tackling extreme poverty in Sub-Saharan Africa (SSA). The 2006 Livingstone Declaration committed the member states of the AU to improve the implementation of Social Protection Programmes. It was agreed at the conference that within a period of three years, African Governments should integrate social transfers in their national development plans and budgets. Ghana has made modest gains through her well-designed development strategies such as the National Social Protection Strategy (NSPS) and the Ghana Poverty Reduction Strategies (GPRS I and GPRS II) which have considered social protection as a key element of poverty reduction and livelihood improvement. Generally, social protection programmes in Ghana are funded from the Government's resources with some support from donors.

The Ghana National Social Protection Strategy and Policy

The Ghana National Social Protection Strategy (GNSPS) started in 2007. The strategy is hinged on three main areas: poverty reduction, reduced inequality and livelihood improvement. These were to be achieved through three strategies: (a) a new social grant scheme to provide a basic and secure income for the most vulnerable households; (b) better poverty targeting of existing social protection programmes; and (c) package of complementary inputs (the need for a policy to bundle all the social protection programmes in Ghana). The NSPS represents the Government of Ghana's (GoG) vision of creating an all-inclusive and socially empowered society through the provision of sustainable mechanisms for the protection of people living in situations of extreme poverty and related vulnerability and exclusion (GNSPS, 2007). The NSPS aims to increase the ability of the extreme poor to meet their basic needs through improving access to livelihood opportunities and to social protection, reduce extreme poverty, related vulnerability and exclusion at the household level through provision of LEAP Social Grants Programme.

The NSPS seeks to spearhead the harmonisation and prioritisation of sector-wide social protection programmes and to facilitate collaborative implementation of social protection in Ghana. It will protect the rights of extremely poor and vulnerable people who will be able to have decent lives through income support, livelihoods empowerment and improved systems of personal safety. The Ministry of Gender, Children and Social Protection (MoGCSP) regards the policy as its main strategy to empower the vulnerable, aged and disabled. Within the framework of the NSPS, the vision of social protection in Ghana was articulated as having an inclusive equitable society in which ordinary, extremely poor and vulnerable citizens are protected from risks and shocks.

They are also empowered with improved capability, to overcome social, economic and cultural challenges to realise their rights and responsibilities and to make meaningful contributions to society.

In 2016, Ghana launched a National Social Protection Policy aimed at delivering a well-coordinated and inter-sectoral social protection system to help co-ordinate all the social protection programmes in Ghana. The policy has three main objectives of: providing effective and efficient social assistance to reduce poverty by 2030, promote productive inclusion and decent work to sustain families and vulnerable communities, and to increase access to formal social security and social insurance for all Ghanaians.

Formal Social Protection Programmes in Ghana

In the quest to improve upon the livelihoods of Ghanaians, the Government of Ghana (GoG) over the last two decades has developed several development strategies and social protection programmes aimed at poverty reduction, livelihood improvement and social safety nets (SSNs) for the poor and vulnerable. The subsequent sections highlight some of the key interventions. These social protection programmes are in the form of social assistance, social insurance schemes and social welfare services. The country's social protection programmes are centred on four key areas: livelihoods improvement, education, healthcare and energy. A number of these programmes are briefly discussed in this section.

Community-Based Rehabilitation Programme for the Disabled (CBRP)

The Ministry of Employment and Social Welfare (MESW), in collaboration with the Ministry of Health, the Ministry of Education, Ghana Education Service, the Ministry of Local Government, non-governmental organisations and organisations of disabled people, initiated a Community-based Rehabilitation Programme (CBRP) for people with disabilities in 1992. The purpose of the programme was to improve the quality of life of babies, children, young people and adults with disabilities, through the mobilisation of community resources, the provision of services and the creation of educational, vocational and social opportunities. CBPR as a social protection measure aims to develop human resources, including the strengthening of social infrastructure and services; it decentralised planning and decision-making, with greater participation of people at grassroots level in development decision making; and develop institutional capacity in the disability service delivery system.

Fertilizer Subsidies Programme

The fertilizer subsidy programme commenced in 2008 and aimed to make fertilizer available to farmers at a subsidised prices of about 64 per cent of the retail market price. The programme used the voucher system to target small-scale farmers. This effort is geared towards increasing the national average rate of fertilizer use from eight kg per hectare to 20 kg to increase crop yields and production. Overall, farmers who were part of the programme obtained higher yields, as well as higher incomes (MOFA, 2011).

Pension Schemes

A nationwide Social Security Scheme was established in 1965 due to the implementation of the Social Security Act. A Provident Fund Scheme was created and which provided money for a lump sum payment for old age, invalidity and survivor's benefits (Abebrese, 2012). The 1950 British Colonial Ordinance (Pension Ordinance No. 42) introduced a pension scheme in Ghana (the then Gold Coast) known as Cap 30. This pension scheme was enjoyed by all civil servants who were on government payroll before 1973. The CAP 30 gave way to the Social Security and National Insurance Trust (SSNIT) pension scheme in 1972 as a mandatory and universal pension scheme for all employees (National Pensions Regulatory Authority, 2010). In July 2004, the GoG started another major reform on the pension systems in Ghana. A committee was set up and finally a Government white paper was released in July 2006 which accepted the recommendations of the committee to introduce a new contributory three-tier pension scheme for Ghana and to be funded by contributions from both the employer and the employee. This new scheme factored in the informal sector which constitutes about 85% of the working population in Ghana with the three-tier pension scheme. A first-tier mandatory basic national social security scheme, which is an improved system of SSNIT benefits, is mandatory for all employees in both the private and public sectors. A second tier, occupational (or work-based) pension scheme, mandatory for all employees, but privately managed and designed primarily to give contributors higher lump sum benefits than presently available under the CAP 30 and SSNIT pension scheme. The tier 3 component of the scheme is essentially a voluntary provident fund and personal pension schemes, supported by tax benefit incentives to provide additional funds for workers who want to make voluntary contributions to enhance their pension benefits and for workers in the informal sector (Abebrese, 2012; SSNIT, 2016). This tier makes it possible for people engaged in the informal sector to contribute voluntarily towards their pension.

Labour-Intensive Public Work (LIPW)

Labour-Intensive Public Work (LIPW) is one of Ghana's national social protection strategies being implemented by the Government under the Ghana Social Opportunities Project (GSOP). Although it commenced in 2010, actual implementation of the programme started in October 2011 to improve essential public-sector infrastructure and help the extreme poor access short term employment (MoGCSP, 2015). The LIPW programme is currently being implemented in 60 districts across the country. In terms of finance, the Government with support from the World Bank has contributed more than 50 million USD to the project, with about 50 per cent of this funding going to the poor as wages (Bentil, 2016). In the past five years, the project has rehabilitated 170 rural roads, a total of 159 small earth dams and dugouts and 386 hectares of plantation. The programme has also created temporary employment for 148,000 unskilled workers out of which 62 per cent are women (Bentil, 2016; World Bank, 2014).

Ghana Luxemburg Social Trust (GLST)

The Ghana Luxemburg Social Trust (GLST) aims at improving maternal and child health status of low income groups. The intervention started in 2009 in two districts and involved 700 women with children under the age of five (GLST Report, 2014). The five-year cash transfer intervention sought to collect evidence about the impact of maternal and child health status of a cash transfer that was conditioned on recipients taking up a certain number of reproductive and child health-related services. As part of the programme, every three months poor pregnant women received 30 Ghana Cedis (In 2014, 1 USD was equivalent to 3, 2525 Ghanaian Cedis), on condition that they access some required services. These services included the utilisastion of pre- and post-natal care, access skilled delivery, do birth registration, carry out immunisation of their children and do periodic health check-ups for the child, including National Health Insurance registration (GLST Report, 2014; GNA, 2014).

Block Farming Initiative

The combined role of agriculture and social protection can play an important role in tackling poverty and hunger in Ghana. With calls for a stronger link between agriculture and social protection policies, the Block Farming Programme was introduced in 2009 as a pilot in six regions of Ghana. As a special presidential initiative, the programme was designed to provide food and money for the socio-economic development of the citizenry (MOFA, 2007). The accrued benefits of the programme included access to low-cost credit in the form of inputs and mechanisation services, which led to greater productivity, production and incomes of participating farmers (MOFA, 2011).

The Livelihood Empowerment against Poverty (LEAP) Programme

LEAP is a social cash transfer programme which initially provided cash and later added health insurance for extremely poor households across Ghana. In March 2008, LEAP started as a trial social protection programme and in subsequent years coverage was expanded to cover more households. The main target groups are extreme-poor households having a household member in at least one of these three demographic categories: households with an orphan or vulnerable child, the poor elderly, or people with extreme disabilities that are unable to work. The main objective was therefore to improve the livelihoods of its beneficiaries through the alleviation of short-term poverty and the encouragement of long-term human capital development. The programme is funded by the GoG with support from some of Ghana's key development partners such as the World Bank and the Department for International Development (DFID), United Kingdom. As of 2016, an estimated number of 146,074 beneficiaries are receiving support under LEAP.

National Health Insurance Scheme (NHIS)

The National Health Insurance Scheme (NHIS) was established by the National Health Insurance Act 2003, (Act 650) to provide financial access to quality basic health care for residents in Ghana. However, prior to this Act (Act 650) there were district mutual health insurance schemes. In 2012 Act 650 was replaced with a more comprehensive National Health Insurance Act, Act 852, which was aimed at integrating hitherto semi-autonomous District wide Mutual Health Insurance Schemes into a Single-Payer

System and thereby transforming into district offices of the NHIA. The new Act also sought to bring some efficiency into the operations and management of the NHIS. Act 650 also established the National Health Insurance Authority (NHIA) which was mandated to take responsibilities of all the operations and the management of NHIS. The authority was also mandated to ensure the attainment of universal health insurance coverage in relation to people resident in Ghana; people not resident in Ghana, but who are on a visit to the country; and to provide access to healthcare services to the people covered by the NHIS.

The School Feeding Programme (SFP)

The School Feeding Programme (SFP) began in late 2005 with ten pilot schools, selected from each region of the ten administrative regions in Ghana. It started as a poverty reduction and social protection intervention, prioritising enrolment and retention in schools and child nutrition, while envisaged to have the potential for the creation of employment and socio-economic development. As a component of an initiative of the Comprehensive African Agriculture Development Programme (CAADP) Pillar 3 of the New Partnership for Africa's Development (NEPAD), the programme is part of Ghana's efforts towards achieving the United Nations Millennium Development Goals on hunger, poverty and education. The programme is also an important component of the short and medium terms development agenda of the country. The SFP is in line with key national and development policies and initiatives such as the Growth and Poverty Reduction Strategy (GPRS II), the Education Sector Plan (2003-2015), Imagine Ghana Free from Malnutrition, Food and Agriculture Sector Development Policy, National Social Protection Strategy and the decentralisation policy of the Government. In the long term, the programme aims to ensure poverty reduction and food security in Ghana, while the short-term objectives include the reduction of hunger and malnutrition; increase in school enrolment, attendance and retention; and to boost domestic food production and employment creation in deprived communities of the country.

Free Compulsory Basic Education (FCUBE)

The Free Compulsory Basic Education (FCUBE) was launched in 1996 by the GoG. The FCUBE programme aimed at providing free and compulsory basic education for every school-age child. Specifically, the main goal of the programme was to provide opportunity for every school-age child in Ghana to receive quality basic education by the year 2005. The Ghana Education Service (GES) under the supervision of the Ministry of Education (MoE) was mandated to successfully implement the programme. To achieve the goals of the FCUBE, the GES defined three broad objectives: To enhance the quality of teaching and learning; to improve efficiency in the management of the education sector; and to provide full access to educational services by empowering all partners to participate in the provision of education to all children. The FCUBE is solely funded by the GoG. To ensure the sustainability of the funding of the programme, the Government introduced legislative instruments mandating the Government to transfer funds into the pool of sources for funding the programme. The programme is funded from the Government's annual budgetary allocations, the Ghana Education Trust Fund (GETFUND), the District Assemblies Common Fund (DACF) and the Capitation Grant. Cost sharing scheme under the FCUBE programme centres on textbooks, stationery, equipment and tools, meals, operational expenses and tuition.

National Youth Employment Programme

Youth unemployment has been the major concern of all the successive Governments of Ghana. Ghana has taken measures to provide some protection for the unemployed youth. The NYEP was created in October 2006 to address the country's youth unemployment with the aim of empowering Ghanaian youth so they could add positively to the socio-economic and sustainable development of the nation through different modules which include youth in security services, youth in fire prevention, youth in immigration, youth in agri-business, youth in health extension, youth in waste and sanitation, youth in paid internship, youth in community teaching assistants, youth in trades and vocation, youth in eco-brigade and youth in information and communication technology. This programme is to explore, recommend and provide additional employment. The NYEP seeks to provide opportunities for the youth in all districts throughout the country and thereby create conditions that will facilitate their economic empowerment. The programme includes a combination of self-employment opportunities, wage earning jobs and voluntary service activities.

Prospects of Social Security Systems in Ghana

The increasing levels of inequality, poverty and vulnerability have increased the relevance of social protection in Ghana. The fact that Ghana remains a lower middle-income country and battles with poverty, hunger, diseases, unemployment and the unavoidable old age means that the country will continue to explore all avenues possible to embrace more social protection programmes. While the need for social protection is widely recognised, and Ghana in the last couple of years has made some modest gains, the fundamental human right to social protection in the country remains unfulfilled for most Ghanaians. Most Ghanaians are employed in the informal sector where contribution to contributory social security pensions is voluntary. Hence, few people in the informal sector contribute towards their social security pension. In other words, the majority of people have no or unsecured future financial security. Social security programmes must therefore be expanded to incorporate more of the informal sector. The current three-tier contributory pension scheme is a brilliant initiative. However, coverage must be extended to more people in the informal sector, with enticing programmes, that will attract them to contribute to their future financial security. Ghana must learn from the ILO Social Protection Floors Recommendation (2012) which has been a masterpiece to many social protection programmes in the world. The NHIS, which is mostly funded with Government taxes and monthly contributions of employees in the formal sector, struggles with funding because of the fewer number of contributors. Annual premiums paid by the employees in the informal sector constitute of a minor proportion of the scheme's funds.

In Ghana, social security programmes not only tackle income poverty, but also provide effective support for broader developmental objectives, including better nutrition, health and education outcomes. Social protection measures promote empowerment and more balanced gender relations. These programmes therefore offer promising avenues for operationalising the sustainable development goals (SDGs) in ways that promote pro-poor growth and country-led national and regional development strategies. It is increasingly recognised that social protection can offer a powerful tool for the GoG and donors to strengthen their responses to emerging global challenges and aggregate shocks, including recent economic crises. Social protection programmes in Ghana will help to create an effective and secure state, promoting growth by building social cohesion, a sense of citizenship and minimising social conflicts.

A motivation for the expansion of social protection programmes is that they have many advantages which include economic growth, food security and political stability. They also play a key role in preventing child labour, malnutrition and child and maternal mortality. For instance, available reports on the impact of the Ghana School Feeding Programme (SFP) reveal that the programme has significantly improved enrolment in basic schools. However, this achievement notwithstanding, there are still thousands of children of school going age who are hawking in the urban centres, breaking stones in quarries, fishing, cocoa farming and working in other sectors of the economy. The SFP needs to be revised and expanded to cover all public schools in Ghana and incorporate all social welfare centres into the programme. Parents should actively support the programme and willingly allow their children to enjoy this social service. Government should release the statutory payments to this programme in time to enhance the efficiency and effectiveness of the programme. Social protection programmes have received a legal backing to compel successive governments to continue to fund and seek funding from international and domestic sources to fund them.

Challenges of Social Protection Programmes in Ghana

Like many other developing countries, Ghana's social protection programmes continue to face various political, financial, institutional, social and sustainability challenges. Supporting social protection programmes in developing countries particularly becomes complicated during periods of global crises. The principal challenges of social protection programmes in Ghana are briefly discussed in the next sub-sections.

Political Challenges

Getting the required political will and commitment to support social protection programmes is a significant challenge in Ghana. Ghana's national budgets over the years continue to depend partly on donor support. Funding of development programmes and projects become a horrendous task on Government because of unavailability of funds. The Government is always handicapped when the inflows from foreign donors are frozen or delayed due to economic or social challenges. To be able to continue to support social protection programmes in situations of limited funds, therefore requires strong governmental commitment. Hickey (2007) correctly argues that the aim of donor agencies should be to strengthen and extend political contracts for social protection where they exist and to work towards their establishment where they do not. There should also be permanent and reliable sources of funding for these programmes and politicians must ensure these sources are always resourced.

Institutional/Organisational Challenges

The slow expansion of Ghana's social protection programmes cannot be dealt with without considering institutional and organisational constraints. The institutional architecture for the social protection programmes in Ghana is complicated, with responsibilities divided among various ministries, departments and agencies through to the Metropolitan, Municipal and District Assemblies. Weak institutional capacity at various levels makes co-ordination of an effective response to demands for social protection difficult. Ghana has a portfolio of social protection programmes which need legislative backing to serve as part of the development agenda of the country and which should be executed by any political party in power.

Economic/Financial Challenges

Financing is one the major challenges constraining the delivery of social protection programmes, particularly in low-income countries such as Ghana. Limited coverage and impact have been attributed to scarce financial resources in many countries (Bastagli, 2013). Ghana's poor economic conditions have restricted the release of funding to these programmes, especially that the investments in these programmes will not yield any immediate dividend. Bastagli (2013) argues that spending on social protection policies across countries highlights the higher share of spending on social protection in high-income countries compared with low-income countries. Ghana is also faced with financial constraints in financing her social protection programmes. For instance, the NSPS estimates that Ghana will need annually an amount of 23 million USD – 27 million USD (about 0,21% of GDP in 2010 and about 0,07% of GDP in 2015) to fund the LEAP programme. Despite the increases in budget allocation since the start of the programme, the Government has always found it difficult to meet the annual demand of the programme which includes grants. Therefore, external donors continue to play a critical role in supporting national social protection initiatives in the country. A report on the impact of the LEAP programme (2014) indicates that cash transfers were inconsistent with the financing conditions of the programme. The breaks in payment were largely due to lack of funding.

Challenges relating to Selection of Beneficiaries

Another important challenge of the social protection programmes in Ghana is the mode of selecting beneficiaries. As has already been mentioned, there is a narrow gap between social protection programmes and political 'gimmicks' in Ghana. Therefore, the perception that beneficiaries of these programmes are linked to specific political parties continues to persist. Targeting beneficiaries is both more critical and harder to do because of the higher percentage of the population in poverty compared to the limited fiscal space, lower institutional capacity and poor infrastructure. It is therefore necessary to design a more transparent scientific method for selecting the beneficiaries of the programmes and the methods explained to the public to understand the selection process and the eligibility criteria. For instance, the LEAP programme adopts household data from the Ghana Statistical Service Surveys (GSSS) which are used in identifying geographical locations for the final selection of the beneficiaries. In general, there is inadequate relevant scientific data for the selection of the beneficiaries in some of these locations. All social protection programmes need clearly cut and transparent eligibility guidelines to be followed during the selection of beneficiaries.

Sustainability Challenges

The sustainability of social protection programmes all over the world is largely dependent on the availability of permanent funding or a reliable source of funding. Ghana's social protection programmes are faced with sustainability challenges since the Government alone cannot fund the programmes. The dependency on multilateral and bilateral donors for funding larger portions of the programmes clearly indicates that the programmes may not be sustainable in the long run. The political games that are played regarding release of statutory payments – which are the main sources of funding of some of these social protection programmes – also contribute to undermine the sustainability of the programmes. The lack of legislative instruments to back some of the social protection programmes in Ghana is another problem. Most of the programmes were introduced to fulfil political manifestos. Sources of funding of the programmes were not clearly stipulated from the onset. Hence, successive governments always challenge the legitimacy of the programmes and are less committed to funding them.

Despite considerable efforts by the Government to provide social security systems in Ghana, the formal social security systems alone cannot serve as a safety net, since they protect only a relatively small proportion of the population. To achieve its aim of social security, the Government must combine several of these methods, including encouraging Indigenous Social Security Systems. An overall social security system cannot be achieved by applying only the method; pluralism is also required. There is the need for a comprehensive strategy for a social security system and that can be achieved by combining the indigenous and formal social security systems. To ensure sustainability, scaling up existing successful programmes and filling the gaps in social protection, there is the need for provision of adequate and innovative financing for social protection through budgetary reforms.

Conclusion

Over the years, Ghana has deployed both the indigenous and formal social security systems. However, modernisation and urbanisation have weakened the traditional social security systems. Some of these systems serve as safety nets for people in times of crises, shocks, reduction or loss of income and disability. The increasing levels of inequality, poverty and vulnerability have increased the relevance of social protection in Ghana. Government has therefore introduced many formal social security systems in the country and which have been increasingly recognised by donors as important interventions for sustainable human development. The effective delivery of social protection interventions will require a focus on building adequate political will, strengthen indigenous security systems, funding, institutional capacity in terms of planning, co-ordination and the actual delivery of cash, food, inputs and other goods or services to well targeted beneficiaries considering factors such as poverty dynamics, demographic characteristics and vulnerabilities.

Reference

Abebrese, J. 2012. *Social Protection in Ghana: An overview of existing programmes and their prospects and challenges*. http://library.fes.de/pdf-files/bueros/ghana/10497.pdf [Accessed 10 June 2016].

Akor, A.A. 2013. *Emerging New Patterns in Social Security in the Informal Economy in Accra, Ghana.* Accra: University of Ghana.

Andrews, C. 2012. *Social Protection in Low Income Countries and Fragile Situations Challenges and Future Directions, Background.* Paper for the World Bank 2012-2022 Social Protection and Labour Strategy. Washington DC: World Bank.

Bastagli, F. 2013. *Feasibility of Social Protection Schemes in Developing Countries, Directorate-General for External Policies of the Union.* Brussels: European Union.

Bawole, J.N. & Hossain, F. 2015. Marriage of the unwilling? The paradox of local government and NGO Relations in Ghana. *VOLUNTAS: International Journal of Voluntary and Non-profit Organizations*, 26(5): 2061-2083. https://doi.org/10.1007/s11266-014-9503-9

Bentil, N.L. 2016. *Labour Intensive Public Works – Breaking the shackles of poverty.* www.graphic.com.gh/features/features/labour-intensive-public-works-breaking-the-shackles-of-poverty.html [Accessed on 23 December 2016].

Boon, E.K. 2007. Knowledge Systems and Social Security in Africa: A Case Study on Ghana. In: Indigenous Knowledge Systems and Sustainable Development: Relevance for Africa, Boon and Hens (Editors). *Tribes and Tribals,* (1): 63-76.

Chike, E.A. 2012. The Impact of the Extended Family System on Socio-Ethical Order in Igboland, *American Journal of Social Issues & Humanities,* 2(4): 262-267

Decardi, N.I.; Asamoah, O.R.; Ayeh, S.B. & Nduro, K.A. 2012. The Informal Sector and Mortgage Financing in Ghana. *Ghana Journal of Development Studies*, 9(2): 136-152. https://doi.org/10.4314/gjds.v 9 i 2.8

Ghana Government. Ministry of Gender Children and Social Protection (MoGCSP) 2015.*Ghana National Social Protection Policy.* http://mogcsp.gov.gh/mdocs-posts/ghana-national-social-protection-policy/ [Accessed on February 2017].

Ghana Government. MOFA 2011. *Special Initiative Evaluation Report. Evaluation of four Special Initiatives of the Ministry of Food and Agriculture, Government of Ghana.* https://gssp.ifpri.info/files/2011/11/MoFA-Program-Evaluation-Report.pdf [Accessed 24 October 2016].

Ghana-Luxembourg Social Trust (GLST) 2014. *Report.* http://www.ogbl.lu/solidaritesyndicale/files/2015/07/Ghana_Brosch_EN.pdf [Accessed 10 November 2016].

GNA, 2014. *Ghana-Luxembourg Social Trust Project ends.* http://www.ghananewsagency. org/social/ghana-luxembourg-social-trust-project-ends-78044 [Accessed on 15 March 2017].

Handa, S.; Park, M.; Darko, O. R.; Osei-Akoto, I.; Davis, B. & Daidone, S. 2014. *Livelihood Empowerment Against Poverty Program Impact Evaluation, Carolina Population Centre.* Chapel Hill: University of North Carolina.

Hickey, S. 2009. The politics of protecting the poorest: Moving beyond the 'anti- politics machine'? *Political Geography,* 28(8): 473-483.

International Labour Organisation (ILO). 2015. *World Social Protection Report 2014/15 – Building economic recovery, inclusive development and social justice.* Geneva: ILO.

Kalusopa, T.; Dicks, R. & Osei-Boateng, C. (2012). *Social protection schemes in Africa.* African Labour Research Network: Windhoek.

McCord, A. 2012. *The politics of social protection: why are public works programmes so popular with governments and donors?* https://www.odi.org/sites/odi.org.uk/files/ odi-assets/publications-opinion-files/7795.pdf [Accessed on 13 March 2017].

Ministry of Social Welfare. 2009. *National Plan of Action for the Elimination of the Worst Forms of Child Labour.* http://www.cocoainitiative.org/wpcontent/uploads/2016/07/ ghana_national_plan_of_action_for_the_elimination_of_wfcl_2009-_2015.pdf [Accessed on 13 March 2017].

National Health Insurance Authority. 2012. *Annual Report.* Accra: National Health Insurance Authority.

National Pensions Regulatory Authority (2010). An Overview of the National Pensions Act, 2008 http://www.iopsweb.org/resources/48749469.pdf [Accessed 14 February 2016].

Ofei-Aboagye, E. 2013. *Social Accountability Platform for Local Governance Performance in Ghana Policy Paper: Advancing Social Accountability in Social Protection and Socio-Economic Interventions: The Ghana School Feeding Programme.* http://www. ilgsedu.org/Publications/POLICY%20PAPER%20ADVANCING%20SOCIAL%20 ACCOUNTABILITY.pdf [Accessed on 12 March 2017].

Owusu, T. 1993. The Non-Bank Financial Sector. *The Ghanaian Banker.* Social Security and National Insurance Trust (SSNIT). 2016. SSNIT at a Glance. https://www.ssnit.org.gh/ about-us/ssnit-at-a-glance/ [Accessed 12 March 2017].

Steel, W.F. & Andah, D.O. 2003. *Rural and micro finance regulation in Ghana: Implications for development and performance of the industry.* African Region Working Paper Series No. 49. Washington, DC: World Bank.

United Nations. 2012. *UN System Task Team on Post 2015 Development Agenda: Social protection: A development priority in the post-2015 UN development agenda*. New York, NY: UN Thematic Think Piece.

United Nations Children's Fund (UNICEF). 2012. *Integrated Social Protection Systems: Enhancing equity for children: UNICEF Social Protection Strategic Framework*. New York, NY: United Nations.

United Nations Research Institute for Social Development (UNRISD). 2010. *Combating Poverty and Inequality: Structural Change, Social Policy and Politics*. Geneva: UNRISD.

World Bank. 2014. Project Expands to Offer More Opportunities for Ghana's Poorest Women. www.worldbank.org/en/news/feature/2014/08/26/project-expands-to-offer-more-opportunities-for-ghanas-poorest-women [Accessed on March 2017].

08

INDIGENOUS SOCIAL SECURITY SYSTEMS AND GOVERNMENT POLICIES: IMPACTS ON THE DEVELOPMENT OF MICRO, SMALL AND MEDIUM SCALE ENTERPRISES IN GHANA

Emmanuel K. Boon & Elizabeth Yeboah

Introduction and Background

A social security system takes various forms and is an important element of sustainable human development in most countries in the world. Many international conventions and treaties require the countries of the world to provide some form of social insurance scheme to protect people against the risks of sickness, disability, maternity, injury, unemployment or old age; to provide for survivors of natural disasters, orphans and those who cannot afford health care; and to ensure that families are adequately supported. In the developed nations, social security takes the form of social services, services provided by the government or basic security. However, in most Sub-Saharan African (SSA) countries, it is still not well developed. It is mainly a government intervention which takes the form of basic social security, like pensions, that fail to reach the masses, but largely benefit people in the formal sector. Indigenous Social Security Systems (ISSS) are widely practised by people in the informal sector which is predominantly made up of Micro, Small and Medium-scale Enterprises (MSMEs). Using a qualitative research approach, this chapter investigated the impact of indigenous and non-indigenous forms of social security systems (SSS) on the development of MSMEs in Ghana. An extensive literature review was undertaken, and a field survey was conducted on a sample of policy makers and administrators of SSS, as well as owners and employees of MSMEs in Accra (capital of Ghana). These enabled an objective analysis of the key challenges that these enterprises face regarding access to informal and formal SSS. Appropriate measures for mitigating the identified problems, as well as policy reforms and opportunities for integrating the two systems are proposed.

In Ghana and most developing countries, most of the population works in the informal sector, which is dominated by MSMEs (Aina, 2004; Adesina, 2010). These people mostly rely on indigenous forms of social security systems, which unfortunately are not sustainable. Despite the prevalence of these enterprises in both the developed and developing countries, they still do not have a universally accepted definition (Ramsrrun & Dalrymple, 2003). This is because various scholars define them from different points of view. The Ghana Statistical Service (GSS) considers firms with less than ten employees as small-scale enterprises, whilst those with more than ten are categorised as medium and large enterprises. Another criterion for defining MSMEs is the value of fixed assets of the organisation. The National Board of Small-scale Industries (NBSSI) applies both criteria. However, data on MSMEs is not readily available. According to Mensah (2004), these enterprises are defined as:

- ⊳ Micro enterprises: Those employing up to five employees with fixed assets (excluding realty) not exceeding the value of 10,000 USD.
- ⊳ Small enterprises: Employ between six and 29 employees with fixed assets of 100,000 USD.
- ⊳ Medium enterprises: Employ between 30 and 99 employees with fixed assets of up to 1 million USD.
- ⊳ Based on size classification, the Social Security and National Insurance Trust (SSNIT), indicates that the Ghanaian private sector is highly skewed, with 90 per cent of companies employing less than 20 people and a small number of large-scale enterprises. In 2012, Small-to-Medium Enterprises (SMEs) in Ghana accounted for about 85 per cent of manufacturing employment, 90 per cent of existing businesses and contributed 49 per cent to the country's GDP in 2012 (Asare, 2013). They contribute to employment creation, provision of basic goods

and services, generation of export and tax revenues for national socio-economic development, social security, a diversified economy and serve as a feeder line for the corporations of the future.

▷ The informal sector in the country is dominated by MSMEs which largely rely on indigenous forms of social security systems for their welfare. They do not have adequate access to the formal social security systems due to many fundamental difficulties, including limited access to investment capital and high quality affordable business development services, inadequate entrepreneurial, management and technical skills, erratic energy supply and limited access to information on market opportunities (Asare, 2013). These enterprises do not receive the required support from both public and private sector institutions, such as banks, the other financial institutions and the large-scale enterprises. This has significantly hampered the development and ability of MSMEs to withstand competition in the local and global markets.

Problems under investigation

According to ILO (2015), over half of the world's population lacks any type of social security protection. In Sub-Saharan Africa (SSA), only an estimated five per cent to ten per cent of the working population has some form of social security coverage and its lack is concentrated in the informal economies of developing countries, which are a large source of employment for women. MSMEs constitute a significant part of the informal economies in SSA and Ghana in particular. According to the 2000 Population and Housing Census of Ghana, 80 per cent of the working population is found in the private informal sector. Despite the commendable contributions of MSMEs to the growth and development of the economy of Ghana, they have not always obtained the required support from the Government and private sector organisations such as the banks, financial institutions and the large-scale corporate entities. In addition, bureaucratic delays and in the complex maze of rules, entrepreneurs must comply during follow-ups in various government agencies that prevent them from realising their full potential.

Inadequate Government policy to protect MSMEs from the negative impacts of globalisation and the entry of multinational companies in the country over the years has hindered the development of the sector. In other words, successive Governments in Ghana have not sufficiently developed appropriate social support systems to make MSMEs the real engine of growth for sustainable development in the country. For example, general social security for all in terms of social insurance does not exist. Formal social security in the form of pensions comprises of contributions from both the employer and the employee. ISSS are widely practised among people in the informal sector which is predominately made up of MSMEs. A fundamental problem of most MSMEs in Ghana is that the owners and employees after retirement ultimately become a burden on their families, communities and the larger society. Clearly, the sustainability of the sector and its capacity to contribute to the welfare of the population requires serious attention by the Government and all relevant stakeholders.

Objectives of the chapter and assumptions

This chapter investigates the impact of indigenous and non-indigenous forms of social security systems on the development of MSMEs in Ghana. It also examines the key challenges hindering them from accessing and enjoying indigenous and formal social security systems. Specifically, it will be investigated how these enterprises have benefited, and continue to benefit, from these two systems for their development. The guiding premise of the chapter is that the integration of indigenous and formal social security systems will significantly help to promote the development of MSMEs, the welfare of their owners and employees and the sustainable development of Ghana.

Materials and methods

Existing literature on MSMEs and indigenous and formal social security systems in Ghana was extensively reviewed to sieve relevant information for preparing this chapter. A qualitative approach was used to conduct the research. According to Patton (2002), qualitative research pre-supposes examination of processes and meanings that do not gain sufficient description by using quantitative methods or where quantitative methods alone are inappropriate. The results of the literature review informed the design of a research instrument for collecting empirical data in Accra in April 2016. A well-structured interview guide was used to collect and analyse data collected from 45 social security policy makers, managers and administrators, as well as entrepreneurs and employees of MSMEs regarding access to indigenous and formal social security systems. The interview guide was pre-tested to ensure its validity before it was used for collecting information from the respondents. Purposive sampling technique was used in selecting the 45 respondents. Because of their experience in MSMEs management and SSS problems, they were considered appropriate to participate in the research (see Table 1). Their perception of the benefits and challenges of the two systems, how best to mitigate the challenges and ensure the integration and sustainability of the systems were investigated. The collected information was grouped thematically to permit the identification of relationships between concepts, issues and challenges. Codes were assigned to the various groups of concepts, issues and challenges to permit objective analysis, interpretation and integration of the results in the chapter.

Table 1   Interviewees of Indigenous and Formal Social Security Systems in Ghana

Type of SSS	Number	Percentage
Formal SSS	10	22,22
Extended Family Members	8	17,77
Kinship/Clan	3	6,66
Welfare Schemes	7	15,55
Community Associations	3	6,66
Susu Groups	5	11,11
Social Networks	3	6,66
Landed Property	5	11,11
Other	1	2,22
Total	45	100,00

Source: Field Data, 2016

The concept of social security

The delivery of social security benefits in a country is a right and a responsibility of individuals, employers, civil society, organisations and Governments to guarantee income at old age and reduce poverty in the medium term. It is a right of every human being as stipulated under Article 22 of the Universal Declaration of Human Rights which states thus:

> Everyone, as a member of society, has the right to social security and is entitled to realisation, through national effort and international co-operation and in

accordance with the organisation and resources of each State, of the economic, social and cultural rights indispensable for his dignity and the free development of his personality (United Nations, 1948).

Similarly, Article 9 of the International Covenant on Economic, Social and Cultural Rights (ICESCR) which is a multilateral treaty adopted by the United Nations General Assembly on 16 December 1966 and in force from 3 January 1976, recognises the right of everyone to social security, including social insurance. State parties to the ICESCR have the obligation to fulfil the right to social security by adopting the necessary measures, including the implementation of a social security scheme. Ghana signed and ratified this Covenant on 7 September 2000. State parties must ensure that:

> ... the social security system will be adequate, accessible for everyone and will cover social risks and contingencies.

> State parties also have an obligation to facilitate the right to social security by sufficiently recognising this right within the national political and legal systems, preferably by way of legislative implementation and adopting a national social security strategy (United Nations, 1966).

It requires signatories to provide some form of social insurance scheme to protect people against the risks of sickness, disability, maternity, employment injury, unemployment or old age; to provide for survivors, orphans and those who cannot afford health care; and to ensure that families are adequately supported. In the General Comment no. 19 (2007) On the Right to Social Security, the UN Committee on Economic, Social and Cultural Rights clarified that the right to social security encompass the following nine branches:

- Adequate health service
- Disability benefits
- Old age benefits
- Unemployment benefits
- Employment injury insurance
- Family and child support
- Maternity benefits
- Disability protections
- Provisions for survivors and orphans

According to ILO (1989), social security is the protection that society provides through appropriate organisations against certain risks. It is a human right and may refer to:

▷ Social insurance, where people receive benefits or services in recognition of contributions to an insurance programme by the employer, employee or both. These services typically include provision for retirement pensions, disability insurance, survivor benefits and unemployment insurance.

▷ Services provided by Government or designated agencies responsible for social security provision with non-contributory provisions. In different countries, that may include medical care, financial support during unemployment, sickness, or retirement, health and safety at work, aspects of social work and even industrial relations.

▷ Basic security irrespective of participation in specific insurance programmes.

An Overview of Social Security in Ghana

Social security takes different forms in various countries. Some countries have general social security for all people often funded by taxation. Another form of social security is where the employer and employees contribute to the system. In recent years, the Government of Ghana (GoG) has introduced major reforms in the formal social security system to address key challenges of access by the informal sector operators to social security benefits and to ensure that contributors can take control and guarantee income and livelihood security during old age. The National Pensions Act, 2008 (Act 766) allows people in the informal sector to make contributions to their pensions and save for short to medium term needs. Section 107 states thus:

> (1) A personal pension scheme applies to individuals (a) who want to make voluntary contributions to enhance their pension benefits outside the mandatory schemes and any provident fund scheme and (b) in the informal sector who are not covered by any retirement or pension scheme under the mandatory part of the three-tier pension scheme.

> (2) For people under subsection (1)(b) a portion of their contributions may be accessed before retirement in accordance with the Governing rules of the scheme.

Before the arrival of Europeans in Ghana and the implementation of contemporary social security systems and plans, traditional African societies relied on collective social security and mutual help systems to cater for certain major contingencies (Kumado & Gockel, 2003). Also, in existence were other indigenous arrangements that people engaged in as a fall back during old age.

Indigenous Social Security Systems (ISSS)

This section briefly explains Indigenous Social Security Systems (ISSS) in Ghana which include community support systems, kinship, clans and the extended family system, welfare schemes, *susu*, savings and loan schemes, social networks, social groups and associations and landed property.

Community Support Groups

Most people in Ghana depend on various community support groups such as church groups for financial and social support in times of need and during absence of the family. Savings by the members are mobilised and given to one person and the circle goes on until everybody earns her/his turn and the cycle continues again. Others save into a pool and the profits are invested, shared or used to start a business and the profits ploughed back into the business. In some cases, the business activities are stopped when downtimes set in.

Kinship, Clans and Extended Family System

In Ghana, kinship, clans and the extended family had long been an institution that people fall back for their social, emotional (psychological stability and moral development) and economic support, especially during old age, unemployment, sickness and other hardships. However, this system is gradually breaking down because of the emergence of the nuclear family system. In contemporary times, and especially with the decline of the extended family system, there is a gradual shift away from primary reliance on the extended family towards dependence on more semi-formally institutionalised social security systems. The gradual breakdown of the traditional social protection schemes is compounded by the new economic order which emerged in the 1980s and is based on market-led strategies to economic growth. The main drivers for the collapse of this social system include changes in economic, political and the social order (Kumado & Gockel, 2003).

Rapid interviews conducted with a few entrepreneurs of MSMEs indicate that the extended family system is a key asset for their social security. The inadequacy of social infrastructure has obliged the extended family members to step in to provide the social needs of their families. In other words, the resources of the family members are utilised in ways that affect their ability to save towards their upkeep after retirement. This means they would not be able to retire comfortably. When a family member retires, the responsibility of bridging his/her retirement income falls back on the wards he/she supported while in active employment. This puts a toll on the income of the ward as he/she takes care of health, feeding, accommodation and other needs of the retiree. The consequence is a vicious cycle of poverty that must be broken, and appropriate measures taken to improve the welfare of the extended family. Box 1 illustrates the challenges of the social security system in Ghana (The Mirror, November 16, 2002).

In recent times a lot has been reported in both the print and electronic media about the increasing fragmentation of the Ghanaian family... Undeniably, the family in all societies and cultures plays a key role in the development of individuals who constitute the human resource base of the country. It provides the necessary environment where children can be nurtured in love, friendship and discipline. Admittedly, current economic pressures are making it imperative for both parents to work outside their homes from dawn to dusk, thereby leaving children to their own devices with virtually no adult supervision... In days gone by, parents, grandparents, aunts and other extended family members provided good childcare practices, but today even grandmothers are trying to eke out a living. It must be emphasised that family and community arrangements that traditionally provided for old people and the poor are under threat as well. These traditional support networks appear to be weakening with the contemporary market-based approach to economic development worldwide so that formal retirement programmes will become increasingly important.

Kumado and Gockel (2003) argued that the gradual breakdown of the extended family system has serious implications because its members provide for the aged, the disabled, the sick and the unemployed members of the family, the newborn child and the mother, the orphaned and even the stranger.

Box 1   Standing Up for the Family

Welfare Schemes

Welfare schemes exist in Churches to offer help to people when the unexpected happens. However, people who qualify to benefit are expected to be members of the scheme and have contributed to it. There are several welfare schemes that are also set up by employees within various organisations with contributions from only the employees to help them in times of need.

Susu, savings and loans schemes

Savings and loans associations exist in many communities in Ghana. They enable members to contribute money in a pool which is invested to generate more funds to facilitate the granting of loans to members at very minimal interest rates or for investment in businesses and the profits shared amongst members. Some trade unions organise informal sector groups and establish welfare and microfinance schemes to assist their members in the informal sector. For example, the Ghana Private Road Transport Union (GPRTU) operates a welfare fund for members to access in times of bereavement. Other organisations such as the General Agricultural Workers Union (GAWU) have similar schemes. The *susu* savings scheme is a popular system for shop operators, market women, artisans and other groups in the informal system. It serves as a savings system that can be accessed by contributors during the occurrence of life events such as death, unemployment and loss of business capital.

Social networks, social groups and associations

Social networks, social groups and associations have always been common channels for people to save and/or take small loans in the context of self-help to engage in small retail businesses or farming ventures. In some cases, members contribute towards the establishment of a business venture and the proceeds are shared or used to open other businesses. Such organisations make cash contributions when a member marries, gives birth or is bereaved.

Landed property

Many people, especially in the informal sector, prefer to purchase land and houses as a fall back when they grow old. But the problem is liquidity issues when cash is mostly needed for emergencies. Moreover, landed properties are beset by encroachment challenges.

Challenges facing Indigenous Social Security Systems

Over the years, ISSS have been affected by serious challenges that threaten their existence and render their purpose unsustainable. For example, urbanisation has affected the willingness and ability of kinship and families to provide members the needed support during old age, disability, death, etc. More often, members of the family are either too poor themselves or have other competing demands for their resources. Increasing economic constraints and the problems posed by urbanisation are particularly affecting kinship ties and the ability for family members to provide support for the needy. Traditional savings mechanisms are also often characterised by theft and misappropriation. The essence of social security is sometimes missing in ISSS arrangements. Mutual associations and schemes rely on the loyalty and effort of their members to contribute, hence excluding the poor from benefiting (Osei-Boateng, Unpublished). The gradual collapse of family systems and mistrust of the Indigenous Social Security Systems in Ghana have given a lot of support for the development and reforms of formal security systems. Various Government policies and social security schemes have been introduced in Ghana to provide protection in both the formal and the informal sectors.

Formal social security systems in Ghana

The principal formal social security systems in Ghana are briefly described in the next sub-sections.

Microfinance Organisations

Microfinance has evolved over the years in Ghana. It encompasses the provision of financial services and the management of small amounts of money through a range of products and a system of intermediary functions that are targeted at low-income clients (Bank of Ghana (BOG) Paper, 2007). It includes loans, savings, insurance, transfer services and other financial products and services. The system is increasingly providing the poor access to capital which the formal financial sector has failed to deliver (UN, 2000). The former UN Secretary General Kofi Annan (2003), during the launch of the International Year of Micro Credit in 2003, pointed to the benefits of this type of credit thus:

> ... Sustainable access to microfinance helps alleviate poverty by generating income, creating jobs, allowing children to go to school, enabling families to obtain health care and empowering people to make the choices that best serve their needs.

According to Bank of Ghana (BoG Paper, 2007), empirical studies show that microfinance helps very poor households to meet basic needs and protect themselves against risks. It is thus associated with improvements in household economic welfare. Littlefield and Rosenberg (2004) argue that the poor are generally excluded from the financial services sector of the economy so Microfinance Institutions (MFIs) have emerged to address this market failure. By addressing this gap in the market in a financially sustainable manner, an MFI can become part of the formal financial system of the country and therefore be able to access capital markets to fund their lending portfolios. This is enabling them to dramatically increase the number of poor people they can reach (Otero, 1999). Currently, there are three broad types of MFIs operating in Ghana:

- ▻ Formal suppliers of microfinance (i.e. rural and community banks, savings and loans companies, commercial banks).
- ▻ Semi-formal suppliers of microfinance (i.e. credit unions, Financial Non-Governmental Organisations (FNGOs) and co-operatives).
- ▻ Informal suppliers of microfinance (e.g. *susu* collectors and clubs, rotating and accumulating savings and accumulating savings and credit associations traders, money lenders and other individuals).

Policy back-up for non-bank financial institutions

The promulgation of PNDC Law 328 of 1991 allowed the establishment of different types of Non-Bank Financial Institutions (NBFIs), including savings and loans companies, finance houses and credit unions, etc. Many regulatory frameworks have been defined to oversee the functioning of these non-bank financial institutions which include:

- ▻ Rural and community banks - are regulated under the Banking Act 2004 (Act 673).

⊳ Savings and Loans Companies are currently regulated under the Non-Bank Financial Institutions (NBFI) Law 1993 (PNDCL 328).

⊳ Credit Unions, FNGOs and ROSCAS. Policies and regulations are being developed for this category of NBFIs.

Key Stakeholders in the Microfinance Industry in Ghana

The key stakeholders in the microfinance industry may be put in the following two groups:

Microfinance Institutions

⊳ The Rural and Community Banks

⊳ Savings and Loans Companies

⊳ Financial NGOs

⊳ Primary Societies

⊳ *Susu* Collectors Association

⊳ Development and Commercial Banks with microfinance programmes and linkages

⊳ Micro-insurance and Micro-leasing services

⊳ Customers/End users

⊳ Microfinance and Small Loans Centre (MASLOC)

⊳ The Ghana Microfinance Institutions Network (GHAMFIN)

⊳ Development Partners and International Non-Governmental Organisations

⊳ Universities, Training and Research Institutions

⊳ Government Institutions

⊳ Ministry of Finance and Economic Planning

⊳ Ministries, Departments, Agencies and Metropolitan, Municipal and District Assemblies.

Microfinance apex bodies:

⊳ Association of Rural Banks

⊳ ARB Apex Bank

⊳ Association of Financial NGOs

161

- ▻ Ghana Co-operative Credit Unions Association
- ▻ Ghana Co-operative *Susu* Collectors Association

Microfinance policy and programmes

Several policies and programmes driving the microfinance sub-sector in Ghana include:

- ▻ The Financial Sector Improvement Project
- ▻ Financial Sector Strategic Plan
- ▻ Rural Financial Services Project
- ▻ United Nations Development Programme (UNDP) Microfinance Project
- ▻ Social Investment Fund
- ▻ Community Based Rural Development Programme
- ▻ Rural Enterprise Project
- ▻ Agricultural Services Investment Project

Currently, the BoG is strengthening the regulatory framework for institutions operating in the microfinance sub-sector to improve outreach, sustainability, efficiency and security of savings. Although Hulme and Mosley (1996) concluded that "... most contemporary schemes are less effective than they might be", they are seen globally as an effective strategy for poverty reduction with the potential for far-reaching impact in transforming the lives of poor people. It is argued that if microfinance is properly harnessed, it can indeed make sustainable contributions through financial investment leading to the empowerment of people, which will in turn promote confidence and self-esteem, particularly for women. It is also known that loans advanced by microfinance institutions are normally for purposes like housing, petty trade and as 'start-up' loans for farming, for groups and for collective enterprises such as irrigation pumps, building sanitary latrines, power looms, leasing markets or leasing land for co-operative farming. The amount of loans extended by NBFIs increased from GH¢70,63 million in 2003 to GH¢72,85 million in 2004 (1 USD = 4,32820 GH¢, as of 22 May 2017), suggesting 3,1 per cent growth. In 2006 alone, a total of GH¢160,47 million was extended to clients, which represents 48,8 per cent higher than the previous year's total loans and advances granted by microfinance institutions.

In Ghana, microfinance is a means of saving and/or providing loans for investment. However, most companies allow for savings first before loans can be accessed. The major challenge that microfinance companies face, is the poor loan recovery rate which is causing their collapse. The principal problems affecting the performance of microfinance institutions include low cash flow, unreliable energy supply, high cost of energy and non-labour inputs, increasing competition and high cost of credit. Until recently, the sector lacked specific policy guidelines, goals and effective co-ordination between key stakeholders.

Health Insurance Schemes

The National Health Insurance Scheme (NHIS) which is based on premium payment ranging from about 6 USD-36 USD, was established under Act 640 in 2003 with the basic aim of securing the implementation of a national health insurance policy that ensures access to basic health services to all inhabitants in Ghana through mutual and private health insurance schemes. The different types of schemes such as district mutual, private mutual and private commercial insurance, are regulated by the National Health Insurance Authority (NHIA). The object of NHIA is to secure the implementation of the national health insurance policy that provides access to basic healthcare services to all residents of Ghana. In 2008, the GOG established a free maternal care policy through the NHIS. The Act also gives exemption from premium payment to some categories of people classified as indigent, such as residents who are 70 years or older; children less than 18 years of age and whose parents or guardians are contributors of some informal sector; people who do not have any visible source of income, or fixed place of residence; do not live with a person who is employed; has a fixed place of residence and do not have a consistent source of support from another person. The NHIA (2015) currently covers over 95 per cent of diseases. Its sources of funding include the following:

- ▷ Premiums from subscribers.
- ▷ 2,5 per cent National Health Insurance levy.
- ▷ 2,5 per cent Social Security and National Insurance Trust (SSNIT), deductions from the formal sector.
- ▷ Funds from the GoG that are approved by Parliament.
- ▷ Returns from investment.

Micro Insurance Schemes

The insurance industry in Ghana is regulated by the National Insurance Commission (NIC) which now operates under the Insurance Act, 2006 (Act 724) with the objective to ensure effective administration, supervision, regulation and control of the business of insurance in Ghana. There are 11 companies made up of eight life insurance companies and three non-life insurance companies providing micro insurance products which sometimes offer savings, credit and telecom subscription benefits (NIC & GIZ, 2012). Insurance penetration in Ghana is still very low with about 1,25 million subscribers. Currently, geographical penetration is very low especially in the northern region. The industry is still suffering from high distribution and administrative cost which eventually affect contributors. Micro insurance schemes mainly focus on the informal sectors and low-income markets to manage risk and certain eventualities that cannot be covered by savings and other means among this group. However, many insurance companies are now targeting the low-income market with their micro-insurance products.

Formal and Private Pension Schemes

Agblobi (2011) defined a pension as a regular monthly income (benefits) paid to a certain category of people because of old age in Ghana (at retirement), invalidity due to ill-health (permanent disability) or to widows/widower (survivor's pensions or lump sum). In Ghana, pension is both a right and a responsibility requiring contribution by both the employer and the employee. The most reliable income security at old age has been the social security or public pension scheme which reaches the vast majority of people. The scheme had an active membership of 1,120,512 at the end of 2013 with a total fund of GH¢ 5,170.13 million (SSNIT, 2013). When one qualifies for pension benefits, one is assured a constant flow of income no matter how small or big until death.

Pension schemes and systems in Ghana primarily focus on the provision of retirement income to the aged and supplementary income for injured or disabled people who formally held employment positions. The provision of income to the beneficiaries of deceased workers, has been a secondary focus of pension policy makers in the country. Prior to the introduction of PNDC Law 247 in 1991, the 1965 Parliamentary Act on Social Security, and all other reforms were managed and pooled by the GoG. However, this system had very little impact in terms of coverage and did not meet ILO's standards for the contributor and beneficiary coverage (Kumado & Gockel, 2003). The pension system in Ghana almost collapsed due to a large fiscal debt and other debt holdings that the GoG had accrued over the years. This situation forced the Government to enact the PNDC Law 247 of 1991, which gave ownership to the fund contributors (mostly workers in the formal sector) and in effect reduced the burden on the Government. The fund created under this law had more coverage as it included part of the informal sector and created a proper fund investment policy. The SSNIT operates a contributory social insurance scheme where members contribute to a pool of funds throughout their working lives and receive pay-outs when they satisfy the qualifying conditions. SSNIT has a primary duty to collect contributions and pay pension entitlements when due.

Pension Reforms in Ghana: The National Pension Act 2008 (Act 766)

In July 2004, the GOG initiated a major reform of the Pension System in the country, which led to the enactment of the National Pensions Act 2008 (Act 766) on 12 December 2008 with the aim of ensuring retirement income security for all Ghanaian workers and for the creation of a unified pension structure. The Act established a regulatory body called the National Pensions Regulatory Authority (NPRA) which is mandated to regulate both public and private pension schemes in the country. The pensions industry in Ghana is compliance-based and backed by the National Pensions Act, 2008 (Act 766) and other legislations. The effectiveness of pensions is larglye dependent on the powers and independence of the regulatory bodies, as defined in the respective laws, relating to licensing, supervision and enforcement actions. Despite the reforms, the SSNIT pension scheme is experiencing its own challenges. For instance, the following schemes were to be unified with the new SSNIT pension scheme four years after the commencement of the National Pensions Act, 2008 (Act 766), but this has not yet been implemented:

▷ the Pensions Ordinance No. 42 of 1950 (CAP 30) as amended,

▷ Teachers' Pensions Ordinance 1955 as amended,

▷ Ghana Universities Staff Superannuation Scheme,

▷ Ghana Police Pensions Act, 1985 (P.N.D.C.L 126),

▷ Public Legal Officers Pensions Act, 1985 (P.N.D.C L 126),

▷ Immigration Service Pensions Act, 1986 (P.N.D.C.L 226),

- Prisons Service Pensions Act, 1987 (P.N.D.C. L 168),
- Section 34 of the Security and Intelligence Agencies Act, 1996 (Act 529), and
- Section 27 of the National Fire Service Act, 2000 (Act 537).

The NPRA also approves, regulates and monitors Trustees, Pension Fund Managers, Custodians and other institutions relating to pension matters. It further introduced the Contributory Three Tier Pension System consisting of:

- Tier 1 – Mandatory Basic National Social Security Scheme
- Tier 2 – Mandatory Fully Funded and Privately Managed Occupational Pension Scheme
- Tier 3 – Voluntary Fully Funded and Privately Managed Provident Fund and Personal Pension Schemes

The implementation of the new scheme started on 1 January 2010 with private companies having registered schemes under Tiers 2 and 3 and pay directly to their respective custodians, who then make the funds available to be invested by the pension fund manager in consultation with the Trustees. Tier 1, Basic National Social Security Scheme, is a defined benefit scheme whiles Tier 2, occupational pension and personal pension schemes, are defined contribution schemes. The major stakeholders in the reformed pensions industry include:

- National Pensions Regulatory Authority (NPRA)
- Ghana Revenue Authority (GRA)
- Trustees/Administrators
- Employers
- Employees
- Custodians
- Fund managers
- Auditors
- Advisors/consultants.

Contributions to the National Pensions System

Both the employees and the employers are expected to contribute to the scheme. Employees contribute 5,5 per cent of their basic salary, while the employer adds 13 per cent of the employee's salary which adds up to 18,5 per cent. Table 2 shows the distribution of contributions under the mandatory Tiers 1 and 2 structures while Table 3 contains the details for Tier 3.

Table 2 Mandatory Contributions Structure under the New Pension System for the Formal Sector

Recipient Institution	Type of Scheme	Beneficiary	Percentage (%)	Total (%)
SSNIT	1st Tier	SSNIT	11	
	1st Tier	National Health Insurance Scheme	2,5	13,5
Private Scheme Managers	2nd Tier	Private Scheme Managers	5,0	5,0
		Total	18,5	18,5

Source: SSNIT 2014

Table 3 Voluntary Contributions Structure under the New Pension System for the Informal Sector

Recipient	Type of Scheme	Manager	Contribution (%)	Total (%)	Tax Benefits
Private Scheme Manager	3rd Tier (Voluntary)	Private Scheme Manager	35,0	35,0	35,0 (of Income Contribution)

Informal sector includes individuals and MSMEs with four employees or less

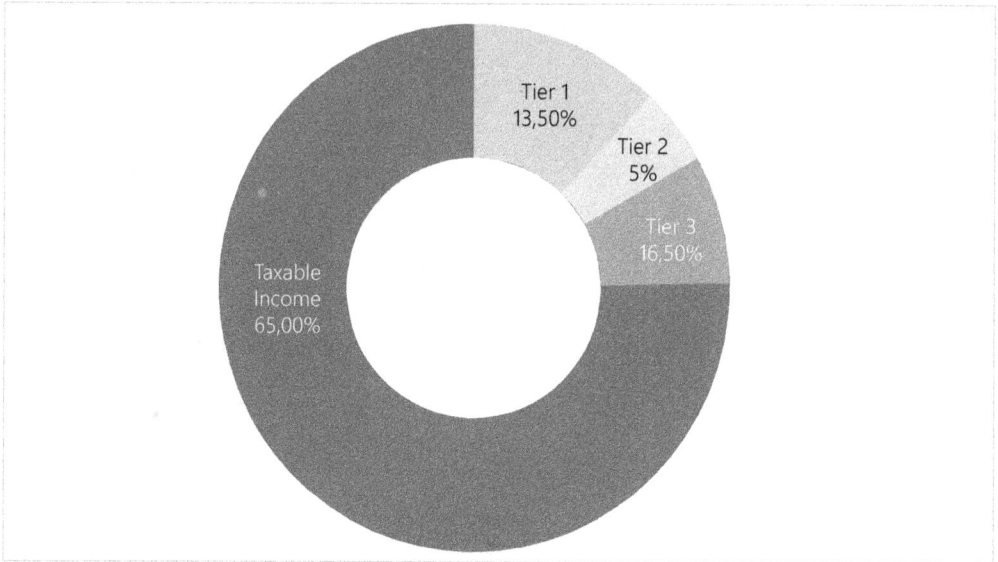

Figure 1   Illustration of Contributions under Tiers 1, 2 and 3

Tax Benefits of the National Pensions System

Schemes operated under the three-tier system enjoy tax reliefs granted under the National Pensions Act, 2008 (Act 766). Contributions up to 35 per cent will be tax exempt for both formal and informal sectors. The first and second tier mandatory schemes will have a full tax exemption of 18,5 per cent of pre-tax contributions. The third tier (voluntary scheme) will have a maximum tax exemption of 16,5 per cent. However, contributors on the third tier who do not contribute to the compulsory scheme (tier 2 and 3) will be allowed the full 35 per cent tax exemption.

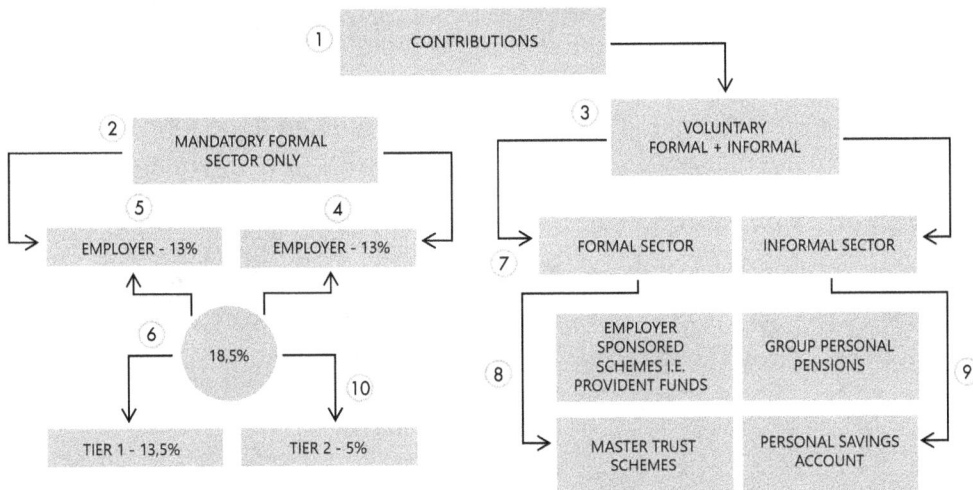

①	Maximum contribution allowed under the new pension's law in Ghana.
②	Mandatory contribution applicable to the formal sector only.
③	Voluntary contributions applicable to people in both formal and informal sector. Ghanaians living abroad can join this scheme.
④	Percentage of employee's basic salary deducted for mandatorily (5,5 per cent).
⑤	Employers contribution on behalf of the employee (13 per cent).
⑥	Employer and employee contribution together (18,5 per cent).
⑦	Voluntary contributions applicable to the formal sector: Maximum allowed is 16,5 per cent because of mandatory contribution of 18,5 per cent to tiers 1 and 2. Note that maximum contribution allowed under the pensions act is 35 per cent.
⑧	Contribution can be put in a stand-alone employer sponsored scheme or a master trust scheme which is a combination of different schemes from different companies.
⑨	Informal sector can save up to 35 per cent of their income in pensions.
⑩	Tier 2 contribution. Tier 3: Voluntary Fully Funded and Privately Managed Provident Fund and Personal Pension Schemes. In May 2010, the NPRA announced transitional guidelines for the commencement of voluntary third tier provident fund (administered in formal sectors with contributions of employer, employee or both) and personal pension schemes.

Figure 2   Tier 2: Mandatory Fully Funded and Privately Managed Occupational Pension Scheme

Tier 1 – Mandatory Basic Social Security Scheme Managed by SSNIT

Under Tier 1, the mandatory scheme administered by SSNIT, contributors are expected to work for 180 months or 15 years in aggregate and must be at least 60 years to qualify for full pension. Pension is paid for old age, invalidity and death. Contributors who do not meet these criteria receive reduced pensions paid as a lump sum. Old age social security pension benefits are calculated based on the age, average of best 36 months payment/three years of salary and earned pension right based on the number of months of contribution to the scheme. Then payment will be made till death. On the other hand, invalidity and death pension payment contributors must have made minimum of 12 months' payments within the last 36 months to qualify for a lump sum payment.

Tier 2 – Mandatory Fully Funded and Privately Managed Occupational Pension Scheme

Tier 2 is a mandatory fully funded and privately managed occupational pension scheme. Contributions to this tier comprise five per cent of the employee's basic salary and is managed by private fund managers, licensed by the Securities and Exchange Commission (SEC) and registered with the National Pension Regulatory Authority (NPRA).

Benefits of a Personal Pension Scheme under the Tier 3 System

The main benefits of a personal pension scheme under the Tier 3 system include the following:

- The pensions industry is highly regulated with stringent operational and reporting requirements.
- Separation of functions of trustees, fund managers and custodians ensure checks and balances.
- Funds are professionally managed.
- Tax advantages exist for both employer and employee.
- Contributors are offered other incentives such as using their funds as collateral to secure mortgages, life insurance options, etc.
- Portability requirements allow transfer of accrued benefits to another scheme by the contributor during change of employment, termination, etc.
- It is an avenue for the informal sector to contribute for their retirement income security.

Discussion of Findings

As has already been indicated, MSMEs constitute an important source of employment and income in Ghana. Moreover, they are more flexible and more effectively adapted to changing market conditions and cyclical downturns. Furthermore, the dispersion of MSMEs across the country can serve as a vehicle for promoting equitable distribution of income, generating additional value in raw materials and products and enhancing domestic market development. The Government and large-scale enterprises, including social security companies in the country, should therefore serve as an effective institutional support mechanism for creating an enabling environment for MSMEs, to forge effective forward and backward linkages and improve their access to markets and social security protection. MSMEs in Ghana have great opportunities for expansion and diversification across various sectors of the economy if the required support is provided. While the developed global markets may be shrinking due to the prevailing economic and financial crises, the steady growth of the market size in Ghana and the increasing business opportunities within Africa are good indicators of the potential of MSMEs to drive prosperity and sustainability.

Clearly, the inherent advantages of MSMEs in Ghana should entice the Government, and other stakeholders, to accord their serious attention. Providing MSMEs easy access to credit will help to establish a more vibrant and successful private sector in the country. Yemoah *et al* (2014) observe that Government institutions mandated to create an enabling business environment in Ghana, but have not succeeded in providing the requisite opportunities for MSMEs development. Unclear national strategies tend to result in poor co-ordination of Government incentive support programmes and failure by these institutions to perform to expectations. In the first place, establishment of institutions and provision of incentive packages alone are not sufficient for ensuring the development of the sector. Secondly, the nature of these institutions can help or harm the development and promotion of MSMEs in each context. For example, the high cost of licensing, legal cost, strict processes and procedures involved in doing business significantly, hinder the development of MSMEs in Ghana. Most MSMEs in the country have limited financial resources and cannot therefore cope with the increasing costs and time needed for licensing their businesses (Abor & Quartey, 2010). In addition, poor administration of laws relating to the issuance of licenses and permits, unequal access to public services and resources, delays in the delivery of public services, poor auditing and tax administration stifle the development of MSMEs (Yamoah *et al*, 2014).

Another major constraint to the development of MSMEs in Ghana is inadequate access to credit (Mensah, 2004). Over the years, finance for these enterprises mostly comes from personal savings of their owners and sometimes from friends and family. This pool of financial resources is limited and cannot therefore ensure the sustainability of MSMEs. Tagoe *et al* (2005) add that the main financial challenge facing MSMEs is access to affordable credit over a reasonable period which is determined by the financing needs of MSMEs and the actions of investors. MSME financing needs to reflect on the operational requirements, while the investors depend on the risk perception and the attractiveness of alternative investments. Most banks and financial institutions in Ghana assess MSMEs to be inherently riskier to do business with because they suffer from insufficient assets, have low level of capitalisation and are vulnerable to market fluctuations and high mortality rates (Asare, 2014). MSMEs also suffer from credit rationing imposed by financial institutions due to insufficient reliable collateral or collateral mismatch between the types of assets held by MSMEs and the type of assets required by banks as collateral.

The strict credit facility assessment system and documentation required by banks and other financial institutions are significant constraints to the development of MSMEs in Ghana. Moreover, the high-interest rates charged by financial institutions are unfavourable to MSMEs' development because all the revenue generated is used to repay their loans and nothing is left for developing new innovative products and expanding their businesses (Aryeetey *et al*, 1994; Green *et al*, 2002; Kayanula & Quartey, 2000). The rapid globalisation of the world in recent years is another big challenge to the development of MSMEs, especially because they do not have the capacity to conduct research and develop new innovative products to compete effectively in the global market. Ineffective marketing strategies, weak capacity to identify new markets, constraints on modernisation and expansion possibilities tend to hinder the development of MSMEs in Ghana.

Non-availability of highly skilled labour at affordable costs is another critical barrier to the development of MSMEs in the country. Most of them have few employees who tend to be mostly relatives of the owner. Hence, there is often lack of separation between ownership and control (Kufuor, 2008). They are often not aware of key developments and changes in the international and domestic markets. The growth and development of the sector is also dependent upon access to new technologies and modern methods of production (Aryeetey *et al*, 1994). The gradual collapse of family systems and mistrust of the informal sources of finance have lent a lot of support for the development and reforms of formal security systems. Various government policies and social security schemes have been introduced to provide protection for people engaged in both the formal and the informal sectors of the economy. The results of a field survey conducted on 45 social security policy makers, managers and administrators, as well as employees and entrepreneurs of MSMEs indicate that 77,80 per cent of the interviewees rely on indigenous social security system while 22,22 per cent depends on the formal system. The most popular formal social security systems are the National Health Insurance Scheme (NHIS) and the Social Security and National Insurance Trust (SSNIT). The majority of MSMEs entrepreneurs and employees indicated they do not participate in the formal SSS for the following reasons:

- Failure by the Government to fulfil its social security promises.
- They are not engaged in gainful employment (informal sector).
- They do not fully understand the formal social security system, policies, regulations and procedures.
- The formal social security systems do not cover all risks, e.g. NHIS.
- The formal SSS are suffering from bureaucratic red tape and long documentation processes.
- Incompetent managers and administrators.
- Delays in payment of benefits.
- Corruption by managers and administrators.
- Ineffectiveness of formal social security systems.

On the other hand, for MSMEs to succeed in establishing adequate trust and confidence, to enable them to gain access to credit and social protection for improving their operations, they need to be more transparent in dealing with banks, financial institutions and social security organisations. The paucity of relevant information, operational skills, including accounting and finance, business planning, among others, are formidable challenges to MSMEs' productivity and ability to pay their social security contributions. To lessen the risk of borrowing to MSMEs, banks and financial institutions need to play a more proactive role in their relations with MSMEs by capacitating and providing them with relevant investment and business management advisory services. To a very large extent by simply granting credit facilities to SSMEs', entrepreneurs who do not have the requisite skills and know-how to make the best use of the funds, are busy with anti-development. Human resource development is fundamental for improving MSMEs performance competitiveness, sustainability and ability to pay social security contributions. The capacity of MSMEs in Ghana to adjust to the competitive pressures that come with globalisation and trade liberalisation will depend greatly on the level of skills available domestically. To make MSMEs in the country efficient and productive, it is necessary to ensure that they have skilled human resources and requisite managerial skills. Ghana should capitalise on her demographic dividend (a large and young workforce) to promote the growth and development of MSMEs through comprehensive training programmes and development of entrepreneurial skills of young people. It is unfortunate that MSMEs in the country tend to shy away from training their staff and rather rely more on external recruitment for boosting their competitiveness.

Another important strategy for promoting the development of MSMEs is access to appropriate technology. With the existing high level of competition, globalisation and market uncertainties, it is important that MSMEs embrace technology. MSMEs in Ghana continuously need to incorporate the latest technological innovations into their production processes, marketing and management functions to gain efficiency and produce the highest quality products for both the domestic and international markets. Educating MSMEs' owners, managers and employees about the importance of indigenous and formal social security systems and encouraging them to subscribe to existing schemes will significantly help to ensure the welfare of their families in the long-term. To ensure an effective integration of the two social security systems in Ghana, 77,80 per cent of the participants of a field survey conducted on the integration of the indigenous and formal social security systems recommended the following strategies:

- Government should effectively implement formulated social protection policies and promises.
- More employment opportunities should be created for young people and women.
- The population should be adequately educated on the importance of social security systems.
- Social security schemes should be simplified and made easy to understand.
- Biometric registration system should be used for registering subscribers of social security systems.
- Competent and ethical managers and administrators should engage social security institutions and companies.

- ☞ Social security schemes should be expanded to cover more risks.
- ☞ Payment of benefits should be swift and devoid of bureaucratic delays and corrupt practices.
- ☞ Subscribers should be given the opportunity to withdraw part of their funds before retirement.
- ☞ Social security schemes should be made mandatory for all workers.
- ☞ Social security institutions and companies should be subjected to rigorous accounting and auditing systems and practices.

Conclusion

In conclusion, the potential of MSMEs in Ghana to contribute to sustainable human development of the country is yet to be fully harnessed mainly because of inadequate structural and regulatory support and access to social protection. Building and strengthening the innovation capacity of MSMEs will enable them to create competent management teams to effectively handle their affairs, seize emerging opportunities and strategise for promoting sustainable growth and securing their future. Effective networking and partnerships between public and private sector stakeholders and between MSMEs and the formal sector enterprises and social security companies are vital for guaranteeing the sustainability of MSMEs and the country. To strengthen MSMEs and make them more efficient and competitive requires relevant policies, capacity building and an enabling business environment that facilitates appropriate blending of indigenous and formal social security systems to assure entrepreneurs and employees guaranteed welfare in the future. It is therefore important that stakeholders of MSMEs should continue to vigorously advocate for integration of indigenous and formal social security systems as an instrument for promoting the sustainability of MSMEs and the country.

References

Abor, J. & Quartey, P. 2010. Issues in SME Development in Ghana and South Africa. *International Research Journal of Finance and Economics*, 39: 218-228.

Adesina, J. 2009. Social Policy in sub-Saharan Africa: A glance in the reer-view mirror, *International Journal of Social Welfare*, 18(S1): S37-S51.

Agblobi, M. 2011. *Pension Systems in Ghana*. www.academia.edu/16541455/Pension_Systemsi_In_Ghana [Accessed 2 March 2016].

Aina, T. A. 2010. Beyond Reform: The Politics of Higher Education Transformation in Africa, African Studies Review, Volume 53, Number 1: 21-40.

Annan, K. 2003. *International Year of Microcredit 2005: Building Inclusive Financial Sectors to Achieve the Millennium Development Goals*. www.yearofmicrocredit.org/whyayear/whyayear_quotecollection.asp#kofiannan [Accessed 3 March 2016].

Aryeetey, E.; Baah-Nuakoh, A.; Duggleby, T.; Hettige, H. & Steel, W.F. 1994. *Supply and Demand for Finance of Small Scale Enterprises in Ghana* (Discussion Paper No. 251). The World Bank: Washington, DC.

Asare, A.O. 2015. Challenges Affecting SME's Growth in Ghana. *OIDA International Journal of Sustainable Development*, 7(6): 23-28.

Bank of Ghana. 2007. *A Note on Microfinance in Ghana*. Accra: Research Department of Bank of Ghana.

Davenp ort, R.B. 1967. *Financing the Small Manufacturer in Developing Countries*. New York: McGraw Hill.

Frimpong, C.Y. 2013. *Strengthening SMEs in Ghana*. http://www.ghanaweb.com/GhanaHomePage/NewsArchive/Strengthening-SMEs-In-Ghana-286949 [Accessed 25 September 2014].

Green, C.; Kimuyu, P. & Murinde, V. 2002. *How do Small Firms in Developing Countries Raise Capital?* Evidence from a Large-Scale Survey of Kenyan Micro and Small Scale Enterprises. https://dspace.lboro.ac.uk/dspace-jspui/bitstream/2134/363/3/erp02-6.pdf [Accessed 3 January 2016].

Hulme, D. & Mosley, P. 1996. *Finance Against Poverty*. Routledge, London, UK.

International Labour Organisation (ILO) (2015). World Employment and Social Outlook 2015. www.ilo.org/global/about-the-ilo/newsroom [Accessed 19 May 2016].

Kayanula, D. & Quartey, P. 2000. *The Policy Environment for Promoting Small and Medium-Sized Enterprises in Ghana and Malawi, Finance and Development Research Programme*. (Working Paper Series, Paper No 15). Manchester: IDPM – University of Manchester.

Kufuor, A.A. 2008. Employment Generation and Small Medium Enterprise (SME) Development – the Garment and Textile Manufacturing Industry in Ghana. A Paper presented at Growing Inclusive Forum in Halifax, Nova Scotia, Canada, Dalhousie University's Faculty of Management, 19-21 June.

Kumado, K. & Gockel, A.F. 2003. *A Study of Social Security in Ghana*. www.library.fes.de/ pdf-files/bueros/Ghana/50022.pdf [Accessed 3 January 2016].

Littlefield, E. & Rosenberg, R. 2004. *Breaking Down the Walls between Microfinance and the Formal Financial System*. www.cgap.org/sites/default/files/CGAP [Accessed 3 February 2016].

Mensah, S. 2004. A Review of SME Financing Schemes in Ghana. Presented at the UNIDO Regional Workshop of Financing Small and Medium Scale Enterprises, Accra, Ghana, 15-16 March.

National Health Insurance Authority (NHIA). 2015. *National Pensions Act, 2008 (Act 766)*. www.iopsweb.org/resources/48749441.pdf [Accessed 3 January 2016].

National Insurance Commission (NIC) & Deutsche Gesellschaft für Internationale Zusammenarbeit (GIZ) GmbH. 2012. *Promoting Microinsurance in Ghana as a Means of Insurance Sector Development*. Accra: NIC/GIZ.

Osei-Boteng, C. 2011. *Engendering Social Security and Protection: The Case of Africa*, http://library.fes.de/pdf-files/iez/08207.pdf [Accessed on 3 January 2016]

Otero, M. 1999. Bringing Development Back into Microfinance. *Journal of Microfinance*, 1: 8-19.

Parker, R.; Riopelle, R. & Steel, W. 1995. *Small Enterprises Adjusting to Liberalisation in Five African Countries*. World Bank Discussion Paper, No. 271. Washington DC: The World Bank.

Patton, M.Q. 2002. *Qualitative research and evaluation methods*. Third Edition. Thousand Oaks, CA: Sage.

Ramsurrun, B. & Dalrymple, J.F. 2002. *Global Competitiveness within Small and Medium Manufacturing Enterprises in Mauritius*. http://www.smmeresearch.co.za/SMME%20 Research%20General/Reports/SMEs%20in%20Mauritius.pdf [Accessed 3 January 2016].

Social Security and National Insurance Trust (SSNIT). 2013. *Annual Report and Financial Statement*. Accra: Ghana.

Tagoe, N.; Nyarko, E. & Anuwa-Amarh, E. 2005. Financial Challenges Facing Urban SMEs under Financial Sector Liberalisation in Ghana. *Journal of Small Business Management*, 43(3): 331-334.

The Mirror, 16 November 2002. Graphic Communications Group. Accra: Ghana.

Yamoah, E.E.; Arthur, S. & Issaka, A. 2014. Institutional Framework for Promoting Small and Medium Scale Enterprises in Ghana: Perspective of Entrepreneurs. *Australian Journal of Business and Management Research*, 3(10): 28-45.

United Nation. 1966. *International Covenant on Economic, Social and Cultural Rights.*New York: United Nations. United Nations. 1948. *Universal Declaration of Human Rights.* New York: United Nations.

09

NON-GOVERNMENTAL ORGANISATIONS (NGOs) AND SOCIAL PROTECTION IN GHANA

Justice Nyigmah Bawole

Introduction

Within a wider study on the role and importance of Indigenous Social Security Systems and their relationship with formal social security arrangements, this chapter reports on the role that Non-Governmental Organisations (NGOs) are playing in the provision of safety nets for families in poor regions in Ghana. The chapter is based on interviews with NGOs operating in rural districts in the north of Ghana, where extreme poverty incidence rates are higher than the national rate and in the Western Region, where oil and gas production has raised civil society concerns about environmental degradation. This activity is likely to significantly contribute to the destruction of sources of livelihoods in the six coastal districts of the region and lead to increased vulnerability, insecurity and poverty in the coastal communities. An opinion leader in a peri-urban community near Accra, the capital city of Ghana, also shared her experience and perspective on the safety net role of NGOs. This chapter also reviews the state of social protection in Ghana, the challenges of state social protection interventions, the rise of NGO welfarism in Ghana and the scope of NGO social safety net activities and the future of NGO social interventions in the country.

In many countries in Sub-Saharan Africa (SSA), formal social security systems remain beyond the reach of the poor and vulnerable. Poor families in rural and sub-urban communities tend to rely on informal support systems in moments of need such as the loss of a family member and the accompanying burial costs, illness, school fees to enable a child to continue his or her education and the destruction of property and livelihood through natural or man-made disasters. Through informal systems of mutual assistance, they pull together to support each other, providing safety nets that are themselves fragile and sorely stretched. NGOs are also regarded as providers of social safety nets (SSNs) for poor families. In filling gaps created by the failure of the state to meet the needs of the poor (Banks & Hulme, 2012), they provide diverse forms of assistance such as microfinance with relatively flexible conditions and payment terms; agricultural and food security support; and alternative income generation and entrepreneurial support activities, which serve as protection for the poor and vulnerable.

As observed by Conway and Norton (2002), there is a need for Governments and other relevant stakeholders to understand better ISSS and work with those informal systems in the design of social protection programmes. These authors suggest that in carrying out needs assessments of the poor and designing programmes to provide for those needs, the state can benefit from knowledge and insights from NGOs. For the purposes of this chapter, two definitions are important. One definition is of social protection, while the other touches on safety nets. With the first, it was proffered by Devereux and Sabates-Wheeler (2004) which describes social protection as involving all initiatives that transfer income or assets to the poor, protect the vulnerable against livelihood risks and enhance the social status and rights of the marginalised. The second one is advanced by Mathauer (2004) which defines safety nets as mechanisms that mitigate the effects of poverty and other risks on vulnerable households.

The role of NGOs in providing safety nets for the poor and vulnerable

From the view point of NGOs working and living within poor communities in Ghana, vulnerability and food insecurity persist as a key characteristic of families in poor communities in Ghana. Some weakening of the traditional social systems of mutual support and welfare seems to be occurring, making the safety net role of NGOs even more important for the poor and vulnerable. For instance, in the northern regions of Ghana there is only one rainy season which also is sporadic. However, farmers continue to depend on rain-fed agriculture. This situation contributes to their vulnerability and food insecurity in the region. Changes in climate patterns and farmers' slowness to adapt farming methods to these changes seem to be contributing further to low productivity, poor harvests and periods of food insecurity. In this regard, NGOs are providing programmes of support that respond to these issues and other causes of vulnerability and insecurity of the poor. Furthermore, NGOs are playing much broader roles in the provision of safety nets to the poor.

Some NGOs play direct safety net roles through programmes which provide direct welfare support to the poor, while others play more indirect roles through programmes which facilitate access to knowledge, skills and empowerment to enable them to lift themselves out of vulnerability. They also provide programmes that mobilise the poor to demand social protection as a right and the government to provide for the basic needs of the poor through advocacy. The argument that governments can benefit from the resources, knowledge and experience of NGOs providing safety nets to the poor is corroborated by this chapter. However, under-resourcing of government agencies seems to limit their capacity to adopt lessons from the best practices of NGOs and their safety net programmes. Again, Government uptake of NGO programmes and strategies seems to depend upon the policy and focus of the Government regarding community development. Nevertheless, the safety nets provided by NGOs are themselves vulnerable to the availability and direction of donor funding. Hence, NGO safety net programmes are often designed as short-term projects and tend to introduce new structures at the community level, rather than being designed as integral parts of on-going community processes that feed into pre-existing structures and systems.

Major factors contributing to insecurity and vulnerability of rural communities in Ghana

In terms of research process, NGO safety net programmes were found to address the three determinants of involuntary income or consumption poverty as presented by Devereux (2002: 658-659):

▷ Low productivity from inadequate returns to labour and other productive inputs.

- Vulnerability from risks and consequences of collapses in income and consumption.
- Dependency from inability to generate an independent livelihood due to the inability to work.

Agriculture was the focus of many NGO safety net programmes, particularly in the northern regions of Ghana. Its importance emerged in relation to the first two determinants of involuntary income or consumption poverty. This was largely due to the agrarian nature of rural communities in the northern regions of Ghana, the rainfall pattern in the area and the type of farming methods practised by rural communities – all of which tended to increase their vulnerability and insecurity. Recent changes in rainfall patterns are also further contributing to their vulnerability. An apparent weakening of traditional systems of welfare and support is further exacerbating the insecurity and vulnerability of rural families.

As earlier pointed out, the northern parts of Ghana experience only one main rainy season during which most farming activities in rural communities are undertaken. Therefore, families rely on the harvest from one farming season by selling and consuming their produce. The tendency by families to consume and sell almost all their produce ahead of the dry season, leaving very little food and seeds for the next rainy season, significantly accounts for their insecurity and vulnerability. As commented by the Executive Director of an NGO in the Bole district of the Upper West Region: "You would have thought that by now they would have known better, but they still eat everything and sell all the rest, then very soon they are hungry and it affects the children the most" (NGO 1). Farming communities' reliance on rainfall for farming means that they are unable to farm during the dry season. A traditional farming practice of mono-cropping increases their vulnerability, as the failure of a crop leaves them with nothing.

In the past, traditional systems of welfare and support apparently enabled families to get through the dry seasons, as families with excess grain supported their neighbours with food, under a tacit agreement that the same support would be offered to them should they someday be in need. This system seemed to be dissipating: "In those days, if your crop failed, or you would run out of food; your neighbour would help you. But now it is not like that. It is each man for himself" (NGO 1). Against this backdrop, NGOs' projects and interventions may be regarded as providing safety nets for poor and rural farming communities. Some NGO programmes provide support that may be regarded as direct safety nets as they provide welfare support directly to families. Others provide support that eventually leads to the strengthening of the food security and social protection of families and may therefore be regarded as an indirect provision of safety nets.

Direct Provision of Safety Nets

Direct provision of safety nets seemed to be provided largely by international charities, International NGOs (INGOs), Faith-Based Organisations (FBOs) such as the Catholic Relief Service, the Presbyterian Agricultural Station and World Vision International and NGOs set up by churches. Their programmes are reported as a regular feature of the agricultural landscape in the three northern regions. Mention was also made of occasional welfare events organised by Churches and philanthropists to provide agricultural produce to poor families during the dry season. In the words of the manager of a local NGO, the programmes of support offered by agriculture-focused INGOs serve in effect as a bridge over the gap created by the farming and consumption patterns of rural communities. "They bridge the gap between one rainy season and the next" (NGO 2). These "bridges" have a wide spectrum, taking different forms, including the following:

1. Programmes that provide welfare to the poor: The Food for Work programme of the World Food Programme (WFP) may be described as an example of direct welfare to the poor. This programme targets farmers, inviting them to work on community development projects at the start of the farming season when food supplies may have run out and they cannot feed their families. Farmers who work on community projects are given food in return for the hours they spend on these projects. Again, another organisation targets school children, providing them with packages of corn and oil to take home. The WFP started a school feeding programme before Ghana's national school feeding programme. Other programmes such as World Vision International provide clothing and funds for education of poor children in rural communities in the three northern regions. These programmes may be said to fall into the category of interventions that protect the minimum living standards of the poor, but do not have a noticeable effect in promoting long term living standards (Devereux, 2002: 662).

2. Programmes that support income generation: These programmes are provided by both international and local NGOs. Within the programmes of this nature,

a wide spectrum again exists, including provision of seeds, agricultural inputs and facilities to farmers; community level credit unions and village banks with relatively soft terms, seed capital; and setting up of farms that both employ and feed the very poor. Irrigation dams have been built by INGOs in some areas in the north of Ghana to encourage farmers to cultivate vegetables during the dry season. Hyfer International's "Spreading the Gift" programme was said to present to each beneficiary a cow. When the cow delivers, each beneficiary is required to give one of the offspring to a neighbour, who must also give away one offspring when her/his cow delivers. Credit Unions and village banks have targeted women's groups, seeking to empower them to engage actively in petty trade. As is the practice with such programmes, the women contribute capital to the bank or credit union through regular savings and the NGO provides counterpart funding. This offers them with a financial safety net. Under CARE International's Co-operatives Programme, farmers' organisations put monies together which are lodged with the co-operative. CARE International provides additional funding and farmers may draw on their monies during difficult times. Yet, another NGO provides farm centres, where farmers store their produce from bountiful harvests. During the off-season, they may return to get grain or food to sell. These programmes may be described as falling into the category of interventions that both protect minimum living standards of the poor and promote long term living standards (Devereux, 2002: 662).

3. Community development projects: Projects that provide community facilities such as bore-holes in remote communities were also described as safety nets, since they provide facilities, without which families and communities would struggle to meet their basic needs.

Indirect provision of safety nets

Local NGOs seemed to be in the forefront of the provision of services described as indirect safety nets, although some INGOs are also providing such services. The indirect safety nets include the following:

1. Education and sensitisation: Programmes of education and sensitisation stood out as one of the key indirect safety net programmes. Through education and extension services, farmers were being empowered to adopt farming methods

and practices more suited to changes in climate. They were being sensitised about the risk of vulnerability associated with some traditional farming practices due to changes in rainfall patterns, the risks of vulnerability involved in mono-cropping, the need for multiple cropping and the need to change planting times. Education on the risks involved in their consumption patterns was also being offered. "We try to make them see that they must start gauging the amounts of food that will last to the next season and keep some for the lean season as food security, rather than selling the entire crop. This is an indirect, but critical safety net" (NGO 1).

2. Information: Some NGOs were providing rural communities with information to enable them access to Government social protection programmes. In the peri-urban locality of Abokobi, an NGO had apparently facilitated the formation of a community association that ensured that community members received information about the existence of LEAP programme [Livelihood Empowerment Against Poverty (LEAP)] requirements for registration and access to the LEAP funds. "My own mother is benefitting from LEAP. She did not know anything about it, because she has been depending on me. But when the association was formed, now she knows how to get access to the funds. She has been going to collect it" (Opinion Leader).

3. Capacity-building: NGOs are equipping the poor with skills to pull themselves out of poverty, while others provide them with knowledge so that they may demand the basic services that Local Government authorities ought to provide them with, as a matter of rights. An example is of an NGO that supports people with disabilities to self-mobilise themselves to demand their right to a legislated percentage of the district assembly common fund.

4. Advocacy: Other NGOs, mainly local NGOs, are advocating at the national level for the rights of the poor to basic services and for the protection of their livelihoods. "We protect them; they are poor and yet even the little they have, they [the multinationals] want to take that away from them. See what is happening to their farm lands and even their fishing activities now that the oil and gas production has started. So, we are speaking for them" (NGO 4).

5. Institutional strengthening: Some INGOs are building the capacity of Government institutions to meet the basic needs of the poor and vulnerable.

Linking NGO safety net interventions to formal social protection programmes

The NGO safety net interventions are taken as representing Indigenous Social Security Systems in this chapter. Therefore, the participants from NGOs who were interviewed for this chapter's purposes, pointed to a great need for NGO safety net programmes to be adopted or mainstreamed into the formal social protection programmes of the Government. They indicated that particularly with NGOs' agricultural programmes, there was already an appreciable level of collaboration with district level agricultural offices and extension officers. "Already, the NGOs work with them [district level agricultural extension officers], but once a project is over, that ends it. The agric officers will tell you there is no money to continue what the NGOs were doing" (NGO 1). There is also the need for NGOs themselves to be supervised and monitored to ensure that the funds they received for the provision of safety nets to the poor were used effectively and efficiently. According to most of the interviewees, the nature of NGO funding significantly made their own safety net programmes vulnerable to the availability and direction of donor funding. Due to an increasing difficulty in accessing donor funds, and long-term funding, NGO programmes are often designed as short-term projects, which only provide safety for a short period.

The short-term nature of NGO projects was seen, in a sense, as a defeat of the concept of a safety net or security. Again, NGO projects tend to be designed as start-up projects, which tended to overlook on-going community-led development/empowerment processes and District Level Government structures, instead of building on existing processes and structures, and tended to introduce new structures and processes. These new structures and processes would have accompanying costs covered by the NGO programmes that would be largely unsustainable to the local communities and district assemblies. Efforts at mainstreaming their projects into on-going community or district structures tended to be hurriedly done at the tail end of the projects and were usually unsuccessful. Therefore, at the end of a project, the support provided by the NGO abruptly comes to an end. A second major challenge was with the provision of Government resources for and commitment to the uptake of NGO safety net programmes. "They always do not have money to continue what the NGOs have started" (NGO 4). Government interest in the uptake of these programmes seemed also to depend on the focus and policy of the Government of the day.

Social protection in Ghana

The 1992 Constitution of Ghana, under the direct principles of the state policy, has categorically made provision for the protection of human rights; equality of economic opportunities to all citizens; safeguarding the health, safety and welfare of all people in employment; equality of rights, obligations and opportunities before the law; provision of social assistance to the aged such that they can maintain a decent standard of living; "guarantee economic security for self-employed and other citizens of Ghana" by "ensuring that contributory schemes are instituted and maintained"; and "the protection and promotion of all other basic human rights and freedoms, including the rights of the disabled, the aged, children and other vulnerable groups in development processes" (Article 37) (Republic of Ghana, 1992). In line with the constitutional requirements, the state has introduced developmental strategies taking into consideration social protection. The strategies include the Ghana Poverty Reduction Strategy (GPRSI), the Growth and Poverty Reduction Strategy (GPRS II) and the Ghana Shared Growth and Development Agenda (GSGDA). All these aim at reducing poverty and inequality and improving the livelihoods of Ghanaians. The state therefore has a herculean task of ensuring that the citizenry is provided with the necessary support and assistance.

It can be argued that social protection in Ghana started during the ancestral era with the traditional forms of social protection. Each person was each other's keeper and hence there was absolute protection of every member of a community. This system of social protection has gradually given way to formal forms of social protection which have placed a huge responsibility on the Government. Everyone now looks up to the Government for social security and assistance. All over the world, social protection has become a global phrase and has taken different dimensions in different countries. However, key among its different dimensions is the fact that the concept's aim is to improve the livelihoods of ordinary citizens irrespective of their status in society. Social protection has also received recognition from several international organisations, international and regional conventions and private sector participation. The International Labour Organization (ILO, 2014) regards social protection, as measures put into place, to provide benefits. Whether in cash or in kind, to secure protection, due to insufficient income caused by sickness, disability, maternity, employment injury, unemployment, old age or death of a family member; lack of access or unaffordable access to health care; insufficient family support, particularly for children and adult dependants; general poverty; and social exclusion. As much as the ILO wanted to be exhaustive in its definition or explanation of social protection measures, there are still areas of concern that need the attention of all sectors, including the Government and private sector.

In the eyes of the World Bank (WB), social protection is not just about providing benefits, but also creating opportunities for people to upgrade themselves from the status quo. Therefore, the WB defines social protection as policies and programmes designed to reduce poverty and vulnerability by promoting efficient labour markets, diminishing people's exposure to risks and enhancing their capacity to manage economic and social risks such as unemployment, exclusion, sickness, disability and old age (World Bank, 2001). The discussion on social protection programmes such as panacea for poverty reduction and livelihood improvement gained more grounds during the last couple of decades. ILO is currently spearheading discussions on social protection as a panacea for development. Other organisations such as the International Council on Social Welfare (ICSW) and other United Nations (UN) agencies through the UN Chief Executives Board (UNCEB) are supporting the discussions. The UN Global Social Statistics indicated that the global food, fuel and economic crises between 2007 and 2009 had impacted negatively on the welfare of children, women and the disabled and marginalised in society. This, according to the report, resulted in the inability of some countries to meet the Millennium Development Goals (MDGs) on poverty reduction, education and quality healthcare (UN DESA, 2011). To meet these goals therefore, there is the need for support from NGOs and Public-Private Partnerships (PPPs).

In her efforts to work within the frameworks of these broad definitions and development discourse, Ghana has come out with several social protection programmes aimed at bringing relief to the needy and the less privileged in society. The country can boast of several social protection programmes. Whilst many of them are not well recognised by the people, a few have received both national and international recognition and are benefiting from inflows from international donors. Key social protection programmes in Ghana include the LEAP programme, Pensions Schemes Programme; Free Compulsory Basic Education (FCUBE) programme; the School Feeding Programme (SFP); the National Health Insurance Scheme (NHIS); the pro poor exemptions for indigents aged 70 and above; and Free Maternal and Child Health Care programme. Equally important, but less publicised social protection programmes in Ghana include programme to reduce nutrition and micronutrient deficiencies; the electricity cross subsidy programme; the Community-Based Rehabilitation Programme for the Disabled (CBRP); Labour Intensive Public Works (LIPW) programme; the elimination of the worst forms of child labour programme; Ghana Luxemburg Social Trust (GLST) programme; the Block Farming Initiative programme; the fertilizer subsidies programme and many more. Government continues to increase the number of social protection programmes in Ghana amidst economic challenges. Free distribution of school uniforms and footwear has recently been introduced in some districts in Ghana.

To co-ordinate the activities of the social protection programmes in Ghana, the Government through the Ministry of Gender, Children and Social Protection (MoGCSP) has developed a programme called the National Social Protection Strategy (NSPS) programme which aims at reducing inequality, ensuring poverty reduction and improving the livelihoods of Ghanaians. The NSPS is expected to be further developed into a National Social Protection Policy in Ghana. Work toward the realisation of this dream has started and is being spearheaded by the MoGCSP. Social protection programmes in Ghana are receiving support from international organisations such as the World Bank (WB), the World Food Programme (WFP), European Commission (EC), the United Nation's Children Fund (UNICEF) and the ILO.

Challenges of the state social protection programmes in Ghana

Like any development programme in the world, the state's social protection programmes in Ghana are facing several challenges ranging from financial, political, social and institutional. Notable among the challenges facing social protection programmes in Ghana is the lack to adequate fund and sustain them. Financing these programmes requires large sums of money which the Government alone cannot provide. For instance, the numbers of LEAP beneficiary households increased from 1,645 in 2008 to 146,074 (185 districts) by 31 December 2015 and it is expected to increase to 200,000 by 31 December 2016 and to 250,000 by 31 January 2017. There is therefore the need for donor support to augment Government's efforts to provide relief to the vulnerable. Another challenge is the political will to continue to source for funding to finance these programmes. With the fragile political system in Ghana, one must be circumspect in writing about commitment of politicians to social protection programmes. However, it is a fact that social protection programmes in Ghana have been used as political bait for 'grabbing' political power. The programmes have been coloured with political colorations which have negative impacts on their sustainability. For instance, the names of political parties are associated with social protection programmes. This tends to make it difficult for opposing political parties that might find themselves in power to exhibit their willingness to sustain such programmes. The remedy most politicians resort to is to introduce their own programmes, try to change the concept of the existing programmes or rebrand them to suite their political manifestos. The sustainability of these programmes therefore requires the commitment of politicians to the welfare of their people, instead of seeking to remain in power.

Another key challenge is the institutional capacity of the country to support these programmes. The country lacks credible data to permit an objective selection of the beneficiaries of social protection programmes. Ghana does not have a single biometric registration which can be shared by all institutions in the verification of the eligibility of beneficiaries of the social protection programmes. The decentralisation of Government business prescribed by the decentralisation policy requires that there should be well resourced Government departments and agencies in all local jurisdictions to ensure good governance. However, this is yet to be achieved as many departments and agencies, especially the Metropolitan, Municipal and District Assemblies (MMDAs), do not have well-resourced offices. Social protection programmes could have been decentralised to ensure effective implementation. While there has been some improvement in recent times in some of the programmes, others are yet to enjoy institutional improvement.

NGOs' social safety net interventions

In many countries in Sub-Saharan Africa (SSA), NGOs have become major providers of social safety nets (SSNs) for poor families. Many families are unable to provide the required support to their members, especially when it is not the farming season. For example, many rural and sub-urban populations in Ghana face extreme poverty during this period. For these people to survive, there was the need for the state and private sector organisations to provide some SSNs to support the needy. Without the participation of private organisations such as NGOs, the Government alone could not have shouldered the welfare responsibilities of the citizenry. Globally, according to the

World Bank (2015a: 43), "only one-third of the poor are covered by any type of social safety net." As a result, many international and local NGOs are playing significant roles in the implementation of the SSNs in many countries to deepen the agenda expanding coverage. The scope of NGO social safety net in Ghana is quite wide. NGO intervention areas in the country are so varied and complex, ranging from development and relief work to charity or philanthropic work.

NGO social safety net interventions are therefore multidimensional and multi-sectoral in nature. A synthesis of a couple of definitions of SSNs *vis-à-vis* the role of NGOs in Ghana clearly reveals the complexity of their interventions. The World Bank (2015b) defines SSNs as non-contributory measures designed to provide regular and predictable support to poor and vulnerable people. They are also referred to as safety nets, social assistance, or social transfers and are a component of larger social protection systems. Awal (2003: 63) describes SSNs or socio-economic safety nets as "social welfare services which are geared toward eliminating poverty in a specific area". These SSNs include cash and in-kind transfers focusing on the poor and vulnerable households, with the goal of cushioning families from the negative effects of economic shocks, natural disasters and other crises; ensuring quality education and health services for children; gender advocacy and empowerment; and creating jobs. NGOs in Ghana operate in almost all sectors of the economy: agriculture, education, health, environment, mining, energy, food security, etc. However, their focus is on short-term poverty reduction and livelihood improvement of the vulnerable and in some cases ordinary citizens. While NGOs are concentrating on short-term measures, they enable the Government to concentrate on long-term development interventions (Bawole & Hossain, 2015). As Ghana's population keeps increasing and as demand for new interventions keep popping up, the demand for SSNs from NGOs will keep expanding.

According to the World Bank (2015a) countries at all levels of income are investing in SSNs. Low-income and middle-income countries devote approximately 1,5 per cent and 1,6 per cent respectively of their Gross Domestic Product (GDP) to SSNs compared to 1,9 per cent by the rich countries. According to the World Bank (2015a), countries are investing in SSNs to reap the benefits of human capital development and income-generating activities. Globally, welfare states are experiencing many challenges, but private organisations continue to provide public goods and basic welfare. For instance, while many

Governments in SSA continue to cut subsidies for healthcare delivery, NGOs continue to launch welfare programmes to support the needy (Cammett & MacLean, 2014). The SSN programmes in Ghana have the potential to help promote sustainable development in the country.

Conclusion: Future of NGO social interventions in Ghana

Current global economic challenges point to the fact that the sustainability of NGO social intervention programmes in Ghana is debatable. Almost all NGOs in Ghana are in one way or the other depending on sponsorships from either local or international donors. However, with the economic challenges facing donors, it is quite difficult to predict the inflows of foreign donations towards the provision of SSNs. Even though the World Bank (2015a) has indicated that globally countries are investing more in the social services sector, it is also important to follow the prioritisations of the countries. Countries are investing in SSNs to reap the benefits of human capital development and income-generating activities. Therefore, the issue of cash transfers and in-kind transfers, such as clothing and shoes, may suffer in the future. Even Government led social safety net programmes, which depend on donations from international NGOs, have a fragile future. The lack of financial capacity by the Government and NGOs to finance SSN programmes requires that the state and NGOs seek foreign donations to execute their SSN programmes. However, the global economic challenges are forcing development partners, including international NGOs, to prioritise donations and back them with stringent measures to ensure effective utilisation of funds.

However, in their quest to ensure proper use of funds, donors tend to influence policy directions which might not be in the interest of the citizens of the country. For instance, in Ghana the invitation by the Government to the International Monitory Fund (IMF), which is commonly referred to as a "Bailout Programme" to help the Government, both in cash and in kind, to implement her "home-grown" programmes, is met with opposition by the Trade Unions and other organised bodies in the country. The rationale behind the opposition is because of the "stringent measures" attached to the conditions of the IMF, such as the restrictions imposed on the Government in the areas of employment and public expenditure. The future of NGO interventions will also depend on the relations between NGO intervention programmes and those of the Government and social services policy directions. The continuous success of NGOs in Ghana demands that there should be a good rapport between them and government. Devereux *et al,* (2010: 2) advocates that:

> "... there is a need to understand both the political drivers of the policy processes and the opportunities for future engagement – by identifying where the energy for social protection is strongest and how external actors might best engage with this, particularly where domestically driven programmes have succeeded."

The sustainability and success of NGO social protection interventions will depend of how well they relate to Government social services policies and interventions. Globally, a stable political environment, rule of law and political commitments on the part of governments are some of the factors that determine the smooth operation of NGOs. However, NGOs need to ensure that they understand why governments have opted for SSNs; the success or otherwise of these safety nets; and how they can dovetail their SSN programmes with those of the Government. This will help to illicit a government support and strengthen its commitment to political stability and rule of law and ultimately the success of NGOs' interventions. Fusing NGOs' social intervention programmes into those of the government will also facilitate the flow of donor funding and the sustainability of NGO programmes and projects.

In analysing the way forward for social protection programmes in Africa, Devereux *et al,* (2010: 2) proposed five approaches for development partnerships to:

▷ learn from Government-driven programmes and work with Governments to monitor, evaluate, improve and extend them;

▷ work through appropriate institutional mechanisms, at regional and national levels;

▷ learn lessons for national implementation from existing national programmes, rather than from pilot projects;

▷ be driven less by instruments and locate social transfers within a broader national social policy agenda, by paying more attention to social protection objectives; and

▷ find new levers for supporting African Governments, based on a more sophisticated understanding of national political contexts.

Regarding the future of NGOs' interventions in Ghana, these five approaches are equally relevant. As has already been mentioned, collaboration between NGOs and Government will help to ensure the former's safety and sustainability of their interventions. However, the collaboration should not lead NGOs to compromise their objective of providing SSNs to the needy. Collaborations should be based on the key principles of social safety net programmes. Again, NGOs, whether local or international, should not operate in isolation without the involvement of public institutions. This is particularly important because data management systems in Ghana are mostly in the hands of public institutions such as the Ghana Statistical Services (GSS); Ministries, Departments and Agencies (MDAs); and Metropolitan, Municipal and District Assemblies (MMDAs).

It is therefore imperative to liaise with all the relevant institutions for quality information to inform NGOs of real time challenges and the impacts of their interventions. Learning lessons from existing national SSN programmes will provide NGOs with the real challenges and solutions. While pilot projects cannot be discredited entirely, it is necessary to consider national social interventions programmes to understand the realities on the ground. It is also an opportunity for NGOs to study Government implementation failures or successes to serve as guide to their operations. Nationals SSN programmes have a broader base and this makes it possible to draw varied experiences from them. Furthermore, while global economic challenges cannot be downplayed as key determinants of the sustainability of donor inflows, NGOs should be reminded of finding other ways of sustaining their operations. As Ghana continues to depend heavily on the global economy and struggle to cut down her budget deficits, NGOs' intervention programmes will continue to supplement the Government's development efforts. NGOs should pay attention to interventions that will ensure capacity building at all levels of development, ranging from government institutions to the vulnerable in society. These interventions will help to adequately capacitate the country, enable it to be self-reliant and to engage in sectors of the economy where it enjoys significant comparative advantage.

References

Awal, M.A. 2013. Social Safety Net, Disaster Risk Management and Climate Change Adaptation: Examining Their Integration Potential in Bangladesh. *International Journal of Sociology Study*, 1(4): 62-72.

Banks, N. & Hulme, D. 2012. The role of NGOs and civil society in development and poverty reduction. (BWPI Working Paper 171). Manchester: The Brooks World Poverty Institute.

Bawole, J.N. & Hossainm F. 2015. Marriage of the unwilling? The paradox of local government and NGO relations in Ghana. *Voluntas: International Journal of Voluntary and Nonprofit Organisations*, 26 (5): 2061-2083. https://doi.org/10.1007/s11266-014-9503-9

Cammett, M. & MacLean, L.M. 2014. Introduction: the political consequences on Non-State Social Welfare in the Global South. In: M. Cammett & L.M. MacLean (eds.). *The Politics of Non- state Social Welfare*. Ithaca: Cornell University Press: 1-21.

Conway, T. & Norton, A. 2002. Nets, Ropes, Ladders and Trampolines: The Place of Social Protection within Current Debates on Poverty Reduction. *Development Policy Review*, 20(5): 533-540. https://doi.org/10.1111/1467-7679.00188

Devereux, S. 2002. Can Social Safety Nets Reduce Chronic Poverty? *Development Policy Review*, 20 (5): 657-675. https://doi.org/10.1111/1467-7679.00194

Devereux, S.; Davies, M.; Sabates-Wheeler, R.; McCord, A.; Slater, R.; Freeland, N.; Ellis, F. & White, P. 2010. *Social Protection in Africa: A Way Forward*. https://www.odi.org/sites/odi.org.uk/files/odi-assets/publications-opinion-files/6147.pdf [Accessed 3 February 2016].

Devereux, S. & Sabates-Wheeler, R. 2004. *Transformative Social Protection*. (IDS Working Paper). Sussex: IDS.

Elliot, R. 2012. *Positive News from Africa: Africa is a Country*. http://africasacountry. com/2012/04/26/positive-news-from-africa [Accessed 3 February 2016].

Howell, J. 2015. Shall we dance? Welfarist incorporation and the politics of state- labour NGO relations in China. *The China Quarterly*, 223: 702-723. https://doi.org/10.1017/S0305741015001174

International Labour Organisation (ILO). 2014. *World Social Protection Report 2014/15, Building economic recovery, inclusive development and social justice*. Geneva: ILO.

Jones, N.; Ahadzie, W. & Doh, D. 2009. *Social Protection and Children: Opportunities and Challenges in Ghana*. https://www.unicef.org/wcaro/wcaro_3798_unicef_odi_Social_Portection_Ghana-full-report.pdf. [Accessed 27 April 2017].

Lambert, M. (Undated). *Evaluating the Impact of Non-Governmental Organisations Assisting with Girls' Education in Ghana*. http://www.bluekitabu.org/blue-kitabu-research-instit/evaluating_the_impact_of_no.pdf [Accessed 12 April 2017].

Lazar, H. & Stoyko, P. 1998. The future of welfare State. *International Social Security Review*. 51 (3): 3-36. https://doi.org/10.1111/1468-246X.00015

Lidzén, L. 2008. A Comparative Study of the Social Welfare Provided by Three Christian Churches in Accra, Ghana. *Institutionen för humaniora och samhällsvetenskap, Rel C fält ht* 2007: 1.

Mathauer, I. 2004. *Institutional Analysis Toolkit for Safety Net Interventions.* http://siteresources.worldbank.org/SOCIALPROTECTION/Resources/SP-Discussion-papers/Safety-Nets-DP/0418.pdf [Accessed 12 April 2017].

Milbourne, L. & Murray, U. 2011. Negotiating Interactions in State–Voluntary Sector Relationships: Competitive and Collaborative Agency in an Experiential Workshop. *VOLUNTAS: International Journal of Voluntary and non-profit Organisations*, 22(1): 70-92.

Osodo, P. & Matsvai, S. 1998. *Partners or Contractors? The Relationship between Official Agencies and NGOs: Kenya and Zimbabwe.* (Occasional Paper no 16). Oxford: INTRAC.

Park, Y.S. 2008. Revisiting the welfare state system in the Republic of Korea. *International Social Security Review*, 61 (2): 3-19. https://doi.org/10.1111/j.1468-246X.2008.00307.x

Petras, J. 1999. NGOs: In the Service of Imperialism. *Journal of Contemporary Asia* 29(4): 429–40. https://doi.org/10.1080/00472339980000221

Republic of Ghana. 1992. *Constitution of the Republic of Ghana.* Accra: Government Printer.

Shivji, I.G. 2007. *Silences in NGO discourse: the role and future of NGOs in Africa.* Nairobi and Oxford: Fahamu.

Tiwari, P.I. 2013. State Welfarism and Social Welfare in Asia. *Journal of Arts and Humanities.* 2(2): 64-78.

United Nations Department of Economic and Social Affairs (UN DESA). 2011. *The Global Social Crisis: Report on the World Social Situation 2011.* New York: UN DESA.

World Bank. 2015a. *The State of Social Safety Nets.* Washington DC: The World Bank Group. World Bank Group.

World Bank. 2015b. *Social Safety Nets Expand in Developing Countries, But Majority of the Poorest Still Lack Coverage.* http://www.worldbank.org/en/news/press-release/2015/07/07/social-safety-nets-expand-in-developing-countries-but-majority-of-the-poorest-still-lack-coverage [Accessed 12 April 2017].

World Bank. 2001. *Social Protection Sector Strategy Paper: From Safety Net to Springboard.* Washington DC.

10

THE CHALLENGE OF HIV/AIDS ON THE INDIGENOUS SOCIAL SECURITY SYSTEMS: THE CASE OF CAMEROON

Agnes Ebotabe Arrey

Introduction

This chapter examines the challenges of HIV/AIDS and explains how the former impact Indigenous Social Security Systems in Cameroon. In most rich countries today, social security systems are taken for granted. Although they differ in their generosity across countries, in most cases they provide a minimum of compensation in the event of illness, unemployment or retirement (Gerkens & Merkur, 2010; Helleberg, Haggblom & Sonnerborg, 2013). However, in Cameroon, the implementation of these kinds of safety nets are limited to the public and private sectors (Sorèle, 2015). Moreover, they often only cover a small share of the total population in need. The lack of insurance against risks such as illness, disability, unemployment, natural disasters and crop failures can have serious short and long-term consequences for the concerned households. Most life-threatening illnesses including HIV/AIDS still pose a huge societal challenge especially to Indigenous Social Security Systems (ISSS) in most Sub-Saharan African (SSA) countries.

Successful socio-economic development patterns of the industrialised countries, especially in the domain of social security, to cover loss of income caused by a chronic illness, death or unemployment are still to be replicated in most of SSA. The infrastructure in most SSA countries is not based on a chronic care model. Most of these countries provide only minimal social security personal coverage to employees. In Cameroon, more than half of the population, including HIV/AIDS patients, are excluded from any type of social security protection necessary to make households and communities more resilient to the negative impacts and effects of the HIV/AIDS epidemic. The lack of a viable nationally-led social security scheme has put great challenges on the ISSS, particularly on families and friends. With the exception of Mauritius, Seychelles, Kenya, Botswana and South Africa, most countries in SSA do not have nationally-led social security schemes that cover vulnerable populations including people with HIV/AIDS (Plamondon, Cichon & Annycke, 2004). Formal social security programmes that are necessary to achieve a reduction in new HIV infections, stigmatisation, discrimination and AIDS-related deaths, never reach the rural or urban poor in most SSA countries. This situation was exacerbated especially after the introduction and implementation of the International Monetary Fund (IMF) and the World Bank (WB) backed Structural Adjustment Programmes in the late 1990s (Kalasa, 2001). Due to this deficit, most HIV/AIDS-infected people and families in Cameroon resort to indigenous protection, where the typical African tradition relies on family members to provide care for the sick, ailing and aging relatives. In this chapter, the existing ISSS in Cameroon and the challenges facing the former in respect to the HIV/AIDS pandemic are discussed.

It is important to point out that HIV/AIDS still poses enormous threats to human development. Globally, about 37 million people are living with HIV/AIDS. More disturbing is the fact that SSA, with only about ten per cent of the world's population, has about 25 million (67,6 per cent) people living with HIV/AIDS (UNAIDS, 2015). This sub-region bears the brunt of the global HIV/AIDS epidemic and grapples with the social, economic, ethical and political complexities of HIV/AIDS (UNAIDS, 2014). Since the advent of the HIV/AIDS pandemic, there has been a new wave of infection each new decade, though extraordinary progress has been achieved in the understanding, treatment, care and prevention of HIV/AIDS. However, the challenges of effectively controlling and eradicating the HIV/AIDS pandemic remain. Previous studies on the socio-economic impact of HIV indicate that the financial burden on families of people living with HIV/AIDS is the most visible impact of HIV at the household level (Schur, Mylne, Mushati, Takaruza, Nyamukapa & Gregson, 2015; Wouters, Vermeiren, Katabaro & Van Damme, 2010).

Traditional communities and families still experience severe economic and financial hardship and in most cases very young people, and the elderly, are left to care for the sick and ailing family members. The younger siblings have the disadvantage of not attaining their educational and vocational goals. Thus, the extended family remains the main source of support for the vast majority of people when additional responsibilities of caring for HIV/AIDS family members arise. The extended family system has made it possible for the effects of HIV/AIDS to be mitigated, as distant relatives and unrelated caregivers have the tendency to care and support people living with HIV/AIDS. There is also evidence of the changing dynamics of the population and household structure impacting on the demographic structure of the population as a result of the pertinence of HIV/AIDS epidemic for socio-economic performance and growth (Floyd, Crampin, Glynn, Mweebabu, Mnkhodia, Ngwira, Zaba & Fine, 2008). Therefore, the focus of this chapter is to explore the challenges of HIV/AIDS and how it impacts on existing ISSS and the major issues confronting many people living with HIV/AIDS in Cameroon. The chapter begins with an examination of contemporary social security systems, Indigenous Social Security Systems and the extent of prevalence of HIV/AIDS in Cameroon. Then the chapter casts light on the findings that emanated from a qualitative study which was carried out by the author and that had focussed on the challenges of HIV/AIDS and its impacts on Indigenous Social Security Systems in Cameroon. It concludes by discussing the findings and draws some recommendations and implications for healthcare guidelines and practices in Cameroon.

Examining social security systems

The term "social security" was first used in the early 1930s by Edwin Witte in the book *The Development of the Social Security Act* (Farr, 2011) to describe the United States' social legislation. It was generally meant to cover secured individuals and dependants in case of disability, loss of employment, sickness, occupational disease or employment injury. Sometimes it made payments to partially offset the consequences of financial burdens associated with life events like birth, death and marriage. In later years, the International Labour Organisation (ILO) in Convention 102 identified the following social security benefits: medical care, employment injury, sickness, unemployment, old age, family, invalidity, maternity and survivors' benefits. The ILO promotes the centrally administered insurance-funded programmes (ILO, 2009). Within the framework of the

ILO, social protection will mean "the entire institutions, measures, rights and obligations whose first objective consists in providing or to try to provide each member of the society with income security and medical care on the basis of specified regulations" (ILO, 2009).

This definition can be interpreted with reference to all societies or countries; to social groups; and to the formal and informal sectors of the economy (ILO, 2009). Some scholars are of the opinion that social security is too expensive to be replicated in most Sub-Saharan African countries given the size of the economies (Kalasa, 2001). Thus, there is need to search for alternative approaches to address poverty and vulnerability that might achieve similar results at lower cost (Garcia & Gruat, 2003). Elements of a social security structure exist in most modern independent countries in the world and in a few African countries. These social security programmes had been created by the Governments and for African countries, a legacy from colonial powers. This legacy, in most cases fragmented, has become expensive, complex, burdensome and even controversial to most African Governments. Many financial, political, philosophical and administrative obstacles plague this system from functioning as in most Western countries (Midgely & Sherraden, 1997). The expansion of social security to African and other developing nations was intended to promote modernity and industrialisation as labour moved from the agrarian economy to wage employment. Thereafter, pressure for a formal system of social protection increased in the developed countries. Similar trends some scholars believed were to occur in the developing countries to insure the general population (individuals) against any contingency of life events, growing old and when they were unable to earn a living (Cockburn, 1980).

In Cameroon, the social security scheme is run by the National Social Insurance Fund (NSIF) for private sector workers, while the state runs the retirement pension scheme for civil servants and other state employees. These schemes are not inclusive of the informal labour force that makes up the majority of the labour market. Before 2015, only about ten per cent of the population was covered despite the fact that the informal sector makes up more than 51 per cent of the economy (ILO, 2009; World Bank, 2015). The insufficiency of the current benefits, which is due to the differences observed among the existing schemes, the insufficient coverage in terms of health as well as the bottlenecks inherent in the access procedures governing regulatory benefits, remain major challenges in Cameroon's social security schemes. The insufficient support actions directed towards vulnerable groups also contributes to the weakness of the social security system. Furthermore, the weak correlation and co-ordination in the elaboration and implementation of social protection programmes is due to ministerial bureaucracies as several ministerial departments are involved in social protection programmes (Barbone & Alvaro Sanchez B, 1999). Nevertheless, it is important to mention that in Cameroon traditional societies have had indigenous mechanisms to deal with these uncertainties and efforts hereafter are made to describe them.

Re-visiting Indigenous Social Security Systems (ISSS)

ISSS are the traditional forms of social security that protect people not covered by the formal social security systems. Contrarily, the belief that economic modernisation will transform ISSS in the developing countries, had not really taken place. Instead, many traditional rural agrarian sectors have remained unchanged. Instead, there has been rapid growth of the informal sector in Africa. The proportion of people covered by the formal SSS remains small in Africa and other developing countries. It can be argued that the down play of Africa's social security system constitutes the social dilemma of Africa's current social policy failings of ensuring the existence of bureaucracies in most African countries that continue to produce highly centralised systems of administration (Sherraden, 2001). MacPherson (1982) contends that prior to colonialism, most African states were small and self-sufficient and reliant. Community solidarity and mutual aid were unplanned and essentially part of the communities of the people (MacPherson, 1982). Inequalities existing in the informal domains of social relationships and cultural expectations limit the capacity of the state to act in a compensatory way. These informal domains are either organised around churches, Non-Governmental Organisations (NGOs), mosques or personalised arrangements like kin and friends. However, Dean (2002) is of the opinion that everyone in the community should contribute towards the social security system and that the state will then act as a regulator of provisions of services (Dean, 2002). Some scholars support the contention that most of everyday health and social tasks take place in the household and most people first turn to family for help (Beresford & Croft, 1995). The next section briefly describes Cameroon and the prevalence of HIV/AIDS.

Cameroon and HIV/AIDS

Cameroon had an estimated population of 24,360,803 million people in 2016 (Central Intelligence Agency, 2017). English and French are the official languages, but the country has about 250 dialects spoken by more than 250 ethnic groups. According to the World Bank, there are wide regional disparities in poverty. Chronic poverty stands at about 26 per cent (World Bank, 2015). Like most African countries, Cameroon suffers from an insufficient rate of contemporary social security coverage (Andrews, Das & Elder, 2012; Hodges, 2008) The population of Cameroon is young and works mostly outside the formal sectors. Cameroon has a generalised HIV epidemic. In 2015, there were about 620,000 people living with HIV/AIDS and 33,000 deaths due to AIDS. The adult HIV prevalence rate is about 4,5 per cent which is the highest in West and Central Africa. The National AIDS Control Committee/Central Technical Group estimates that there are about 141 new HIV infections per day in Cameroon, averaging six new infections each hour, every day. Furthermore, an estimated 340,000 women are living with HIV and 310,000 children have been orphaned due to AIDS. Of the 620,000 people living with HIV/AIDS, about 28 per cent received antiretroviral therapy as of 2015. The main mode of transmission is through heterosexual contact (90 per cent), while mother to child transmission account for six per cent and four per cent from blood and accidental transmission respectively. In 2010, about 7,300 babies were born HIV-positive due to mother-to-child-transmission. Young women represent seven in ten of the youth – 15-24 years who are HIV positive (UNAIDS, 2015).

The Study

This chapter draws on findings from a qualitative study that explored the impact of HIV/AIDS on Indigenous Social Security Systems in Cameroon. An in-depth account of what participants said about HIV/AIDS and existing ISSS in Cameroon is reported. Telephone interviews were conducted with participants resident in four towns in the South West Region of Cameroon. Interviews were carried out between July and August 2016. The region has an estimated population of 1,481,433 inhabitants and covers about 25,410 km^2 of the total surface of Cameroon. Unemployment rates are very high in the area. Even though there is good awareness of HIV/AIDS, nevertheless, HIV/ AIDS prevalence rate is high (5,7 per cent), as compared to the national prevalence of

4,5 per cent (Institut National de la Statistique (INS) & Ministry of Public Health, 2011). Despite this high prevalence, social security protection for people living with HIV/AIDS remains minimal.

Research approach and process

To examine the challenges of HIV/AIDS on ISSS in Cameroon, participants were recruited through snowballing techniques, also called 'chain sampling' by some authors (Hennink, Hutter & Bailey, 2011). This method was suitable to help identify study participants who met the study's criteria stated in the paragraph. The number of participants increased with each new recruitment. Snowball sampling entails a process where identified participants refer other potential participants based on the researcher's interaction with the identified participant and it ensures a more efficient means of data collection (Marshall & Rossman, 2006). The researcher had contacted three people in her network and informed them about the objectives of the study. None of these initial contacts participated in the study. These people, in turn, contacted participants who agreed to be interviewed. Consistent with previous studies on creating rapport with participants, the researcher also contacted each participant without formally asking questions related to the subject matter. Although it may be more convenient to conduct face-to-face semi-structured interviews, telephone interviews were used because of the inability of the interviewer and interviewee to be at the same place. Telephonic interviewing allows respondents to feel relaxed and able to disclose sensitive information (Novick, 2008). Oral consent for tape-recording interviews were obtained from participants at the start of the interviews. All the participants invited were adults, aged 18 years and above, speaking French, English or Pidgin (a common intercultural language spoken by many Cameroonians). Inclusion criteria also hinged on people infected with HIV/AIDS, caregivers of people infected with HIV/AIDS, an agent of the national social insurance fund, members of social associations and NGOs.

Qualitative semi-structured telephone interviews were conducted with the participants in their preferred language (English or Pidgin), using an interview guide comprising open-ended questions on issues related to the study's objectives. All interview recordings were transcribed. The transcriptions were then reviewed and coded in preparation for thematic analysis. Thematic analysis was used to retrieve themes in line with the study's objectives and significant to participants, as well as those of interest from an indigenous social protection perspective. Themes were identified as they emerged from the data. This is also known as the "bottom-up approach" (Miles & Huberman, 1994; Pettigrew 2000). Themes related to the topic were identified by constant comparison until saturation was reached. In this study, the use of thematic analysis was important in the identification of themes that recurred in the data and that could eventually produce a bigger picture leading to general explications (Braun & Clarke, 2006). There were no attempts to quantify the occurrence of themes. Following a qualitative paradigm, the intention was to highlight themes that were common across participants, as well as less common themes which could reflect ideas that were not often expressed, but are nonetheless significant in social sciences. Selected quotations from the data are presented with any potential identifiers removed and are used to illustrate the themes described in the chapter. In some cases, quotations are rephrased for better comprehension.

Ethical considerations

In terms of ethical considerations, ethical approval was obtained only from the participants and not from an internal review board. Participants were informed of the objectives of the study and permission was obtained to audio-tape record interviews. Interviews were conducted after oral consent was obtained from all participants. There was no financial reward to any participants who were willing or agreed to participate in the study. Due to the sensitive nature of the study, confidentiality and anonymity of participants was guaranteed by refraining from releasing data to third parties and withholding the residence of participants living with HIV/AIDS. For example, initials were used to identify the participants.

Characteristics of participants

With regards to participants' sociodemographic characteristics, the sample (n=7) was all women aged between 29 and 60 years. There were diverse levels of annual income of less than 5000 Euros. Two participants were self-employed. Of the two participants employed by the Government, one was a senior social security employee and the other a higher education lecturer. One participant was a farmer, one was retired and one a cleaner at a village health centre. Three participants were HIV positive and one HIV-positive participant had just lost a sibling to AIDS at the time of the interview. A minority (2/7) had a university education and the rest of the participants had secondary education. Of the seven participants, three reported their civil status as single; two were married and two were widows. All seven participants had children living with them. Two participants reported that their husbands recently died from an AIDS-related illness. All participants were members of a social and tribal association, locally called *Njanjis* and *Tontines*. Only one participant had complete social security coverage, like what exists in most developed countries.

Discussion

The family network, social and tribal associations locally called Njanjis and Tontines, Church-based organisations and local NGOs are the main Indigenous Social Security Systems existing in Cameroon. It must be noted, however, that ISSS have suffered a decline in recent decades because of falling commitment to traditional systems of support. Their effectiveness has been further eroded by the HIV/AIDS pandemic and thus reducing the numbers of younger people able to contribute to family welfare. Traditionally, informal social security has been effective in reaching the poorest and most vulnerable in rural, as well as urban areas. The potential for strengthening the characteristically weak, resource bases of these systems and the re-energising of commitments to family and community responsibilities, are areas for action on HIV/AIDS disability and death. In Cameroon, as in most of the African countries, formal systems of social security capable of absorbing the increasing numbers of HIV-infected people do not exist. Currently, less than ten per cent of Cameroon's workforce is covered by social security programmes. Former civil servants and formal sector employees may receive pensions from contributory social security schemes, but the vast majority of people across the country involved in informal sector activities are not covered by any form of social security. One participant, had this to say:

> It was not easy. It was difficult for me because on the other hand my husband was not working. He was at home and if he could not do it, I had to go an extra mile because it is difficult for people to come in and assist. Family can just be there, but you must foot your bills. You must go to the hospital even if I don't have to. I must go to [the hospital], anyway. My husband had to go to the hospital every month and it cost about 75.000 FCFA (about 115 Euros) each visit. You must check the liver so that it is not overloaded, you must. It was difficult (EA caregiver and widow, 55 years old).

The labour market is dominated by the informal sector in Cameroon. Therefore, informal sector workers and those working in subsistence farming continue to be socio-economically excluded and consequently, they face increased chances of living in poverty and obtaining suboptimal care if they are living with HIV/AIDS. The task of caregiving exerts so much pressure on survivors and HIV/AIDS sufferers that they often receive inadequate medical treatment and food. Despite global and regional policy aims of introducing non-contributory pensions for all, there is no clear-cut solution to improving and extending coverage of formal social protection systems in Cameroon. Given the structure of the economy, scaling up coverage in Cameroon is not straightforward. Over 75 per cent of the workforce is involved in agriculture, while the informal economy of non-agricultural employment is about 78 per cent (National AIDS Control Committee Central Technical Group, 2010), making social protection of people living with HIV/AIDS problematic. Another participant reflected on family support in this way:

> That is where the problem really lies. They have free medications, but it becomes a problem when they must take care of their families. If family members are not there to help, the children or the people [with HIV/AIDS] become vulnerable. People with HIV/AIDS are vulnerable in social matters.

In Cameroon, there is a long-standing tradition of people forming self-help groups where they meet regularly, contribute money and give to a member or members (depending on the agreed rules and regulations). This enables the beneficiary (ies) to invest that money in education, health, business and/ or other projects for the economic and social betterment of the recipients. Most of the *Njangis* or *Tontines* have no legal status. They are based on trust. These *Njangis* and *Tontines* may also act as credit houses to their members and sometimes non-members, who can borrow money and repay with interest, depending on the amount borrowed. People without formal social security protection rely on this form of Indigenous Social Security Systems in times of need to care for their sick, pay for funerals, pay for education, travel, start new businesses or expand existing businesses. Hence:

> In Cameroon, as in most African countries, we count on families to give us assistance and some people depend on meetings, what we call Njanji for assistance. This is a one-time assistance. For example, if you are sick, they may give you a small amount to help you, but in the long run, it is not sufficient. They don't give the assistance every time. It is a one-time assistance. For HIV/AIDS, we have programmes in the hospital where you can receive antiretroviral therapy at a lower price, but you must cover your cost. We depend on families. If you die, you can have a coffin from your

meeting [social group] or your family contributes for the burial (National Social Insurance Fund agent, 52 years old).

Njangis and *Tontines* contribute towards poverty alleviation in Cameroon. They must be encouraged as they complement the lack of universal social security coverage of the poor in the community. This is what one of the participants said:

> We have a contribution of 2000 FCFA (about three euro) a week, but those who can't meet up, pay 1000 FCFA (about 1,50 euro). We also have another Njangi of 10,000 FCFA (about15 euro) per month. Those who can't pay 10,000, pay 5000 FCFA (about 7,5 euro) per month. This is what we do in our group to help ourselves and meet up with our family needs including education for our children, feeding, buy things for ourselves and pay for healthcare cost (NGO coordinator of a Women's social group).

Although coverage is sporadic, community-based organisations, including church organisations, also play an important role in providing services in the absence of public healthcare options for people living with HIV/AIDS (Cameroon Baptist Convention, 2010). Such responses are particularly valuable in Cameroon where the incidence of HIV/AIDS is high and where frequent high prices have threatened food security for many, including older people caring for PLWHA. Besides directly offering support to PLWHA, these organisations have also improved the assistance they give to families caring for PLWHA. Such interventions have reduced the distress of sale of productive and household assets, such as livestock and land. This often occurs as families try to cover expenditures incurred due to either illness or death (Kaplan *et al*, 2006). Organised Churches like the Catholic and Baptist Churches have moved a step further in trying to put into place a sort of health coverage for vulnerable populations.

> Religious organisations have their own [social security schemes]. The Catholics, for example have an insurance fund. I will talk for the Catholics because I'm a Catholic. The Catholic church has a small project they call BEFA. Weeh! [The participant exclaims] I don't know the full meaning, but people contribute some money. They too [The Catholic Church] provide free antiretroviral therapy. Let me ask a friend, but it is mutual... [weeh...exclamatory sound of distress] it runs like an insurance. They [subscribers] pay contributions to the scheme. They have a contribution rate. They have grouped the members. They group their members who pay according to their level. You pay every month. Some people contribute quarterly, some contribute annually. They cover 75 per cent of your treatment, whether the patient is an HIV/AIDS patient or not (National Social Insurance Fund agent, 52 years old).

HIV/AIDS has profound implications on the Indigenous Social Security Systems in the management of the epidemic, now and in the future.

The HIV/AIDS pandemic is one of the most dramatic challenges that the Indigenous Social Security Systems (ISSS) have to face in Cameroon, like most countries in sub-Saharan Africa (Heymann et al, 2007). The implications for the ISSS are still far from fully known or understood; especially as the pandemic underline the inadequate nature of social security systems in Cameroon (Beresford & Croft, 1995; Gerdes, 1975; National AIDS Control Committee Central Technical Group, 2010). Many of the individuals who have been affected have no formal social security coverage. A 52-year-old national social insurance fund participant confirms this assertion:

> Unfortunately, in Cameroon, the social security system does not cover illness, diseases, sickness. It covers old age, pension, invalidity, family allowance, maternity leave. In Cameroon, even though they signed the ILO charter 102 of ILO, Cameroon does not cover sickness. The Social Security Systems in Cameroon does not cover sickness [repetition for emphasis purpose]. The National Social Insurance Fund has nothing to do with HIV/AIDS patients. Apart from the fact that they are running a hospital where they have these free antiretroviral drugs [therapy] that they give to HIV/AIDS patients who come and register in their hospital. That is all they do.

Because of inadequate coverage, they lack quality access from the medical care that they require. Replacement income is unavailable to breadwinners or their families when they are unable to work or die. The many costs associated with the HIV/AIDS epidemic are lives lost; suffering of families; extreme social, economic and emotional burdens on caregivers and orphans left behind; loss of productivity and food security; and the staggering costs and overwhelming demands on health systems. One of the most critical effects is that it robs the family of their only "social security" system, that is, productive members are taken out of the equation when they become ill and die, leaving children and the elderly to fend for themselves (Tsala, 2004; Van & Meekers, 2011). The traditional family institution, with its notions of intergenerational commitments, used to care for all family members, including older people. This familial sense of responsibility has been eroded by forces including migration of younger people, particularly from rural to urban areas, urbanisation, social and political instability and the impact of the HIV/AIDS pandemic.

HIV/AIDS has had a significant social impact upon the Indigenous Social Security Systems. Generally, people with HIV/AIDS can no longer expect to be recipients of family care. The incidence of death among the middle generation has multiple impacts upon the traditional family institution. Alongside bereavement, they lose people who might have once been a possible source of external financial support in their old age. The ongoing income-generation responsibility is often coupled with active care responsibilities for adult children and grandchildren, which heighten the financial burden. Many HIV/AIDS people do not receive the support they need as this woman said:

> I do not have any help from anybody except my brother. I try to take care of myself and the children. (LT, HIV positive woman)

People living with HIV/AIDS remain alive for long periods of time with severe and cumulative financial and social consequences, not only at the personal and household levels, but also at community and national levels. In many instances, family resources become depleted, family relationships are strained and family resilience itself is seriously tested. The lack of comprehensive health insurance and inadequate healthcare facilities in Cameroon is compounded by a lack of financial assistance for families caring for PWLHA.

> I do not have insurance. I have my small shop that I run and I make sure that I have money for my testing. I also play Njangi. It [antiretroviral therapy] is free. Now, we do not buy the medications. They are given without charge. But you pay for testing. I do not really have difficulties except when I have to go for testing because it is expensive (JK, HIV/AIDS patient, 42 years old).

The indigenous social security mechanisms including the family and local community are overstocked by the numbers of adult breadwinners now being struck down in their prime. It has never been clearer why Indigenous Social Security Systems must be organised to ensure the necessary help to families that are most affected by HIV/AIDS to receive proper care in the appropriate setting.

> Most often when you have crisis, they [the Njanji group] can bring to you a tin of milk etc. They do not really assist that much. They only do what we call 'solidarity'. Just like for any illness. But when it is bad like the case I cited (a group member with HIV/AIDS and blindness), they can go out of their way to help. We bought a bag of rice, oil, soya beans since she must eat nutritious things [food]. Most often in their rules and regulations, it [HIV/AIDS] is not there (National Social Insurance Fund agent, 52 years old).

People with HIV/AIDS may also receive benefits from local, national and international NGOs and Churches. However, the effectiveness of ISSS is undermined by weak resource bases. They may therefore fail to adequately protect large numbers of HIV/AIDS patients from having a good quality of life. In addition, as noted throughout this chapter, the strength of familial and informal support systems has been diminishing in Cameroon and across many countries for reasons associated with modernisation. Therefore, supplementing intra-family and community support with public social protection programmes, is essential for people living with HIV/AIDS in Cameroon. Familial and informal/indigenous support networks provide social protection to seriously HIV/AIDS affected people in Cameroon. The transfer of resources in cash and in kind from financially well-off relatives to sick relatives has been a mainstay of traditional social protection systems. The transfer of these resources has prevented large numbers of HIV/AIDS infected people from sliding into destitution as evidenced in this quotation:

> I know a girl who is infected. She comes here and tells me 'sister I am not well'. She is not from a family that can support her. She comes and asks for assistance (transport money) to go to the hospital. This means that there are people out there who do not have family that can assist them. So, they go to see people who can help them one way or the other. They beg to go to the hospital – I want to go for check-up, but I do not have transport money. You give the transport money because you know that they will get the ART there free (EA, Former HIV/AIDS caregiver, widow, 55 years old).

There is need for an integrated approach at the national level that provides linkages between different sectors, mechanisms and policies and avoids the danger of having a system that includes some and excludes others from the national system. According to the World Bank (2015), costs to companies through losses of human capital due to AIDS include absenteeism, loss of production, need to train replacements and/or increase the size of the work force. Cameroon is bearing an extraordinarily large health burden as the epidemics of HIV/AIDS and opportunistic infections, associated with HIV/AIDS related diseases place increasing demands on the healthcare sector (UNAIDS, 2015). Health risk is one of the severest challenges confronting poor households. Apart from the personal suffering it brings, illness can cripple a poor household's income earning capacity. For instance, seriously sick individuals may no longer be able to contribute to household income. In addition, households must allocate resources to provide care within the family and cover the expenses of treatment.

The surge of HIV/AIDS-related illnesses and deaths only exacerbates this problem. In the absence of access to free and good public care or health insurance, households are forced to resort to alternative coping strategies. However, for low-income households the depletion of savings, assets, or human capital may lead to a further eroding of their already poor asset base. For example, children might have to decrease their time in school and start working for income, care for their ill household member or take over domestic chores.

Considering the case of HIV/AIDS, a severe illness, where a household must finance the costs for treatment out of current income, patients can be confronted with a transient period of poverty, whereby other expenditures on food, energy, children's education or clothing must be scaled back. Financing such costs with meagre revenue can reduce future earning capacity or make the household more vulnerable to future shocks. If the household decides to forgo treatment altogether, the health status of the HIV/AIDS patient will decline and probably also adversely affect their earning capacity. The implementation of social security is particularly difficult in Cameroon, especially as the country faces serious budget constraints, making it almost impossible to finance rather expensive insurance systems. In addition, the implementation and management of social security systems requires quite complex institutions which, again, are not available in most regions in Cameroon. Therefore, it is important to explore how these problems can be tackled and to think about alternatives which could be used.

The International Monetary Fund (IMF) and the World Bank's (WB) Structural Adjustment Programmes (SAPs) have produced large vulnerable groups that cannot contribute to social insurance schemes. The IMF and the WB imposed SAP on the Government of Cameroon in the 1980s that resulted in increased poverty through lower wages, high food and housing prices, fewer employment opportunities, diminished access to education and medical care (World Bank, 2015). These conditions generated various degrees of vulnerability in people living with HIV/AIDS where individuals faced fewer choices of generating enough income to take care of their medical treatment and families. With the implementation of the SAP, women and girls became even more vulnerable because they were the first to be withdrawn from schools, either to take care of sick family members, or to work and sustain the family when the sole breadwinner of the family became incapacitated by HIV/AIDS. People with HIV/AIDS who can no longer count on family support and who have not been able to make provisions for their pension are the most vulnerable group of people outside the labour force.

Another consequence of the SAP is the fact that women have fewer employment options and lower wages. When an income earner succumbs to HIV/AIDS, the family must find resources for medical care and fees. According to UNAIDS about a quarter of households in Cameroon is expected to lose an income earner to AIDS and the incomes of the poorest households are expected to fall to about 13 per cent (UNAIDS, 2015). To help alleviate this situation, international organisations are resorting to debt cancellation, for they have realised the detrimental effect of SAP on communities. Instead of spending money on HIV/AIDS intervention, the Government had been preoccupied with debt repayments with serious repercussions of the population (National AIDS Control Committee Central Technical Group, 2010; ONU/SIDA, 2014).

Cameroon is experiencing a growing number of households headed by women and grandparents. These households are already generally poorer and less able to provide for the children in their care.

> I have not started receiving help. I am single and have three children to care for. I was diagnosed six months ago when I was sick and went to the hospital. I was given free antiretroviral medications and asked to take them every day at 8pm (LT, HIV-positive, 33 years old).

A report of the United Nations Children's Fund UNICEF shows that many of the most severely affected countries in Sub-Saharan Africa have no national policies to address the needs of orphaned children, including children orphaned and made vulnerable by HIV/AIDS (UNICEF, 2014). The on-going failure to respond to the orphan crisis will have serious implications not just for the children themselves, but for their communities and these nations. HIV/AIDS infected or affected people not only have the financial burden, they must also deal with the persistent HIV stigma and discrimination in their families and communities. ISSS may not be fully exploited because of fear of HIV stigmatisation and discrimination.

HIV Stigmatisation

The culture of silence continues to reign even when people with HIV/AIDS are ill, dying and need assistance from families and friends – their main source of social security coverage. Since HIV/AIDS is the name for a cluster of diseases that immune deficient people develop, patients and their care-givers can simply choose to view their illness just as tuberculosis, diarrhoea or pneumonia. A report by UNAIDS and World Health Organisation (WHO) cited an instance from Cameroon where, in a study of home-based care schemes, fewer than one in ten people who were caring for HIV-infected patients acknowledged that their patients were suffering from HIV or AIDS. Patients themselves were only slightly more likely to acknowledge their status and several patients would not disclose their status to anyone, including the person caring for them or their adult children. The self-imposed silence is hard on the patient and it can also be hard on caregivers, particularly when they are children or adolescents and ignorant of the danger they live in (UNAIDS, 2014):

> Well when we look at the Indigenous Social Security Systems, in my observation, is basically the family that is involved. The family takes care of the sick person. It is difficult for the church to come in our society because people do not feel free to come out and say that they have this disease [HIV/AIDS]. I am suffering from this. People do not talk about the illness [HIV/AIDS]. I do not know but I think it is the stigma. You know stigmatisation. It depends on the individual, if he or she can be open to let the family know because back in the family you have individuals who hide it from their family. I think this depends on the knowledge and the acceptance of that individual. Basically, what I observe is that in my own situation, the family bears the load (EA, former caregiver, widow, 55 years old).

Stigma, and the fear it engenders, fuel the spread of HIV, as those with risky behaviours may be reluctant to change their behaviours in case the change is interpreted as an admission of infection. For example, the fear of acknowledging HIV/AIDS infection can stop a married man from raising the subject of condom use with his wife. The fear of disclosing her HIV status may prevent an infected woman from giving her baby replacement feeding to avoid transmitting the virus through breast milk. The stigma attached to HIV/AIDS affects both sexes. However, the consequences may be more severe for women, who risk being beaten and even thrown out of their homes if their statuses are revealed. This may still be the case even when the husband was the source of the woman's infection. An HIV-infected woman may be blamed for the death of her children or be deprived of care of her children. Many people simply do not want to know if they are HIV-positive, even when counselling and testing are offered:

> The families assist a lot financially. They pay for your drugs [medications], food, housing and give psychological comfort. Here in Cameroon there is still that

> stigmatisation and it is only the family that can keep you, welcome you, embrace you and give you the psychological balance that you need – the financial assistance – it is only the family (National Social Insurance Fund agent, 52 years old).

The Government has recently spoken out loudly, clearly and repeatedly about HIV/AIDS and has sought to demystify it by encouraging discussions about safe sex everywhere, from the classrooms to the boardrooms and Churches. In Cameroon some progress has been made not only in keeping the number of new infections down, but also in ensuring the well-being of those people who are already living with the virus (ONU/SIDA, 2014).

Conclusion and Recommendations

Formal social security institutions are unable to cover most Cameroonians and the culture of social solidarity extended throughout the continent provides the basis to build a broad social protection umbrella. The family, social and ethnic networks, the community and church based organisations are the main forms of ISSS in Cameroon. People living with HIV/AIDS can complement the antiretroviral therapy they receive with the contributions and protection from ISSS to sustain the life-long struggle with HIV/AIDS. The Government has not responded with a formal social protection system to the phenomenon of HIV/AIDS that is decimating the population of Cameroon. Most HIV/AIDS people still rely on indigenous systems of family and community support, which though traditionally robust, are now being undermined by modernisation, individualism, migration and the life-long impact of HIV/AIDS. The performance of the Cameroonian economy and competing demands for public investment from other sectors of the economy, as well as strong lobbies from a range of disadvantaged groups make this a difficult decision for the Government. Yet acting now will relieve the suffering of many people with HIV/AIDS, with the aim of establishing effective systems to cope with their growing numbers.

The potential for developing links between formal and indigenous interventions to scale up effective community initiatives may offer a way forward. Nonetheless, all options require the Government to mainstream HIV/AIDS issues and introduce a supportive policy and institutional framework that prioritises people living with HIV/AIDS rather than overlooking them. Indigenous Social Security System (ISSS) still must protect people whose lives depend on agriculture for their livelihood and in most systems in

Cameroon, ISSS provides adequate protection. Traditional family obligations and other institutions insure those in need. The question for future research is how to ensure adequate social security coverage against sickness, disability unemployment, old age and death of people living with HIV/AIDS in Cameroon. Improving governance is the most critical challenge. Given the problems in the past, often 'business as usual' is not the best option and new institutional set-ups must be found. Some aspects of the indigenous social security system should be incorporated in the existing social security system to protect the rights of the beneficiaries by providing better services, reducing administrative costs and contributing to overall development by carefully considering the links with the rest of the economy.

Acknowledgements

I would like to thank all the women who accepted to participate in the study. I am also grateful to Ms Sarra Ndedi Nnoko and Mr Thomas Enowtanya Arrey who were my points of contact and introduced me to some of the participants.

References

Andrews, C.; Das, M. & Elder J.O.M.Z.G. 2012. *Social protection in low income countries and fragile situations: Challenges and future directions.* World Bank: Washington DC.

Barbone, L. & Alvaro Sanchez, B.L. 1999. *Pension and social security in sub-Saharan Africa: issues and options.* The World Bank: Washington, D.C.

Beresford, P. & Croft, S. 1995. It's our problem too! Challenging the exclusion of poor people from poverty discussion. *Critical Social Policy,* 15 (2-3): 75-95.

Braun, V. & Clarke, V. 2006. Using thematic analysis in psychology. *Qualitative Research in Psychology,* 3(2): 77-101.

Cameroon Baptist Convention. 2010. *HIV/AIDS care and Prevention.* Bameda: Cameroon Baptist Convention Health Board.

Central Intelligence Agency. *The World Factbook: Cameroon.* 2017. Washington DC: CIA.

Cockburn, C. 1980. The role of social security in development. *International Social Security Review,* 33: 337-3358.

Dean, H. 2002. Manageable Discord: Fraud and Resistance in the Social Security System. *Social Policy & Administration,* 31(2): 103-115.

Farr, G.N. 2011. *The Development of the Social Security Act.* By Edwin E. Witte. Madison: University of Wisconsin Press.

Floyd, S.; Crampin, A.C.; Glynn, J.R.; Mwenebabu, M.; Mnkhondia, S.; Ngwira, B.; Zaba, B. & Fine, P.E. 2008. The long-term social and economic impact of HIV on the spouses of infected individuals in northern Malawi. *Trop.Med.Int.Health*, 13(4): 520-531.

Garcia, B. & Gruat, J.V. 2003. *Social Protection: A Life Cycle Continuum Investment for Social Justice, Poverty Reduction and Sustainable Development.* Geneva: International Labour Organisation (ILO).

Gerdes V. 1975. Precursors of Modern Social Security in Indigeneous African Institutions. *The Journal of Modern African Studies*, 12(2): 209-228.

Gerkens, S. & Merkur, S. 2010. Belgium: Health System Review. *Health Syst. Transit*, 12(5): 1-266.

Helleberg, M.; Haggblom, A.; Sonnerborg, A. & Obel, N. 2013. HIV care in the Swedish-Danish HIV cohort 1995-2010, closing the gaps. *PLoS.One*, 8(8): 72257.

Hennink, M.; Hutter, I. & Bailey, A. 2011. *Qualitative Research Methods.* First Edition. London: SAGE Publications Ltd.

Heymann, J.; Earle, A.; Rajaraman, D.; Miller, C. & Bogen, K. 2007. Extended family caring for children orphaned by AIDS: balancing essential work and caregiving in a high HIV prevalence nations. *AIDS Care*, 19(3): 337-345.

Hodges, A. 2008. Perspectives for social protection in West and Central Africa. In: UNICEF (ed.). Social Protection for the Poorest in Africa: Learning from Experience Conference. *Entebbe*: UNICEF: 8-10.

International Labour Organisation (ILO). 2009. Social Protection: Social Security Convention, 102 (1952). Geneva: ILO.

Institut National de la Statistique (INS) & Ministry of Public Health. 2011. Cameroon Demographic and Health Survey and Multiple Indicators Cluster Survey. Yaounde: INS.

Kalasa, B. 2001. *Population and Ageing in Africa: A policy dilemma.* UNFPA: Addis Ababa.

Kaplan, S.A.; Calman, N.S.; Golub, M.; Ruddock, C. & Billings, J. 2006. The role of faith-based institutions in addressing health disparities: a case study of an initiative in the southwest Bronx. *J.Health Care Poor Underserved*, 17(2 Suppl): 9-19.

MacPherson, S. 1982. *Social Policy in the Third World: The Social Dilemmas of Underdevelopment.* Brighton: Wheatsheaf.

Marshall, C. & Rossman, G.B. 2006. *Designing Qualitative Research, Fourth Edition.* Thousand Oaks: Sage Publications.

Midgely, J. & Sherraden, M. 1997. *Alternatives to Social Security: An International Inquiry.* Westport: Greenwood Publishing Group.

Miles, M.J. & Huberman, A.M. 1994. *Qualitative data analysis: an expanded source book, Second Edition.* Thousand Oaks: SAGE Publications.

National AIDS Control Committee Central Technical Group. 2010. The Impact of HIV and AIDS in Cameroon through 2020. Paris: UNESCO.

Novick, G. 2008. Is there a bias against telephone interviews in qualitative research? *Res. Nurs.Health*, 31(4): 391-398.

ONU/SIDA. 2014. Rapport National de Suivi de la declaration Politique sur le VIH/SIDA Cameroun: *Global Aids Response Progress (GARP).* Geneva: UNAIDS.

Pettigrew, S.F. 2000. Ethnography and Grounded Theory: a Happy Marriage? *Advances in Consumer Research.* 27: 256-260.

Plamondon, P.; Cichon, M. & Annycke, P. 2004. Financial Effects of HIV/AIDS on National Social Protection Schemes. In: M. Haacker (ed.). *The Macroeconomics of HIV/AIDS.* Washington DC: International Monetary Fund. 259-286.

Schur, N.; Mylne, A.; Mushati, P.; Takaruza, A.; Ward, H.; Nyamukapa, C. & Gregson, S. 2015. The effects of household wealth on HIV prevalence in Manicaland, Zimbabwe – a prospective household census and population-based open cohort study. *J Int.AIDS Soc*, 18(1): 20063.

Sherraden, M. 2001. *Assets and the Poor: Implications for Individual Account and Social Security.* Center for Social Development: Washington DC.

Sorèle, G.A.B. 2015. *Cameroun: Vers un accès universel à l'Assurance maladie, Cameroon Tribune.* SOPECAM, Yaounde,Cameroon.http//ct2015.cameroontribune.cm/index. php?option=com_content&view=article&id=87724:assurance-maladie-vers-un-acces universel [Accessed 2 February 2017].

Tsala, J.P. 2004. The lift and the stairs: the fight against AIDS in Cameroon. *SAHARA.J.,* 1(3): 139-156. Available from: PM:17601002

UNAIDS. 2015. *HIV and AIDS estimates 2015.* Geneva: UNAIDS.

UNAIDS. 2014. *Global Report 2014: UNAIDS report on the global AIDS epidemic.* Geneva: UNAIDS.

UNICEF. 2014. *HIV/AIDS in the region: West and Central Africa.* New York: UNICEF.

Van Rossem, R. & Meekers, D. 2011. Perceived social approval and condom use with casual partners among youth in urban Cameroon. *BMC Public Health*, 11: 632.

World Bank. 2015. Country Overview: Cameroon. World Bank: Washington DC.

Wouters, E.; Vermeiren, P.; Katabaro, M. & Van, D.W. 2010. Modelling social reality: limitations to measuring the impact of HIV/AIDS on rural households. *Trop.Med.Int. Health*, 15(8): 955-957.

CONCLUSION

Indigenous Social Security Systems for Policy Development in Africa

Ndangwa Noyoo & Emmanuel Boon

The research work that resulted in the publication of this book brought together experts from Southern and West Africa to proffer insights into Indigenous Social Security Systems (ISSS) which have often been referred to as 'informal' systems in Western literature. In this regard, the book also endorses the work of Devereux and Getu (2013: 3) that also brought together African social protection experts to discuss pertinent issues related to the conceptualisation and status of 'informal' and formal social protection in Sub-Saharan Africa (SSA). These two authors and their colleagues recognised the fact that the literature on social protection systems in SSA is not robust enough to facilitate the identification and understanding regarding 'informal' and 'formal' social protection systems and therefore the designing of sustainable social protection programmes based on local values and capacities. This book hopes to contribute towards the discourse on ISSS in SSA. In this sense, it has veered away from the usual approach that characterises ISSS as 'informal'. This was deliberately done to raise ISSS to the formal platform where public and social policies should ideally adequately respond to the needs of Africans.

The book sought to ascertain the levels and depth of ISSS in Africa's public and social policies by focusing particularly on the two regions of Southern and West Africa. The authors from the two regions were able to ferret out many issues in their chapters and discussions. Almost all of them seemed unanimous on two main points:

- ISSS have always existed in Africa and in the two regions. They have also remained parallel to the so-called formal systems which are basically derivatives of the former colonial systems in the respective SSA countries.
- ISSS are heavily relied upon by the mass of poor people in Africa; both in the urban and rural settings. In most cases, despite the importance of ISSS in offsetting external shocks and extreme needs, they are not taken on board by politicians and policy-makers when public policy and social policy programmes are developed to provide adequate protection for the people.

The above-mentioned issues were teased out by the different authors in their respective countries. It is important to note that the essence of this work lies in the fact that most ISSS issues and their utility in the SSA context remain anecdotal and therefore necessitated this objective scientific enquiry which resulted in the publication of this book. Another objective of the research was to generate valid and reliable information on ISSS to facilitate informed discussions on the subject. As has already been mentioned, the research approach adopted by the contributing authors was exploratory in nature. As far as was possible, interviews were conducted on samples of relevant ISSS stakeholders to collect data and information for analysis and to interpret and present the findings in the various chapters of this book. In most chapters, the authors have shown that policy-makers are aware of ISSS and their importance, even though ISSS are not accorded any significance in the formal policy-making processes. Another issue that clearly emerged from the findings of the various chapters of the book is that political will on the part of national governments to mainstream ISSS into public and social policies continues to be illusory. This challenge seems to resonate with most countries in the two regions, thus raising serious questions as to what governments are doing to find 'African solutions to African problems' as we are constantly reminded by African Union (AU) officials.

Devereux and Getu (2013) echoed this challenge and noted that there have been many initiatives on the African continent that sought to raise the profile of social protection/social security in different countries, but none of them gave adequate attention to the potential of 'informal' social protection systems. This book goes beyond the nomenclature of prominent social protection literature, which tends to equate Indigenous Social Security Systems with 'informal' social security systems, by positing that *indigenous* is not equal to *informality*. It is important to note that this juxtaposition is fraught with contradictions and it may even be argued that it is Eurocentric. When scholars and policy-makers become engrossed in defining Indigenous Social Security Systems as 'informal', they are most probably reinforcing the 'otherness' of the former and thereby advocating its peripheral character. Therefore, this book considers the terminology of informal social security or social protection systems unhelpful regarding its premise of exclusion and marginalisation of those systems that are indigenous. In fact, if one approaches ISSS from this perspective, it would probably be very difficult to argue for their inclusion in the so-called formal systems which are largely championed by governments.

Another significant emerging issue from the discussions in the different chapters of the book is that despite the relegation of ISSS to second class status, when formal economic systems in the two regions are challenged by global crises, it is usually ISSS that step into the breach and 'cushion' individuals, families and communities from socio-economic hardships. In fact, over the past few decades, ISSS have helped to offset the dire consequences of failed economics in the two regions and yet they have never been given due credit by politicians, policy-makers and even some academics. Nevertheless, the preponderance and relevance of ISSS, both in the urban and rural settings of the two regions, have been clearly confirmed in this book. For the urban and rural areas in Africa, social security systems are nuanced differently. However, their primary role remains the provision of social protection to individuals, families and communities. Another important issue raised in the book is the fact that despite the 'informal' status of ISSS, they have stood the test of time and have evolved from the pre-colonial era to the present time. Their continuous resilience is a clear indication of their relevance to SSA. Furthermore, the organic and intrinsic nature of ISSS in African societies, in comparison to the so-called formal social security systems which are essentially a forced affair in SSA, should make policy-makers and academics seriously rethink the appropriateness of existing development policies, strategies and programmes. In response to this anomaly, this book calls for a reassertion, reification and integration of ISSS into mainstream public policy-making efforts in SSA. It is also necessary to review and recalibrate the formal social security systems to fit the SSA context and allow the integration of ISSS in the formal development policy design and programming.

References

Devereux, S. & Getu, M. 2013. The conceptualisation and status of informal and formal social protection in Sub-Saharan Africa. In: S. Devereux & M. Getu (eds.). *Informal and formal social protection systems in Sub-Saharan Africa.* Addis Ababa: Organisation for Social Science Research in Eastern and Southern Africa.

INDEX

L

M

N

O

P

www.ingramcontent.com/pod-product-compliance
Lightning Source LLC
Chambersburg PA
CBHW080043280326

41935CB00014B/1770